Germany in the Modern World

Germany in the Modern World

A New History

Sam A. Mustafa

ROWMAN & LITTLEFIELD PUBLISHERS, INC.
Lanham • Boulder • New York • Toronto • Plymouth, UK

Published by Rowman & Littlefield Publishers, Inc.
A wholly owned subsidiary of The Rowman & Littlefield Publishing Group, Inc.
4501 Forbes Boulevard, Suite 200, Lanham, Maryland 20706
www.rowmanlittlefield.com

Estover Road, Plymouth PL6 7PY, United Kingdom

British Library Cataloguing in Publication Information Available

Library of Congress Cataloging-in-Publication Data

Mustafa, Sam A.
  Germany in the modern world : a new history / Sam A. Mustafa.
    p. cm.
  Includes bibliographical references and index.
  ISBN 978-0-7425-6802-0 (cloth : alk. paper) — ISBN 978-0-7425-6803-7 (paper : alk. paper) — ISBN 978-0-7425-6804-4 (electronic)
  1. Germany—History. I. Title.
  DD89.M87 2011
  943—dc22

                                                                                2010033758

∞™ The paper used in this publication meets the minimum requirements of American National Standard for Information Sciences—Permanence of Paper for Printed Library Materials, ANSI/NISO Z39.48-1992.

Printed in the United States of America

For my students.

~

Contents

~

Acknowledgments

It would be impossible for me to thank all of the German friends and scholars who have helped me with my work over the past fifteen years, but I must single out Ursula Soyez and Markus Schirmer for their hospitality, enthusiasm and interest, and for reading and discussing large sections of this text. And I am always grateful to Oliver Schmidt, for the generosity with which he shares his research.

I am grateful to Dr. Michael Leggiere of the University of North Texas, Dr. Katherine Aaslestad of West Virginia University, and Dr. Alexander Mikaberidze of Louisiana State University for their detailed and insightful analysis of the manuscript.

I am always grateful to Susan McEachern of Rowman & Littlefield for her enthusiasm, patience, and accessibility. This is now the second book of mine that she has brought in from the cold.

I thank the United States Holocaust Memorial Museum and the Moravian Archive of Bethlehem, Pennsylvania, for permission to use various images from their archive.

Unless otherwise cited in the captions, all images were created or photographed by the author.

Illustrations

Preface

"My pity is too deep, my grief and sympathy are with this unhappy nation, when I think of the exaltation and blind ardour of its uprising, the breaking-out, the breaking-up, the breaking-down."

—Thomas Mann, *Doktor Faustus*

Throughout much of the nineteenth and twentieth centuries, most history was *national* history. Scholars wrote the stories of nations almost as if writing biographies. It is hard to imagine today, but most middle- and upper-class European and American families had history textbooks in their homes as general references or coffee-table books, and thus not simply students but educated people in general learned the history of France, or England, or Russia, or Italy. They read, knew, and discussed these histories the way that we today discuss news, politics, or entertainment.

After the Second World War scholars began to question the emphasis on history as a story of separate nationalities. After all, is there really something uniquely "Italian" about people living in Italy? Isn't the creation of the Italian nation-state simply the story of migrations and wars, of customs and religion, of shifting boundaries and politics? Why should historians draw an arbitrary line down a political border? Things like culture and religion, lifestyle and work habits, and even political ideas and social movements don't necessarily stop at borders. And the creation of a nation-state doesn't suddenly make all the people within its borders the same. Thus national histories fell out of favor as scholars sought new and original ways to organize the telling of the human past.

But national history never completely went away. In fact, for most American colleges and universities, it is still the normal way to organize undergraduate history courses. The course catalogs of most history departments still offer the traditional British History, French History, Russian History, and so on.

This is a textbook of German history, designed to introduce students and any interested readers to the fascinating, tumultuous, and often tragic story of the largest nationality in Europe. Although our story begins in ancient times, it focuses, as the title suggests, on the modern era: the past three centuries. Along the way we will consider issues of culture, faith, politics, nationality, and race. Although every national story has something to offer on these topics, the way the Germans dealt with them has often had global consequences. Struggles and Big Ideas that began in Germany had a tendency to echo like shock waves around the modern world, sooner or later affecting much of humanity.

Sonderweg: A Special Path?

Shortly after the Second World War, when most of the world was astonished and horrified by the spectacle of what the Germans had done, scholars groped in vain for some kind of explanation. How could such a sophisticated society, which had produced so much of Europe's great literature, music, and art, have descended into the madness, cruelty, and violence of the Nazi regime? It is a natural human tendency to seek simple, clear answers to immensely complex and confusing questions, and many people after 1945 were looking for a *monocausal* explanation for Germany's catastrophe.

What Does *Monocausal* Mean?

A monocausal explanation is one in which all parts of a complicated event or series of events come from a single root cause, such as "The American Revolution happened because of a dispute over taxes." Obviously, most monocausal explanations are far too simplistic, and in many cases not even accurate, and historians usually try to avoid them.

The answer formulated by many historians has come to be known as the *Sonderweg Thesis*. The word *Sonderweg* is German for "special path." The thesis, articulated by historians both inside and outside Germany, was that the Germans had not followed the same path toward modernity that the rest of western Europe had. At some point in their past, the Germans had "detoured" from the path of liberal democracy that countries like England, Holland, France, and others were following, and instead of becoming more free and progressive, Germans followed a uniquely undemocratic and authoritarian path that inevitably led to the Nazis, the war, and the Holocaust.

Historians could not agree on where, exactly, the detour had been. Some suggested that it happened in 1848, when liberal and middle-class Germans failed to create a democratic German republic at the Frankfurt Parliament. Some suggested that it happened when German conservatives led the fight against Napoleon by harnessing ethnic and xenophobic fears and resentment. Some went all the way back to Martin Luther to note the famous Protestant leader's anti-Semitic harangues. But all the Sonderweg historians agreed in principle that the Germans had made fundamental developmental errors that rendered them more susceptible to the sort of dictatorship and genocidal racism embodied by Hitler and the Nazis.

In recent years, most historians have rejected the Sonderweg thesis as being too simplistic, not to mention broadly flawed in its analysis. For one thing, history is not a train on a track. There are no "paths to modernity," and "modernity" isn't a destination in any event, since it can't be defined precisely or nailed down in time or place. Nations aren't vehicles, with all the passengers along for one common ride. More to the point, Germans were arguably less war-, violence-, and conquest-prone than the British or French, who spent the second half of the nineteenth century conquering much of the world and ruling native peoples in conditions approaching slave labor. Belgian colonial rule in the Congo resulted in the death of somewhere between 5 and 8 million native people, possibly greater in number than the victims of the Nazi Holocaust. Germans were certainly no more anti-Semitic in the nineteenth and twentieth centuries than the Spaniards or Italians and were arguably much less so than the Poles or Russians. And any concept of the Germans as abnormally preferring authoritarian government over democracy not only calls into question the development of so many German political movements and parties in the nineteenth and twentieth centuries but also forces a comparison of German behavior to that of other European nationalities that were grappling with the same political issues, often in very much the same ways. (The French, arguably one of Europe's most democratic and republican peoples, nonetheless created three empires in the course of the nineteenth century, two by coups d'état within France and the third by global conquest and colonization, in each case with broad popular support.)

To put it bluntly, most European nations had a lot of blood on their hands in the nineteenth and twentieth centuries.

Nonetheless, even if there was no single, clear "special path," the idea of the Sonderweg remains potent for many people. It is of course a *teleological* concept. It is always tempting to search the past for answers to the questions of the present. But there is no single explanation for the crimes, tragedies, and mistakes of German history, any more than there is for any other nation. Nor should we consider any nation's history as simply a path toward any one event, no matter how staggering the event. The Nazi era and the Holocaust remain crucial elements of the German national story, but they are not the end of the story.

What Is Teleology?

Although it means different things in different disciplines, for historians *teleology* is the practice of searching in the past for "why things turned out the way they did" in the present. Historians usually reject it because it assumes two fallacies: (1) that we could all agree how things "turned out" in the present, when obviously we each have very different understandings of our world and (2) that there is ever a single cause or chain of causes somewhere in the past that can be traced directly to the present, which is obviously not true.

If German history can't promise you a set of simple, clear explanations for terrible things like the Nazi era, then why study the history of this one nation? Why study any national history at all? I would like to propose a few reasons, addressed by this book.

The Nation and the State

For centuries, European peoples had only vague concepts of nationality. Kings often ruled over people who did not speak the same languages they did. This did not usually trouble rulers, since loyalty to the state was what mattered. In a hereditary monarchy, the state was embodied by the king, his family, and his immediate subordinates in the ministries. A king didn't want his subjects to think of themselves first as belonging to a nationality, but rather to think of themselves first as *his subjects*.

One of the most important changes in Western history was the merging of the state with the concept of nationality. This had been underway slowly for a long time but accelerated dramatically in the French Revolution at the end of the eighteenth century. By the end of that period, a new entity existed on the map of Europe: the *nation-state*.

Having a nation-state meant a new kind of identity and loyalty. A person who lived in a nation-state had the duties of a citizen to the national community, not just to the king. Throughout the eighteenth and nineteenth centuries, many European nationalities began to create nation-states, or transformed old state identities into national ones, as subjects became citizens, and loyalty to the state meant loyalty to one's own nationality—or, as they would have said in the nineteenth century, one's race.

The Germans, Europe's largest nationality, were very late in creating a nation-state. The process was fitful and often stumbled on the fact that the German nation seemingly had no center point around which to unify. And when Germans finally did create a nation-state, as a byproduct of a European war, that new entity appeared so large and powerful that it alarmed most of Europe.

Religious Conflict and Identity

People in the English-speaking world do not often consider that Germany was one of the most important places in the history of Christianity. It was in Germany that the Protestant Reformation began, was defined, and was initially sustained. Germany bore the brunt of the ensuing Wars of Religion. At the height of the Protestant-Catholic conflict in the seventeenth century, Germany became a vast landscape of misery and suffering, a perpetual battlefield. Entire cities were destroyed, entire communities annihilated.

Most of western Europe (and increasingly the New World) felt the impact of these struggles, but no place was as damaged or as divided as Germany. Indeed, a central component of the final peace settlement in 1648 was the religious division of Germany into an astonishingly complex arrangement of hundreds of tiny principalities. The religious divide cut through politics and society in almost every part of the German-speaking lands. It forces us to consider whether any kind of national identity can survive such a fundamental rift.

From Democracy to Dictatorship

German schoolchildren spend a great deal of time in history class studying the fall of democracy and the rise of dictatorship. Their textbooks pass very quickly over much of the national story to focus overwhelmingly upon two periods: the Weimar Republic and the Nazi regime. This is a story that fascinates people all over the world.

Many other nationalities have witnessed the decline and collapse of constitutional government and its replacement with dictatorship, but the German case is special, if for no other reason than that we have collectively chosen to make it special. The historian Richard Evans has noted that writing about the Nazis has never been more popular, with an average of three new books on Hitler or the Nazis being published *every day* for the past decade. For better or worse, the world is fascinated by what happened in Germany in the 1930s and 1940s. Germany offers one of history's most compelling case studies in the fall of constitutional government and the rise of dictatorship. And along the way, it forces us to consider the fragile nature of democracy and its relationship to nationality, patriotism, and bigotry.

A Window into the Cold War

Germany was one of the few nations physically divided by the Cold War. For decades more than a million soldiers faced off along the so-called German-German border and in particular at the flash point of divided Berlin. The German experience thus provides us with a view of that conflict like no other Western nation. Germans were the only Europeans on both sides of the Cold War simultaneously, and they developed a unique perspective on the great rivalry between East and West.

The Stepchildren of Western Civilization?

Germany was for centuries a crossroads of European cultural and intellectual achievement. It produced the most prodigiously creative composers and musicians in Europe and did more collectively than any other nationality to create what we now call classical music. Germans were pioneers in philosophy, psychology, physics, chemistry, and engineering. They were probably Europe's most literate population, producers and consumers of literature from periodicals and poetry to novels and stage plays. World-changing ideas like Socialism and psychoanalysis emanated from German thinkers, and for much of the nineteenth and twentieth centuries Germans defined the cutting edge of military science.

And yet history texts rarely associate Germany with any of the great sociocultural movements of Western civilization . . . except the bad ones. Italians are usually credited for the Renaissance, despite the great impact of German artists and astronomers and of course the German creation of printing presses that enabled Renaissance thought to travel as it did. The French are usually the focus for the Enlightenment, despite that period being the golden age of German music and literature and despite the fact that the most famous essay on the meaning of the Enlightenment was written by a German philosopher. The nineteenth-century industrial revolution is usually depicted as a British phenomenon, and the concerns over its ills a British social question, despite the fact that Germany surpassed Britain in industrial output and despite Britain's most famous critics of industrial capitalism being a pair of exiled Germans.

Indeed, most high school and even college students do not learn much about Germany until the history survey course reaches the twentieth century and the rise of fascism. Then, as if waiting for their cue, the Germans appear as the perpetrators of what is usually described as the worst atrocity in Western history.

This book will not attempt to answer the question of how the people that gave the world Bach, Mozart, Beethoven, Schiller, Goethe, Kant, Einstein, and Freud also gave the world Hitler, Himmler, Mengele, and the whole dreadful cast of the 1930s and 1940s. That is because the question is not worth asking. No nationality has a monopoly on genius or brutality, and the presence of one does not mitigate against the presence of the other.

Rather, this book will offer—insofar as a short text can—an appreciation for the rich complexity of the German national story, and the German people who wrote it.

CHAPTER ONE

~

Germania

Most nationalities have some sort of foundational myth. It is perhaps even impossible for people to consider their own nationality without conjuring some romanticized version of the past. Often these myths are genesis stories of some kind: explanations of how the nationality came together in this place under a semimythic leader, and often in the face of some great foreign enemy. The degree to which people internalize these stories and take them seriously varies from place to place and time to time. For Germans today, their genesis story (if they even remember it from school) provokes little more than a chuckle. But there was a time, lasting several centuries, when Germans took it very seriously indeed. And it is fitting for us, therefore, to begin with that legend, and to try to pull the roots of history carefully out of the surrounding soil of mythology.

Hermann the German

In the decades before Christ, the Roman Republic convulsed in civil wars and finally was transformed to an autocracy by one man: Augustus, the first emperor of Rome. Augustus ruled an empire that controlled the entire Mediterranean area and western Europe to the Rhine River.

The Rhine is a very large and fast-flowing river, running north from the icy lakes of the Alps. For much of its length it cuts through dramatic hills and mountains, whose steep cliffs come right down to the water. As it moves north it gradually broadens and the land becomes flatter. For centuries

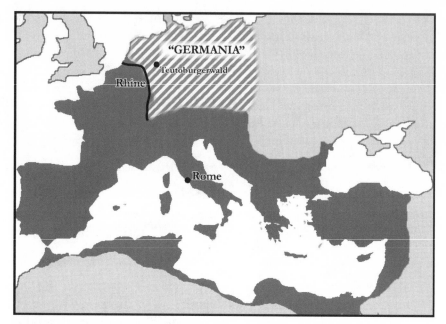

Figure 1.1. The Roman Empire and Germania

Germans had a romantic attachment to "Father Rhine," one of the few rivers written in the masculine gender. It certainly is a beautiful and romantic landscape to this day, but the attachment stems also from a mythological source: the idea that the Rhine is the "father" river of the Germanic peoples, the line where the Roman Empire ended and "Germania" began.

In fact, the Romans had already colonized both banks of the river. Many modern German cities, such as Düsseldorf, Cologne, Bonn, Mainz, and Trier, began their existence as Roman outpost towns. Roman settlements in some cases reached seventy miles or more to the east of the Rhine. But for Romans, the Rhine was effectively the frontier region, if not precisely the line of the frontier. Beyond the Rhineland, to the east, lay *Magna Germania*: greater Germany.

As far as the Romans were concerned, "German" people were a broad collection of northern tribes. They included the Gauls, whom Julius Caesar had conquered a generation earlier and who were now assimilating into the Roman state in present-day France. The Romans knew that Germanic tribes moved around, sometimes in large numbers, and they had an ongoing relationship with several tribes in the frontier region, where trade and migration were tolerated as long as the Roman state and military were not directly threatened. Sometimes German tribes launched raids for plunder inside the Roman borders, usually resulting in a retaliatory strike by the Romans to wipe out or drive away the offending tribe. But as to the precise number and demography of the Germans, or the extent and cartography of Germania, the Romans could only guess.

A visitor to Germany would be hard-pressed to imagine the country as it must have looked in Roman times. Germany, today so thoroughly populated, developed, and paved, was once an endless frosty forest, scarcely inhabited in many regions, whose deep woods gave way to occasional sandy bogs and marshes or mountains. Why the Romans ever seriously considered conquering and ruling it is something of a mystery, since it was a difficult, cold, and (they thought) unproductive landscape. But in the early days of the Roman Empire, the state was still expansionist by implicit design, and often by explicit assignment.

If later writers like Tacitus are to be believed, the Romans found the Germans to be a fascinating collection of contradictions. Big, hairy, pale-skinned, blue-eyed giants with tremendous physical strength, the Germans were also lazy and prone to sleeping away an entire day because they had been up all night feasting and drinking. They were individually brave warriors who loved a good fight, yet were disorganized and made poor armies. They were illiterate and came in such a variety of tribes that many couldn't understand each others' languages, although many tribes did apparently have some common words, values, and symbols. The tribes appeared to share many of the same gods and goddesses and religious myths and had imported a fair number of Greco-Roman ones as well. Although some tribes were settled, others were still seminomadic and rarely built any settlement bigger than a town.

The Roman historian Tacitus, writing almost a century after the Emperor Augustus, made these observations after the Romans had had more than 150 years of contact with Germanic tribes, and yet he still could only guess at the nature of the people beyond the frontier. Nor did he have a clear understanding of the origins of these "German" people: some were from modern-day Scandinavia, others from eastern Europe and Russia, and the ancestors of others had lived there for hundreds, perhaps thousands, of years. The Romans identified the tribes individually, but also referred to them collectively as Germans because they all lived in Germania.

In 16 BCE a coalition of German tribes ambushed a Roman legion and dealt it a serious defeat, capturing the sacred eagle, symbol of the legion and the empire. Augustus authorized a plan of gradual invasion and colonization. The Romans courted alliances with some Germanic tribes while building up armies to crush others. Augustus appointed his stepsons Drusus and Tiberius to command the conquest. Their record was mixed. Roman forces did advance deeper into Germania than they ever had before, but actual control of the region proved elusive. Drusus died on campaign and Tiberius was forced to leave in 6 CE to put down a rebellion in another region. That left command of the campaign to Publius Quinctilius Varus.

Varus was a controversial commander, and negative opinions from his colleagues and subordinates indicate a lack of trust in his honesty or competence. That may well be after-the-fact rationalizing, given what was about to happen. Varus had a sizable force at his disposal: three legions (about fifteen thousand professional soldiers), plus perhaps another fifteen thousand auxiliary soldiers and supporting units. Although he was aware that launching this large army headlong into the uncharted wilderness of Germania was a risky venture, Varus believed that he had sufficient local support from loyal tribes, particularly the services of a young man whose advice he trusted completely: a chieftain from the Cherusci tribe whose Latinized name was Arminius, and who has been remembered in German as Hermann.

Arminius was twenty-six years old when Varus confided in him for the crucial role of organizing local support for the campaign. The Romans had every reason to trust him. Arminius and his brother had been taken hostage during an earlier Roman pacification campaign and "Romanized." This was a common practice in regions that the Romans wanted to assimilate: re-educating the children of local chieftains and aristocracy as Romans. Thus Arminius spoke and read Latin and spent years in Roman military service. He was even granted the title of an *equestrian* (the lower rank of the Roman nobility). At some point in 7 or 8 CE he returned to Germania to marry a young woman of the Cherusci tribe, whereupon he became not only a recognized chieftain in his own right, but also a diplomat between the Roman and Germanic worlds.

Arminius? Or Hermann?

The name "Hermann" became attached to him during the Renaissance, when the story became widely popular, but his Germanic name was probably something like Irmin or Irminus, perhaps indicating a different tribal origin than the Cherusci. Given that most educated people—on both sides of the frontier—used Latin, or at least many Latin words, it is likely that he was "Arminius" for his whole life, even when speaking to other Germans.

Unfortunately for Varus, however, Arminius had for at least a year been in the process of assembling a coalition of Germanic tribes specifically to oppose the Romans. He had made peace with six of the larger settled tribes, as well as getting agreements from perhaps hundreds of little villages and settlements in the region, all of whom pledged to contribute warriors for a campaign. How he kept all of this a secret remains a mystery, but he must have been very persuasive. His motivations are also somewhat mysterious. Some writers believe he had specific grievances against the Romans, others that his complaints were against Varus personally, and others that he may have wished simply to advance himself as a regional warlord and then deal with the Romans on his own terms.

In the summer of 9 CE, Varus's army was already well east of the Rhine, and he believed that he had pacified a large area of Magna Germania. What he had actually done was march his men into a gigantic trap. Arminius left him, allegedly to confer with Germanic tribal chiefs, but in reality to raise his army. Varus pressed on confidently, allowing the Roman forces to stretch out in a column almost ten miles long. In this unwieldy formation, and in the midst of densely forested, unfamiliar terrain, the formidable fighting power of the legions was drastically reduced.

It must have been a dreadful campaign for the Roman soldiers as evidence mounted that they had been abandoned, and little skirmishes with unfriendly locals indicated that the countryside was not pacified after all. Most alarming to Varus must have been the desertion of many of his *auxilia* (militia) troops, who were local tribesmen themselves and who now appeared on the opposite side. Finally, on September 9 the Roman advanced guard was stopped by a blocking force of Germanic warriors, then ambushed from the marshes and forests as they tried to deploy.

The event has ever after been known as the Battle of the Teutoburg Forest (in German, *der Teutoburgerwald*), although "massacre" is more accurate than "battle." The fighting on the first day probably only lasted an hour or two, during which more than half of the Roman soldiers were killed, captured, or wounded. Groups of Romans fought on for another two days before they were finally overwhelmed. Varus committed suicide. Handfuls of dazed survivors emerged in small groups later that autumn, spreading word of the worst Roman military defeat in living memory.

According to legend (probably embellished by the Roman historian Suetonius), the normally stoic Augustus suffered a rare loss of composure when a messenger brought him the news. He went pale, then tore at his hair and clothes in anguish, howling, "Quinctilius Varus, give me back my legions!" True or not, we know that he lost his enthusiasm for the conquest of Germania.

And thus we have the genesis story of the German people. The barbarian leader Arminius—Hermann—united the Germanic tribes against the mighty invader from the west. The arrogant Romans advanced deep into the primeval forests of Germany, only to be ambushed and massacred. And the Roman emperor declared that there would be no more attempts to conquer them. The Rhine would be the border. The Holy Rhine, Father Rhine, guarded the German people from conquest and assimilation into the Roman Empire. Thus the Germans evolved pure and strong, their language and written script preserved and evolving as a uniquely German thing, not absorbed into Latin; their race distinctly different, tall, blonde, and blue-eyed in contrast with those small, dark, swarthy Latins of the south and west.

That's the legend. Like all good legends, it has grown around a skeleton of documentable fact. But of course like all creation myths, it is a better story than history.

For one thing, the Romans weren't done with Germania in 9 CE. Five years after the disaster the new emperor Tiberius ordered his nephew Claudius Drusus (known, ironically, as "Germanicus," because of his father's victories over the Germans in a previous war) to lead a punitive invasion. By this time one-third of Rome's mobile army was deployed on the Rhine. This was a huge

Figure 1.2.   The Mountains and Rhine Valley, South of Koblenz

operation, more than twice the size of Varus's expedition, and it moved into central Germania, supposedly assisted by Arminius's own brother, who was still loyal to the Romans. Germanicus devastated several Germanic war bands, but Tiberius ultimately called off the operation as too costly. Nonetheless, the Romans considered it a success, and Germanicus received a triumph in Rome. Thus, it was Tiberius, not Augustus, who gave up on a conquest of Germany, and not because of the defeat at the Teutoburgerwald.

Second, there was nothing "pure" about the Germanic tribes, and in fact there was very little "German" about them, if we use that term to mean the direct ancestors of the modern German people. The Roman Empire was already an immense and complex polyglot society by the time of Augustus and only became more so with the following centuries. Germanic peoples came and went across the Roman frontiers in both peace and war, mixing with Romans (who could have been from Spain, Africa, Turkey, Macedonia, Syria, or any number of places) in endless combinations. Germanic peoples adopted Latin words into their languages even before Arminius, and certainly did so after him. And while the German language did evolve its own unique script, it was nonetheless based upon Latin letters. By the time of Rome's disintegration, as we shall see, Germans and Romans had so thoroughly mixed in the frontier regions, as well as throughout the Western Empire, that it was almost impossible to distinguish them except at the highest ranks of nobility. When the empire became Christian early in the fourth century, Germans increasingly took Latinized names, making any attempt to separate their ancestry even more difficult.

Third, the people the Romans called "Germans" were only the current inhabitants of a land that had been populated before Rome even existed. Humans had passed through the region for millennia, and Germany was settled long before recorded history. The bones of hominids were found in the Neander Valley (in German, Neanderthal) not far from the modern city of Düsseldorf, indicating settlements at least as early as 30,000 BCE, and an even earlier ancestor that could be half a million years old was found near the modern city of Heidelberg.

Notwithstanding the excellent story of Arminius and the defeat of Varus, the development of most of what became Germany happened only long after the fall of the Roman Empire.

Rome vs. the Germans, Part II: The Great Migrations

The traditional picture of the fall of Rome involves waves of Germanic barbarians shattering the frontiers of the Western Empire, ultimately carving out their own kingdoms in the fifth century as the empire collapsed. For centuries this was a popular way for Germans to imagine their own origins: a circle of historical justice being closed as the Germans who had once defended themselves against Roman invasion now turned the tables and destroyed the corrupted and decaying old empire.

What we know of these centuries, from admittedly scattered and fragmentary sources, indicates a complex process of transformation. The Roman Empire of the fifth century was very different from that of Augustus's time, and considerably more demographically mixed. People living in one province were accustomed to a large imperial bureaucracy filled with people who were probably from somewhere else. Even as Catholicism became the official religion of the empire, the Roman lands were full of different religions and various sects of Christianity. Latin was not in widespread use in many places where the local languages prevailed. It was possible to rise very high up the political and social ladder without coming from a traditional Roman background, and indeed there had been many emperors with barbarian ancestries. The dividing line between Romans and Germans, for example, was often not clear.

The threat of barbarian invasion was not much greater in the fifth century than it had been in earlier times, but the empire was less able to deal with it. This was primarily because the lack of any clear system of imperial succession meant that the death of an emperor usually touched off a civil war. The majority of Roman emperors died violent deaths, or died in the midst of war, or were overthrown by rivals. Most of Rome's military power was usually turned against other Romans. Emperors tried to find military manpower from outside the traditional structures of the empire, and tried to bribe their way to political support from groups that had been previously neglected.

By the fifth century it was common for emperors to grant *foederati* status to groups or entire tribes of barbarian peoples. Germanic people, in particular, were offered this arrangement: they would be settled inside the empire or granted large areas of land, and in return would provide fighting men to support the emperor who had given them the deal. Of course, if that emperor were killed or overthrown, the loyalty of the foederati was often up for grabs. If they felt mistreated, they often revolted and then might be defeated by another group of foederati. But this arrangement meant that almost a century before the "fall" of Rome, the old frontier line of the Rhine provinces was in some ways moot. The Germanic peoples were already settling and mixing into the empire, sometimes peacefully, sometimes not.

As with so much of this early prehistory of Germany, later generations of Germans embellished and elaborated, until the long century of migration and conflict became known as the First Great Migration (*Völkerwanderung*)

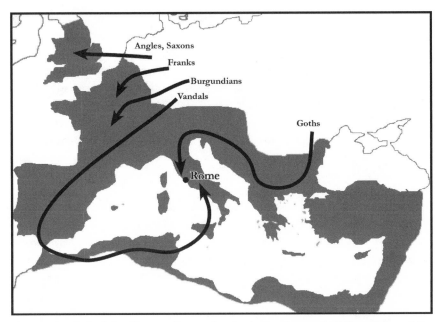

Figure 1.3.   Fall of the Western Roman Empire to the Germanic Tribes: A few of the largest tribes and their major areas of invasion and settlement in the fifth century AD.

of the German people. Yet none of these "ancient Germans" ever called themselves Germans. They apparently had no sense of national identity at all. The German language never existed in ancient times.

In some cases these groups moved rapidly, and they might indeed have thought of themselves as "invading" or crossing a frontier. But in most cases they moved slowly. They might settle in a place for several generations until everybody in the tribe probably thought that was where they were from. And when they did move, they inevitably mixed with other people, many of whom they had already been mixing with and whose religions and languages were probably familiar to them. In many cases, therefore, we are talking about gradual change, not sudden collision.

The Romans had called these people Germans in the first century, but not in the fourth and fifth centuries. Why not? Surely, if they were being invaded by Germans, some Roman officials should have written, "The Germans are invading." But they didn't. Romans wrote instead about specific tribes: Goths, Vandals, Alans, Franks, Saxons, and so on. That is because the Romans considered Germany a place—not a nationality. And it is likely that the "Germans" felt the same way.

Thus the fall of Rome in 476 CE is not a story of Germans "conquering" the Western Roman Empire. It is a story of the Romans tearing themselves apart in fratricidal internal conflicts and the various Roman factions, either through negligence or through deliberate action, allowing barbarian tribes to enter, often in the hope of enlisting them in the struggle. Eventually, Rome became so weakened that it wasn't much more than a collection of barbarian nations loosely held together by the political brokerage of the emperor.

That means that after Rome fell, it wasn't "replaced" by Germanic kingdoms. Those kingdoms were already there. The Romans themselves had allowed that to happen. What fell was much of the imperial superstructure. There was no sudden break from ancient times to Dark Ages, no sudden shift from Roman to Germanic civilization. Rather, there was more than a century of transition, to the point where some Germanic tribes in the fifth century did not even realize that they had adopted Greco-Roman religious myths and legends and believed themselves to be the descendants of Hercules or Helen of Troy.

The Arminius legend was forgotten, then rediscovered in the Renaissance. It enchanted Germans for centuries and gave them their first mythic hero, "Hermann the German." The story of the great migrations added a kind of historical justice to the tale, as Germans returned to wreak vengeance upon the Romans. We will see the themes of these legends recurring over and again in German history, reflected not just in poetry, songs, and operas, but in politics and policy down to Hitler's Third Reich. The events and people were real, but it was not the founding moment of either a German people or a German nation.

Kings, Warlords, and Dreams of Empire

The German word for king, *König*, derives from the verb *können*, meaning "to be able" to do something. Thus, a king is literally "he who is able," or "ableman." In other words: "he who has power."

Up to now we have been speaking of Germanic "kingdoms" replacing the Roman Empire, but the term is misleading. The kings of the Dark Ages had virtually nothing in the way of bureaucracy, no civil service, and very little ability to exert their power beyond their immediate location. In many cases, they were simply the descendants of tribal warlords, and they counted upon their extended family, as well as trusted commanders, to enforce their will. Those other men pledged loyalty to the king, but only in return for a degree of freedom to do as they pleased on their land. Most peasants never saw the king. Instead, the authority figure in their lives was the local lord, who collected taxes and managed the handful of tasks of local government.

Historians disagree, often sharply, about many aspects of the European Dark Ages. Many recent historians have stopped using the term at all, arguing that calling them "dark" prejudices our understanding of the period and leads to simplistic conclusions. But it seems clear that as the Roman Empire vanished, so too did much of its administrative ability. In its heyday, Rome was able to move huge quantities of wealth, goods, food, information, people, and military might tremendous distances and was able to organize vast projects. By the sixth century in western Europe, the remaining institutions— aside from the Catholic church—were local. Most people were born, worked, lived, and died in a tiny radius of perhaps twenty-five miles.

Although recent historians have argued that this era saw more commerce than we originally thought, the conventional wisdom still holds that long-distance transmission of goods and information dramatically decreased. Many local economies were based upon trade and barter, although in a few places new coins were minted. Life was difficult, dirty, and violent for most people. Centers of education became almost nonexistent. While ancient Romans had had a small but influential educated class and an infrastructure for things like sewage, water supply, and public bathing, their successor states had very little in the way of administration or public works.

The handful of written records surviving from these centuries are usually church-related. Baptismal and burial records, for example, indicate that a family might have four or five sons, all with the same name, born within a few years of each other. That was because it was commonplace to keep naming a child—particularly a boy—with the family's traditional name until one of the boys finally survived. A woman essentially stayed pregnant from her teens until menopause, or until one of those pregnancies finally killed her, probably in her thirties. A man was as likely to die from a simple work-related injury such as a splinter that became infected and then gangrenous as he was to be killed because the local lord conscripted him to fight in one of the frequent local wars.

The most important institution to survive the fall of the empire was the Roman Catholic Church. Yet in the Dark Ages most people had very little contact with the church. There were not yet parish churches or local clergy. There might be some rudimentary large church many miles away, and a priest might show up in a town once every few years for some festival, or perhaps to bless the accession of a new local lord (the priest could well have been from the same family as that lord). To use the word "Christianity" for this period is to be too precise. Most people practiced some combination of tribal magic, old Greco-Roman myths, and bits of Christian teachings.

Still, the survival of the Roman church meant that a kind of nostalgia also survived for the old Roman Empire. Many of the terms and institutions of the empire survived within the church. Over and again in early European history we see people keeping alive the hope and belief that somehow they could put the old empire back together again. What they actually knew about the old empire was probably very vague, but they had come to imagine it as a sort of golden past that they could restore with God's help. Almost as soon as the empire disappeared, the Germanic kingdoms began to use it as a historical touchstone. In the late fifth century the barbarian king Theodoric set up his throne in Ravenna, northern Italy, where the last emperors had lived, and assured the Eastern Roman (Byzantine) emperor that he was their legitimate representative of imperial authority in the west. Early in the sixth century the Frankish king Clovis conquered most of old Roman Gaul, and persuaded the Byzantine emperor to call him "consul" and "Augustus," in the hope that one day he would reunify the old Western Empire. When he took baptism in 496, Clovis began the process of catholicizing the Frankish realm. The sixth-century Byzantine emperor Justinian managed briefly to reattach much of the old Western Empire, in a futile attempt to restore the glory of ancient Rome under his power. And then in the late eighth and early ninth centuries, one family came closer than anyone to actually pulling it off. They did it in a tight alliance with the Catholic church, who supported and often funded the venture. But the empire that the Carolingian dynasty of the Franks created was not the old Roman Empire. It was a new empire altogether, and with it came the creation of what we can begin to call Germany.

Karl the Great

The Franks were a large Germanic tribe that settled in the Roman Empire in the fifth century, in present-day Belgium and northern France. They had often allied themselves with the empire against other tribes, and after the empire disappeared, their king, Clovis, converted to Catholicism and began to adopt many Latin words and customs. But his descendants proved to be weak and brutal incompetents, and the real power of the Frankish kingdom shifted to the local lords, known as *dukes*, in cooperation with the Church leadership.

In the seventh century the Carolingians became the most important of these Frankish ducal families, closely cooperating with church officials as they conquered much of central France and spread Frankish control in several directions. By the eighth century the Carolingians were in de facto control of the Frankish kingdom and were cooperating with the Catholic church on two important projects. The first was the resistance to the spread of Islam, which was checked in 732 at the Battle of Tours by the Carolingian leader Charles Martel. The second was the work of spreading Catholicism to the east, across the Rhine, into Germany. In 751 the pope rewarded the Carolingians with the kingship of the Franks, overthrowing the old dynasty founded by Clovis. By this time the process of missionary work in Germany was well underway.

Christianity was already widespread among many of the tribes of Germany, but it was rarely Catholicism. Many German tribes were Arian Christians or belonged to other "heretical" sects. Others used various bits of Christian theology mixed with their tribal religions, and still other tribes, especially in the north and east, were pagans worshipping a variety of gods and goddesses. The credit for beginning the process of conversion usually goes to an English monk named Winfrid, known by the Latin name he chose, Boniface, with which he was sainted by the church.

St. Boniface established himself as bishop of Mainz—the easternmost of the old Roman outpost cities of Germany—sending out missionaries and establishing convents and monasteries across the countryside. In fact, Boniface's work is often cited as the beginning of the transition of the church, not just in Germany but everywhere, to a system of parishes and parish priests who watched over specific local communities. Within a generation, the Carolingians, now the undisputed rulers of a large Frankish kingdom, came to believe that the best way to expand their power and prestige was not by fighting the powerful and well-organized Muslim rulers in Spain, but rather by annexing these newly Christianizing regions across the Rhine.

The Frankish invasion of Germany was overwhelmingly the work of one man, the greatest of all the Frankish kings, Charles, in French and English Charlemagne and in German Karl der Grosse (Karl the Great). His extraordinarily long reign (768–814) saw the transformation of western Europe and Catholic Christianity, and the creation of a people that began to call themselves Germans. As it turned out, Germany was one of Charlemagne's projects, not the only one, but in the long run the most important. He conquered the Lombards and expanded Carolingian power into northern Italy as well, thus going far beyond what the pope had asked or desired of him. He tried, unsuccessfully, to conquer portions of Spain, but was forced to withdraw in the face of Muslim and Basque resistance. It soon became apparent that under Charlemagne the traditional role of the pope as senior partner with the Frankish king had been reversed. The king was now dominant.

The cathedral that Charlemagne built for his new capital of Aix-la-Chapelle still stands in the German city of Aachen. Inside, one can intuit a few things about this man whose reign traditionally ends the Dark Ages and begins the Middle Ages. He was physically immense, probably standing about 6'3" (almost a foot taller than the average man of his time), and was squarely built with a broad chest and thick neck. Like his ancestors and like most Dark Age rulers, he was never entirely out of his role as warlord, and he relished battle and other masculine pursuits, including hunting, eating, drinking, and sex, apparently all to excess. Yet he was also the first European ruler in centuries to make a serious effort to gather scholars in the service of the state and to try to preserve what remained of the advanced Greco-Roman learning of the distant past.

For many German tribes, he must have seemed like a new Attila the Hun. Charlemagne's first major campaign was into northern Germany (the present-day North Sea coast and lowlands), where he conquered Saxon tribes and forced them to accept Catholicism, often annihilating entire villages when their leaders refused to be baptised. Estimates of the numbers killed in these campaigns remain only speculation but surely amount to tens of thousands. In one incident alone, at Verden, the king was apparently angered by a report that the locals had reverted to praying to their old gods, and he ordered over four thousand people beheaded.

Charlemagne's choice of Aix-la-Chapelle (Aachen) for his new capital city is evidence that he considered the conquest of Germany to be his most important mission. Aachen was not just his new residence and administrative and religious center, it was the headquarters of his military operation. The pace of the conquests is fairly astonishing, given the limits of eighth-century technology and transport and the rugged nature of terrain in much of the country. By the mid-790s, the Franks had conquered nearly all of present-day Germany, as well as Holland, Austria, and parts of Denmark and Hungary. Slavic tribes living in the eastern border regions were forced into submission as vassals.

In 799 Pope Leo III fled to Germany as a result of a power struggle in Rome, and he asked for Charlemagne's help in restoring him to power. The opportunity must have amused the king. If it hadn't been for a pope selecting his great-grandfather to be king of the Franks, Charlemagne would never have come to power. Four generations later, it was now the king who could make or break popes, not vice versa. For his support and restoration of Leo, Charlemagne was crowned emperor. It is worth noting that in the brief ceremony, the pope called him "Charles Augustus . . . great and peace-giving emperor of the Romans." Charlemagne was apparently surprised and not entirely happy with the new title, probably concerned that it implied some sort of subservience to the Roman Catholic Church or some sort of direct challenge to the Byzantine emperor in Constantinople (the Byzantines always referred to themselves as the Roman Empire).

But whatever misgivings he may have felt about his new role as a Roman emperor, Charlemagne remained dedicated to the expansion of his own massive new realm. By the time of his death, after nearly five decades of war and conquest, he ruled over a kingdom bigger than anything seen in western Europe since the fall of Rome. It included new territories that had never before been part of any western or Christian state. Charlemagne had moved the center of Europe decisively eastward, hundreds of miles. The Rhine was no longer the border of Europe; it was now simply one of many lines running through the middle of a new Europe.

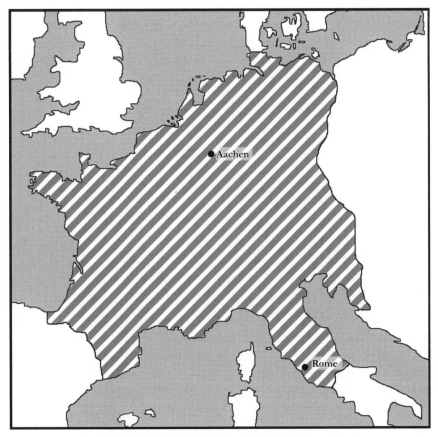

Figure 1.4.   The Frankish Empire at the Death of Charlemagne, 814 AD

It is still much too early for us to speak of states or even a nation. Char-lemagne's realm comprised thousands of small towns and villages. There were simply no real cities yet in western Europe north of the Alps; nothing to compare with Constantinople, Cairo, or Baghdad. The Frankish empire was thinly populated and relatively unproductive, with many, perhaps most, communities routinely unable to produce enough food for everyone. A huge variety of languages were spoken, including Old High German, an ancestor of the modern German language, but the Carolingian conquest was starting to bring together an aristocratic upper class that dealt with each other and with the church in Latin. An equally huge variety of religious practices still existed, but the creation of the Carolingian state began the process by which all these areas would be brought, peaceably or forcibly, into line with Catho-lic dogma. And a large number of semi-independent tribes and ethnicities still proliferated, but the creation of the new empire had begun the process of regional unification from which European nations would arise.

We began this chapter with a look at the mythical genesis story of the German people, only to deconstruct it as myth and legend. We conclude with a real genesis moment: the death of Charlemagne in 814. The great warlord built an empire that was nearly impossible to maintain as a single unitary state. In the following generations it broke apart, and from those divisions came the first states of the German nation.

Suggested Reading

Barbero, Allesandro. *Charlemagne: Father of a Continent.* Berkeley: University of California Press, 2004.

Einhard. *The Life of Charlemagne.* Translated by Samuel Turner [modern translation of this famous medieval biography]. Ann Arbor: University of Michigan Press, 1960.

Goldsworthy, Adrian. *How Rome Fell.* New Haven, CT: Yale University Press, 2009.

Heather, Peter. Empires and Barbarians: Migration, Development, and the Birth of Europe. Oxford: Oxford University Press, 2009.

———. *The Fall of the Roman Empire: A New History of Rome and the Barbarians.* Oxford: Oxford University Press, 2008.

Wells, Peter. *The Battle that Stopped Rome: Emperor Augustus, Arminius, and the Slaughter of the Legions in the Teutoburg Forest.* New York: W. W. Norton, 2003.

CHAPTER TWO

~

Das Reich

A visitor to Germany today seeking historical sites will be struck by the vast proliferation of castles and palaces. Few European countries are so overpopulated with medieval and baroque residences. In some regions they are so close together that a visitor can ascend one castle and from its heights have a clear view of one or two others. Today, in a large unified country, it is difficult to imagine that Germany was once chopped and divided into myriad small states, some quite tiny, but each with its own local aristocracy.

All sizable European nations dealt with regional differences. Even under an absolutist state like the France of Louis XIV, as many as a quarter of the French people did not speak French as a native tongue. The English, later British, monarchs ruled over restive Welsh, Cornish, Scottish, and Irish subjects. The Spanish monarchs did their best to suppress the independence-minded Catalans and Basques. Yet in each of these cases, the trend was steadily toward centralization of royal power and the creation of a unitary state. Unlike other large nationalities of western Europe, Germany did not develop an obvious political or social center point: no Paris, London, or Madrid. For centuries, this regional and local subdivision was the defining characteristic of German political and economic life.

The Second Great Migration

Germany as we know it was created by a wave of settlement pushing east from the Rhineland in the wake of Charlemagne's conquests. This process lasted roughly three centuries, from the early 800s to the early 1100s. By the time it waned, a large population of people speaking dialects or derivatives of Old High German or Old Saxon had settled across all of present-day Germany, Austria, and most of Switzerland, plus Bohemia (the present-day Czech Republic), northern Poland, Lithuania, and many regions of the Balkans. This second "Great Migration" came largely at the expense of local tribal peoples, as well as the Slavs, whose various nationalities were either subjugated and became ethnic minorities or were pushed farther to the east.

Regional differences were important. People in the mountains of Austria spoke very differently from people on the coastal plains of Pomerania. Centuries later, historians gave labels to these different languages, giving them names like Low German, Middle High German, Old Saxon, and so on. But in most regions people spoke some version of a language they gradually began to call *Teutsch*. (The word evolved from an ancient Germanic word for "common" or "folk.") And as the centuries passed they began to refer to themselves as Teutsche people, and the lands of all the Teutsch-speaking peoples collectively as Teutschland. And thus although Germans were always divided by strong dialects, Germany, in the modern spelling and pronunciation *Deutschland*, is one of those rare nations named after a language, and the German people, *die Deutschen*, are literally "the speakers of Deutsch."

Historians disagree on when Germany truly became a separate entity apart from the Frankish empire. Charlemagne had apparently considered splitting his realm among several sons, but in the end he outlived most of his possible direct heirs and thus the whole empire passed to his son Louis (in German *Ludwig*). The new emperor was unable to control the aristocracy of his sprawling empire, who neither feared nor respected him as they had his father. His tenure was plagued by rebellions, frontier wars with the Slavs and other tribes, arguments with the pope, and full-scale civil war. It is not surprising, then, that from early in his reign Louis began to plan for the eventual breakup of the empire by dividing it among his three sons. Upon his death in 840 the conflicts continued for three years until settled in 843 by the Treaty of Verdun. The Carolingian state was subdivided for the first time.

A glance at the Verdun settlement reveals the creation of what will become France. And it shows a German state in the east. The fate of the middle zone, stretching from Holland through the Rhineland and into Italy, is less clear. But Verdun was only the first in what proved to be a series of divisions. By the 860s the Carolingian heirs were at war, and the borders of their kingdoms, as well as the control of the regions within those kingdoms, were in flux.

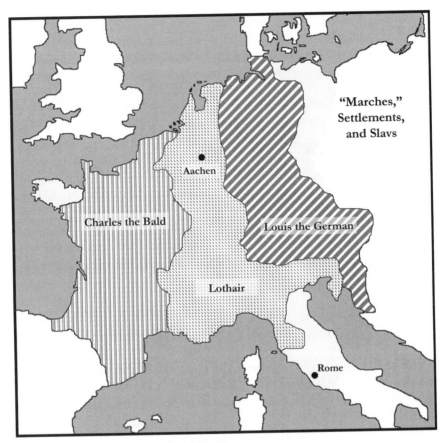

Figure 2.1.   The Treaty of Verdun, 843 AD

The next century of western European history is a bewildering tale of inheritance wars: struggles with Islamic states in the Mediterranean, with Slavic states in the east, with the Vikings from the north, and with the Magyars in central Europe. Average people in much of Europe lived in perpetual fear of violence and the hardships of war. This period, however, was also crucial for the formation of Germany, as the first large German states emerged: Bavaria in the south, Saxony in the north, Thüringia and Swabia in the center, and Carinthia, which eventually became Austria, in the eastern Alps. In almost every case, these states emerged due to aristocratic family conflicts, split inheritances, and/or war. And the subdivision of Germany was just getting started.

The popes went on crowning "Roman" emperors, usually from the descendants of Charlemagne who ruled over that portion of his old empire that included Italy. By the late ninth century, however, conflict raged over control of both Italy and the title of emperor. In Germany a similar struggle developed over the concept of kingship, with several men attempting—almost always unsuccessfully—to assert control over all the German states, from their basis of power in one of those states. A number of local rulers thus tried to become "King of Germany," and some of them also had ambitions to become the "Roman" emperor. The first ruler to succeed, unifying a German kingdom in fact as well as in title, was Otto I of Saxony. By the 950s he had not only subdued the German lands but also defeated the Magyars and stabilized the frontiers. With the imperial title still in turmoil, Otto married into an Italian branch of the imperial family and laid claim to the Roman crown. In 962 the pope conceded, and thus Otto "the Great" became the first man since Charlemagne to rule nearly all the German-speaking peoples under the title Roman Emperor.

Holy Roman Empire

The institution that shaped German politics and society for almost a millennium had an improbable name. The Holy Roman Empire, according to the French philosopher Voltaire, was neither holy nor Roman, and was not much of an empire. However, by the time the great Enlightenment author made this witty observation, the *Holy Roman Empire of the German Nation* had been an integral element of German life for nine centuries. For most Germans, it had always been simply *das Reich*, "the Empire."

Otto the Great is generally acknowledged to be the first German emperor (in German: *Kaiser*). That is, he was the first person to combine the concept of a "King of Germany" with "Emperor of the Romans." This unity between his secular role as king and his religious role as an emperor who defended the Church is the reason that the Reich was a "Holy" Roman Empire. For much of its existence—certainly for most of the Middle Ages—the Reich was troubled by this split personality. The relationship between an emperor and a pope was always complicated, usually tense, and occasionally violent.

The Reich evolved very differently from the emerging kingdoms in the rest of Europe. First, the Reich was a kind of political superstructure that rested on top of existing states; it did not replace them. For example, a ruler of Bavaria was still a sovereign ruler of Bavaria, with all the rights and powers that implies, except that Bavaria was a part of the Reich, with some additional responsibilities to the emperor as a result.

Second, over the centuries the types of different states within the Reich diversified as their numbers increased. There were duchies, grand duchies, principalities, counties, free imperial cities, landgravates and margravates, imperial estates, orders, and a variety of Church lands. In many but not all of these cases, these entities were grouped into regional "circles" that dealt with some administrative questions. But fundamentally, each and every state of the Reich was a fully sovereign entity, with the rights to make its own currency, laws, tolls, weights and measures, and so on.

Examples of States in the Reich

Everyone knows that a duchy is ruled by a duke and county by a count, but some other terms may be more obscure or lost in translation:

Free imperial city: A large number of cities were fully independent states, particularly many of the port cities in the north.

Margravate: This was a county whose ruling family had no feudal obligations to any other higher families, only directly to the emperor. A margrave (from the old word "mark," meaning military border region) also had certain military rights and responsibilities from the emperor.

Imperial estate: This was a single family with its castle or manor house and a small amount of land. These families were later referred to as "free imperial knights."

Orders: In the Middle Ages a number of knightly orders held land (sometimes quite large territories) and acted as sovereign states: the Teutonic Knights, for example, or the Knights of St. John.

Third, the emperor was not an inherited position; he was elected. There were a limited number of *electoral* states in the Reich, and the ruler of each was known as an *elector*. The number of electors rose and fell through the centuries, from as few as six voting members to more than a dozen. The electors did not necessarily represent the largest, wealthiest, or most powerful states of the Reich, but rather the most well-connected families, many of whom were represented in church positions (the Archbishop of Trier, for example, was an elector). Consequently, in order to win election, a certain amount of deal-making had to take place, thus limiting an emperor's freedom of action.

Finally, the Catholic Church was intimately involved in Reich politics. This was certainly not unique to Germany; every king of medieval Europe had to deal with the pope and his representatives in powerful positions in each kingdom. But the fragmented nature of the Reich, and the "holy" nature of the emperor's job description, reflected a more complex relationship with Rome than in any other place. Because the component states of Germany were so numerous and included so many Church-owned lands, the Church had innumerable ways to interfere in German politics. And because an emperor was only truly legitimate with the sanction of the pope (not because he had inherited his job from a long-standing dynasty), a German emperor was more vulnerable to papal control than any king in Europe. Indeed, an emperor was not an emperor until his election had been certified by the pope, and for several centuries new emperors traveled to Rome to make it official under the pope's hand.

The Reich did produce ruling dynasties. At various points in its history, certain families produced one emperor after another. But those families were well aware that it never had to be so. A politically savvy family could control the imperial throne if it knew how to use imperial politics to its advantage, but there was no guarantee.

There was very little an emperor could do to prevent the increasing fragmentation of Germany, and in fact imperial intervention often made problems worse. German states kept subdividing as a result of marriages, treaties, conflicts, and complex inheritances. By the time of the Renaissance, there were over three hundred German states in the Reich, some of which were minuscule. And the ongoing pattern of political disassembly and reassembly meant that many of these states had bizarre and noncontiguous borders, with one family ruling of bits of land widely scattered in separate pieces.

None of these phenomena were unique to the German lands. One could find in France or England or Sweden, for example, powerful extended families who ruled large collections of territory in various places, or special abbeys or knightly orders who controlled castles and land and answered to the pope. But in most of Europe the trend was to bring these entities under the control of a single king and kingdom. An English king, for example, had to juggle all of these factors in his own domestic politics. But a German emperor was at the mercy of them because ultimately he could only have been elected as emperor in the first place by being acceptable to the status quo. The Reich reinforced disunity. It was—at best—a confederation, not truly an empire.

A Holy Roman Emperor had the power to summon an imperial army (*Reichsarmee*) if there was a threat to the Reich as a whole. Each state had its quota of troops it had to contribute in such a case, and for some of these

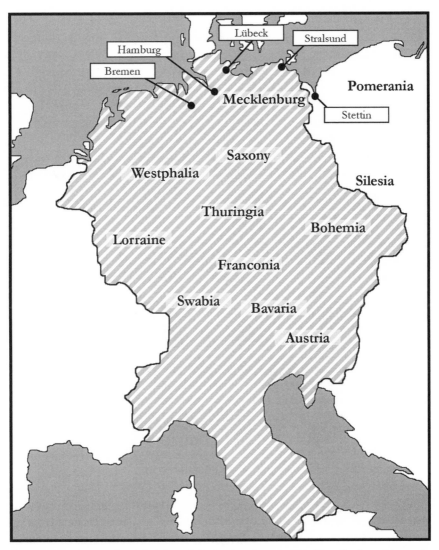

Figure 2.2. The Medieval Reich and the Major German-Speaking Regions: Names in boxes point to major Hanseatic cities.

tiny states the numbers are comical. (The free city of Pfullendorf at one point had to contribute precisely eight soldiers to the imperial army.) Needless to say, with its forces drawn from three hundred separate local governments, the Reichsarmee was generally not a very effective force. It was, however, a highly politicized army, because the emperor had the right to call it up

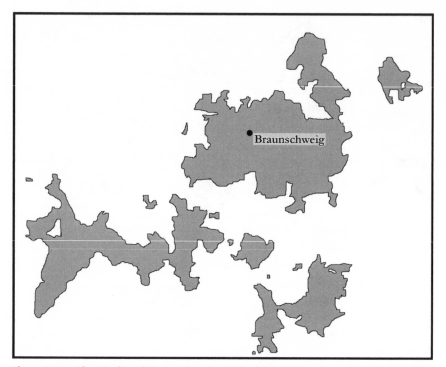

Figure 2.3. The Duchy of Braunschweig-Wolfenbüttel: Like so many other German states, this one owed its existence to a family feud, this time involving a Saxon duke and the emperor himself. The House of Welfen had split into several branches by the fourteenth century, one of which ruled this duchy: a sort of constellation or splashes of territory, some only a few miles long, spread out across north-central Germany for more than seventy miles. This actually made Braunschweig-Wolfenbüttel not only a fairly large state by Reich standards, but also abnormally compact. Some German families ruled territories separated by hundreds of miles.

against an *internal* threat as well as an external one. Thus, German soldiers could be asked to fight against other Germans if one state, or a group of states, was deemed to be grossly out of line. This almost always involved a German-German war with foreign powers meddling on both sides.

The Reich had an assembly of sorts, the Reichstag. All member states were theoretically represented, but in fact the many arcane rules meant that certain rulers had a lot more power than others. The Reichstag was divided between secular and religious leaders, as well as between the aristocratic status of families. The lower-ranking families could only vote as part of their "college." (All the small states in one region collectively had one vote, as a region.) This was a moot point in many cases, since many of these little towns or families could not have afforded a full-time representative at the Reichstag even if they had been allowed to have one.

The Reichstag was supposed to function as a check on the emperor's power, and in fact the Reichstag regarded itself as more powerful than the emperor, because at the top of the Reichstag were the electors who had voted this emperor into power in the first place. But we should not think of the Reichstag as anything like a modern legislative body. It did not represent "the people" in any meaningful way. Instead, as with so many other things in the Reich, it represented the fractious nature of German aristocratic politics and regional rivalries.

The organized chaos of the Reich was not wholly objectionable. In fact, it persisted because it served the interests of most German aristocrats. The strong princes didn't want to be dominated by a strong emperor, and the weaker aristocrats didn't want to be dominated by the strong princes. The empire served the purpose of protecting tiny states from aggression and domination by the larger ones. (Whether this was good in the long run for Germany is another matter, but it was obviously good from the point of view of the small states at the time.) A low-ranking nobleman under threat from some larger state could appeal to the emperor for help via the imperial courts (which were appointed by, and usually controlled by, the emperor himself), and the emperor was usually eager to cut down an aggressive prince. But the emperor had to tread carefully, because the powerful princes in turn dominated the Reichstag.

Between the eleventh and thirteenth centuries, many powerful families established dynasties that would reign over their regions of Germany down to the modern age. It was the high water mark of the power of knights and princes. The popes called them to the Crusades, from which many returned with wealth, fame, and new power. The increasing wealth and power of the aristocrats can be seen by the boom in castle construction of these years. Many of the famous surviving fortresses and residences of medieval Germany date from this period when local lords asserted themselves. A German aristocratic family usually used the preposition "von" to denote their class status, followed by the name of their castle or land. For example, the "von Wittelsbach" family, who ruled Bavaria for centuries, derived their name from the castle of Wittelsbach.

The German emperors were either weak or tried and failed to be strong in the face of Church or regional resistance. The most spectacular conflict was the Investiture Controversy of the late eleventh century, in

Figure 2.4. **"The Cat": One of the many well-preserved castles along the middle Rhine.**

which Emperor Henry IV tried to unseat a pope and get imperial control over the appointment of church officials in the Reich. He failed on both counts and ended up performing a humiliating penance, begging the pope for forgiveness and for a lifting of the excommunication he had placed on the emperor. There were a few powerful emperors in this period. Frederick I "Barbarossa" (red beard) was undoubtedly the most famous, although his power arguably derived more from his foreign diplomacy and his victories in foreign wars than from any inherent political cachet at home. Indeed, his skill at settling disputes between warring noblemen demonstrated that the German emperor was at best a broker of power, not the true source of power.

The final limiting factor upon a German emperor was the fact that he, too, was a nobleman, representing some region of the Reich and elected by his peers. The bottom line for most emperors was the survival and prosperity of their own ancestral lands. A king of Austria, for example, who became emperor was still and foremost a king of Austria. He knew that Austria was his true base of support and was the thing that he had to protect and nourish if all else failed. He was never truly just a "German" monarch.

Von? Von der? Zu? Zum?

German aristocrats occasionally used other prepositions, especially if a split family inheritance or complicated situation required more specificity (such as one branch of the family owning the castle while a cousin's branch owned some or all of the land around it). One might see the preposition zu or zum, instead of or in addition to von, such as the name of the German defense minister at the time of this writing: Karl-Theodor von und zu Guttenberg.

The German Middle Ages

Germany had a good Middle Ages. Agriculture flourished as huge new areas of land came under cultivation. Population boomed, doubling in the four-teenth century alone, increasing the wealth and productivity of many areas. Professional guilds spread across the land, raising the standards of quality for goods and offering protection to craftsmen and their families. Hundreds of convents and monasteries proliferated, offering employment and education to thousands of men and women, many of whom then lived lives of public service or scholarship. The first universities appeared as Europeans took their first tentative steps out of the Dark Ages and toward an era of science and learning.

And Germany had a terrible Middle Ages. Plague was widespread, culmi-nating in the Black Death of the fourteenth century, in which many German towns virtually ceased to exist. Vikings continued to thrash the cities of the North Sea and Baltic coastlines, wrecking havoc and shutting down trade. Princes fought each other and emperors struggled against popes as wars tore up the countryside and consumed human lives and property. The popes of the crusading era declared open season upon Jews, resulting—at best—in their being forced into ghettos, and often resulting in torture and killing. The average person's life continued to be hard, often hungry, and full of fear and superstition.

We have some sense of the intellectual atmosphere of medieval Germany, and especially of the norms for men and women, from the remarkable career of a twelfth-century nun. Hildegard of Bingen was arguably one of the most important thinkers of the German middle ages, and certainly one of the most significant female figures of the entire era. Born to an aristocratic family, Hildegard had religious visions from childhood, and entered a convent as a teenager. She was in her forties when she became *Magistra* (mother superior) of the convent, at which point she also began to have a new and dramatic series of religious experiences, including visions of Christ standing over her, bathing her in light.

Hildegard of Bingen lived to be seventy-three, a remarkably long life in that era, and the second half of her life was a career of astonishing productivity. She wrote extensively about religion, morality, art, medicine, and natural science. She composed a large body of devotional music for Catholic worship. She compiled an encyclopedia of the plants and animals of Germany, including information on uses of herbs and other natural medicines. She learned several languages and even developed an alternative alphabet system. Her huge volume of letters includes regular correspondence with several popes, church figures, and political leaders.

Most controversially, Hildegard wrote on questions of gender, sin, and sexuality: taboo subjects, obviously, for a woman in the employ of the Church. (Aside from condemning adultery and premarital sex, she specifically condemned lesbianism, which has of course intrigued scholars who wondered how commonplace it must have been in medieval society to draw her attention in the first place.) She opposed the Church's official doctrine that because of the original sin of Eve, women were inherently more sinful than men, and thus by default the guilty party in any case of adultery.

Hildegard was also one of the more outspoken anti-Semites of her day. Convinced that Jews were the enemies of Christ, she wrote that they were conspiring with Satan to bring an end to the world. She even claimed that the Garden of Eden was not a Hebrew, but rather a Germanic Christian creation story. Hildegard may have been an intellectual of genius status, but like many Catholic leaders of her day, in the midst of the Crusades, she advocated the killing of Jews and Muslims as the holy mission of all Christians. That was a belief that was widely shared in much of western and central Europe at the time.

The social development of the German lands was not very different from the rest of medieval western Europe. Towns began to grow as centers of manufacturing and commerce. In the towns could be found "free" peasants: common folk who owned little plots of land and/or houses and who did not owe service to any lord. Townsfolk, with their greater degree of social and economic freedom, began to develop differently from peasants in the countryside and soon thought of themselves as not being peasants at all, but people of a different, higher class. The towns began to develop a money-based economy, using silver or copper coins or, much more rarely, gold. The structure of the Reich affected the development of German towns. Generally, the farther north or west that one traveled, the more free cities one found. The diffused nature of the Reich encouraged this type of tiny city-state. To call them cities is to stretch the meaning of the word for modern readers. Most were smaller than the average college campus today, and were home to only a few thousand people. But by the standards of the Middle Ages, they were indeed cities, and thus important centers of commerce, where regional fairs were held and where craftsmen brought their goods to sell and trade.

In the countryside, the lords still ruled the land, with the huge majority of peasants renting from them and working small plots. These families were usually in debt to the lord—a debt that was passed down from generation to generation—and thus unable to leave, or unable to refuse the lord whatever service he desired. These were the serfs that we find all over western and central Europe in these centuries: the large majority of the population, in fact, was locked into basic agricultural labor.

The aristocrats in their castles usually did not have very much cash. Their wealth was based upon their land, and most of their transactions were done *in kind*; that is, in agricultural produce. So a natural tension existed between them and the free peasants in the towns. The townsfolk needed food and animal products, and the lords needed cash and manufactured products, but neither one liked dealing with the other. Aristocrats, in particular, resented having to bargain with peasants for any reason and were suspicious of giving up any of their power to these free peasants in the towns.

In general, the Middle Ages saw a struggle between towns and "princes"— a word which could mean any number of powerful aristocrats ruling hereditary lands and possessing armies. The fear that the townspeople had of the princes is obvious from the existence of the thick walls that every free town built to defend itself. These walls—many of which still stand today, or are at least still partly visible—were not simply to protect Germans from the Vikings or other invaders. Most of the danger came from other German rulers, particularly the rural princes who wanted to conquer and annex the towns and their wealth into their own territory.

For their own protection, the towns often joined together in "leagues" that were usually regional in nature. There were, for instance, a Rhenish League, a Swabian League, and a Lusatian League. The Swiss League was the most successful, ultimately resisting the power of all the princes and establishing a confederation of free towns that evolved into the cantons of modern-day Switzerland.

The largest, wealthiest, and ultimately most influential league of cities was based not on a particular region, but rather upon seagoing commerce.

Considering the size of its interior, Germany has a relatively small and narrow coastline. Only the north of the country touches the sea, and then only touches restricted waters (the North Sea and the Baltic Sea), rather than open ocean like the coasts of Portugal, Spain, or France. However, most of the major rivers in Germany flow to the north, draining from the highlands in southern Germany and ultimately to the sea. Thus a German city did not have to be on the coastline in order to participate in seagoing trade. Unfortunately, that also meant that all of these towns were vulnerable to the attacks of the Vikings.

Because of the Vikings, German free cities on the coast and on rivers began in the 1200s to pool their resources and efforts for collective defense. By the early thirteenth century, these cities were calling their confederation the Hanseatic League (*der Hansebund*), often simply "the Hanse," from the root word meaning trade. By organizing together for defense they also organized a common set of rules and customs for trade and navigation, and within a few decades the Hanse had developed a monopoly on seagoing trade in the North Sea and the Baltic. The Hanseatic cogs were versatile ships; they rarely drew more than six feet at the waterline, making them useful as riverboats as well as seagoing vessels. Although cities in the Hanse did have disputes with each other, they were generally able to cooperate. In the fourteenth century, the Hanse fought a war against the Danes, which they won, thus drawing them into closer cooperation.

And so yet another structure emerged within the Reich. Although most Hanseatic cities were members of the Reich, not all of them were. Some were in Holland or Poland or Scandinavia. In theory, the emperor was their protector, but in reality, because the Reich had no navy or merchant marine, the Hanse effectively filled both of these roles. Yet, as with so many things in German history, the Hanse were not a clearly unified structure. There were dozens of Hanseatic cities, each with its own voice. For much but not all of its history, the Hanse's leading city was Lübeck. But it was not a "capital" city. The Hanse was a *league*, not a nation, not a state.

If anything, the creation of the Hanseatic League caused more diversification in German society and politics. The Hanse was a league dominated by small city-states. (Kolberg, in Pomerania, was a typical example: a city of about four thousand people, give or take another thousand who might be coming and going by ship at any moment, plus half a dozen little hamlets as suburbs in about a ten-mile radius.) Hanseatic cities were small enough that everybody knew everybody else, and government was local and direct. Many of them evolved into republics, with an elected senate and a sort of chamber of commerce that ran the city. Because they had no large areas of farmland, aristocracy was limited or even nonexistent. People rose to high rank because of their wealth from trade, not their land or inheritance. The economies of these cities were based on retailing and wholesaling. That brought them into contact with the wider world, with the goods and people of other nations, which in turn made them more liberal and worldly than farming folk in the interior of the country, who saw little change and rarely encountered strangers or new ideas from abroad.

The Hanse cities of northern Germany evolved a different worldview that tended to be more democratic, more liberal, less religious, and less militaristic. (War, after all, was usually bad for business.) Even though most Hanse cities had a clique of wealthy families who tended to run the place generation after generation, nonetheless it was possible and even common for "new money" to arrive and for families to make and lose fortunes. These cities were therefore much more socially diverse and saw a great deal more change than the rest of Germany. To a certain extent, these stereotypes have persisted to this day: the northerners are perceived as liberal and money-oriented; the southerners as conservative, more religious, and tradition-oriented.

What did it mean to be German in the Middle Ages? Was there in fact a sense of German nationality or identity emerging in these early centuries? The German word for patriotism is *Vaterlandsliebe*, literally "love of the fatherland." (Centuries later, Germans adopted the French word and concept,

Figure 2.5. A Treaty between the Hanseatic League and the Kingdom of Denmark: Note the profusion of wax seals and signatures at the bottom. Doing business or diplomacy with the Reich and its institutions was never simple!

and thus began to speak of *Patriotismus*.) Because of the strange overlapping loyalties of Germans, identity was very complicated. Average people didn't move around much, so their idea of patriotism was usually tied to their town and/or their local ruling family. Linguistic differences also shaped people's ideas of their nationality and homeland. German dialects could be very different, to the point where northerners and southerners could barely understand each other. Two southerners (a Bavarian and a Swabian, for example) might be able to understand most of each other's dialects, but they would both consider someone from Lübeck, a northern Hanse city, to be a "foreigner," and they might not think of that person's speech as even belonging to the same language.

There was also *Reichspatriotismus*: the loyalty people felt toward the Empire. The emperor could summon all the princes to contribute soldiers and money in time of war, and people were expected to show their patriotism in this way, too. Men from one little town who were conscripted into some prince's army and marched off to fight a war against the Swiss, for instance, came home with a new sense for how big and diverse the German lands were and an idea of the extent of the Reich. And later, when the Reformation split Germany between Catholics and Protestants, a religious patriotism developed, so that a Rhinelander (probably Catholic) who had nothing else in common with a Bavarian might feel a kind of unifying Germanness with his fellow Catholics in Bavaria that he wouldn't feel with Hessians, who might be much closer geographically but who practiced a different religion.

But in spite of all these competing loyalties, a sense of being German did in fact begin to emerge by the end of the Middle Ages and the beginnings of the Renaissance. The concept of being German is by definition an identity associated with speaking a certain language, not simply being from a particular place. During the Renaissance and Reformation, two crucial developments ensured that Germans would associate themselves with a single language and thus a national identity: the invention of a printed German script and the creation of a German Bible.

Suggested Reading

Arnold, Benjamin. *Princes and Territories in Medieval Germany*. Cambridge: Cambridge University Press, 1991.

Barraclough, Geoffrey. *The Origins of Modern Germany*. London: W. W. Norton, 1984.

Cantor, Norman. *The Civilization of the Middle Ages*. New York: Harper Collins, 1993.

Fuhrmann, Horst. *Germany in the High Middle Ages*. Cambridge: Cambridge University Press, 1986.

Jeep, John, ed. *Medieval Germany: An Encyclopedia*. New York: Routledge, 2001.

Reynolds, Susan. *Fiefs and Vassals: The Medieval Evidence Reinterpreted*. Oxford: Oxford University Press, 1994.

Todd, Malcolm. *The Early Germans*. Malden, MA: Wiley-Blackwell, 2004.

Wickham, Chris. *The Inheritance of Rome*. New York: Viking, 2009.

CHAPTER THREE

∼

Confessions

For most educated Americans, discussion of the European Renaissance generally brings to mind Italian inventors and scientists, Dutch master painters, and perhaps the England of Shakespeare and Queen Elizabeth I. Germany does not usually figure in the popular imagination as a place of Renaissance science or art. Yet the German contribution to this era was significant, and the Renaissance in turn changed Germans profoundly. We do not have the space, in a brief book such as this, to give this topic the full treatment it deserves. But this chapter will attempt to summarize the impact of the European Renaissance upon the Germans, and vice versa.

Gothic

As western Europeans began to improve the quality of their goods in the late Middle Ages, and especially as a few began to travel to wealthier regions like the Middle East and North Africa (partly because of the Crusades, and partly because of trade), advanced ideas and products began to enter European life along with an influx of metal coins. This benefited the relatively small class of "free peasants" who tended to live in towns and who preferred to do business using cash. Townspeople and their money could circulate more freely than aristocrats or serfs living in the country, whose wealth was based on the land and its products, and was therefore more static.

As some families began to thrive by importing and retailing goods from far-away places, they became the leading citizens in their towns. We still use a French word to describe them: *bourgeoisie*—literally, "town people." The German word is *Bürger*, meaning people who live in a *Burg*, or town—a word which came to mean simply "citizen." The bourgeoisie were helped by another development in the late Middle Ages: the emergence of an increasing number of landless peasants who traveled to towns looking for work. These people became the first real working class as we would understand that term: paid (in cash or other benefits) for their labor on behalf of some business.

As the prosperity of towns increased, wealthy bourgeois wanted larger homes and acquired a taste for expensive and beautiful things. Aristocrats soon followed, wanting to decorate and expand their estates. The Renaissance was probably the first time in a thousand years of European history that it was possible to make a living as an artist. We see such a dramatic flowering of art and architecture because there was finally a market for it, and competition inspired truly talented people to devote themselves to finding wealthy patrons who would be willing to pay for great works of art.

The European Renaissance began in the Italian cities and soon spread north. By the mid-1400s, much of central and western Europe was experiencing the changes brought by a new economy based on cash and credit. The bourgeoisie was never more than a very small minority in most places, but their role in brokering wealth to others meant that they had tremendous influence. The new wealth, for example, enabled new universities to appear, and old ones to expand and thrive, with the result that the Renaissance also became an era marked by intellectual and scientific achievement. That, in turn, caused many educated people to question old Catholic doctrines, resulting in furious controversies between science and faith on matters such as the shape of the earth and the cosmos, or the human anatomy.

The Renaissance is also regarded as the dawn of modern European literature, certainly assisted by a famous invention that began in Germany. Johannes Gutenberg was born to a wealthy bourgeois family in the city of Mainz on the eve of the 15th century. His father and most of his ancestors had been skilled metalworkers, and young Johannes became an accomplished goldsmith. It is not clear when he began working on the printing press, but most likely throughout his late thirties and early forties Gutenberg was experimenting with movable metal type and considering a major new business venture in printing. The fact that a businessman like him could expect to make a good living printing books tells us a lot about the increase in literacy during the Renaissance. It also tells us that foreign ideas (in this case printing itself as well as inexpensive paper, both from China) were now circulating among European thinkers and inventors.

Although nothing like a majority of people could yet read and write, Gutenberg believed that there was a sufficient customer base among the wealthy and educated. Gutenberg's printed Bible appeared in 1455, and indeed earned him enough money that various of his business partners sued him, believing he was not sharing the profits fairly. In fact Gutenberg barely broke even, but by the time he died, printing was a growth industry. It was also one of the great turning points in modern history, allowing Renaissance ideas to travel quickly and relatively cheaply across all of Europe, enabling new learning and study as well as the rapid spread of common information and of course money.

The German lands became, and for centuries remained, the most active marketplace of European printing and publishing. Within a generation of Gutenberg's death, most German cities had presses and multiple publishers. Printing and literacy evolved differently in the Reich than in much of western Europe. In many nations the capital city became the center of the publishing industry in that country. The huge majority of French books, for example, were published in Paris, the majority of English books in London, and so on. But Germany had no capital city. Instead, hundreds of German cities and towns evolved their own printing houses and markets. The disorganized nature of the Reich actually helped Germans to develop one of the highest literacy rates in Europe. Visitors from other places frequently commented upon the proliferation of libraries, book markets, and presses and the huge selection of newspapers and journals.

This profusion of printing also made literature in Germany more diverse and unpredictable than in other places. In France, for example, the centralization of the French printing industry in Paris made it easier for the government to control and censor books and periodicals. French writers who wanted to publish controversial works had to break the law or have them printed and distributed in secret. In the Reich, by contrast, it was easy to get around the local censorship in one's small state because somewhere, not too far away, there was most likely some other state or free city where the author could find a willing printer. German princes tried in vain for centuries to stifle the free press, but the huge variety of book printers and dealers made it almost impossible to do.

German type and script from centuries past is very distinctive in appearance and difficult for our modern eyes to read. Many people today misunderstand the multitude of different German script and type styles, and think of them all as a single "Gothic." But in fact German evolved its own cursive alphabet, very different from the Latin script used by the western European languages. Although the symbols were representative of Latin letters, many of them evolved from ancient runic (pre-Roman) writing, and others were organic to certain German regions.

Because the handwritten language was cursive, and so variable from region to region, it did not lend itself to a single typeface. Thus in the Renaissance the early German printers sought a new German typeset. They turned to a much older style of writing from the Middle Ages and based the typeface we have ever after thought of as Gothic upon the ninth-century handwritten texts of the Frankish Empire. Early German printing shows that the language was full of Latin words and idioms, which were printed in a completely different typeface to make them stand out as foreign. Thus educated Germans grew accustomed to no fewer than three alphabets simultaneously: the handwritten cursive, which was a unique alphabet; the Gothic typeface developed in the Renaissance; and the Latin alphabet in use in most other western European countries. To be literate in those days was therefore quite an accomplishment.

When Gutenberg printed his Bible, he did so in Latin. It was a faithful Vulgate (Catholic) text, to be used by Church officials and those wealthy and educated people who could afford their own private copy. Common folk did not read the Bible and indeed most had no idea what it contained, other than word-of-mouth stories they had learned in church and from local folklore. And when they attended Mass, they probably understood very little apart from the familiar rituals of the catechism, because common people could not understand Latin.

Gutenberg did print a few short German texts, apparently as early experiments, but there was not much money to be made printing in German. That was because German was considered by most educated people to be a peasants' language, variable by region and not suitable for upper-class discussion or religious services. Men (and it was only ever men) who received a university education during the Renaissance learned the classics of Greek and Latin in those languages.

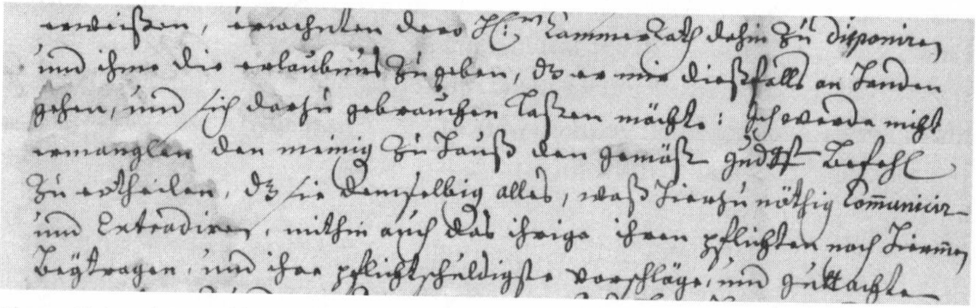

Figure 3.1. A Letter in German Script, Early Eighteenth Century. Used with permission of the Moravian Archives, Bethlehem, Pennsylvania.

From the Renaissance, and for centuries thereafter, one of the striking things about German history has been the ambivalent feeling that Germans have had toward their own language. Educated Germans have often expressed a sort of inferiority complex about the supposed roughness or ugliness of German speech, or the supposed awkwardness of its grammar. During the Renaissance, cultured Germans wrote and spoke Latin to each other in formal settings like a university. The Holy Roman Emperor Charles V, who ruled over a huge empire including Spain, parts of France, Holland, Italy, Germany, Hungary, and Croatia, supposedly quipped: "I speak Spanish to my priest, Italian to women, French to my ministers, and German to my horse." (It cannot be proven that he definitely said this, but it conveys a common sentiment.) By the time of the Enlightenment, French became the preferred language for German intellectuals, even in private letters to their own families. The Emperor Joseph II initially laughed at Mozart's suggestion of a grand opera performed in German; surely only a beautiful language like Italian was suitable for this art form. Prussia's most famous king, Frederick the Great, always spoke French at court and even when relaxing in private and only slipped into German when he was angry, or when shouting commands at his soldiers. For centuries, one way that educated Germans showed off their education was to insert foreign words and expressions into their daily speech, first Latin, then French, and now American English.

This is why the great scholarly and scientific works of the German Renaissance appear overwhelmingly in Latin. The brilliant mathematician and astronomer Johannes Kepler, for example, from a respectable south German bourgeois family, enjoyed a spectacular career in several important German cities, including working directly for the Holy Roman Emperor. Yet all of his groundbreaking works on light, vision, and of course the planets and the solar system, were available only in Latin: the language of intellectuals. The geographer Martin Behaim of Nürnberg, who created the first spherical globe, covered it with place-names written in Latin. The great German Renaissance painter Albrecht Dürer was an exception, specifically because he made his fortune as an artist without ever having a classical education. Later in life, as a wealthy and admired master, he wrote in common German, although his two books on geometry and anatomy are full of Latin idioms and references to classical texts.

Revolution

In the first two decades of the sixteenth century, the German lands—like much of Europe—were ablaze with excitement over the extraordinary discoveries being made in the Americas. Books appeared, filled with fantastic stories of monsters and half-naked Amazon women and rivers of liquid gold. A handful of Germans did actually get to see some of the New World, taking part in the missions of exploration and conquest, but for the most part Germans experienced this crucially important chapter of history as spectators, and distant ones at that.

Why didn't the Germans participate in the European discovery and conquest of the Americas? Why, for instance, didn't the Hanseatic League send their ships to the New World?

Germany is of course awkwardly situated for such a mission. Not only were German ports several days more distant, but any German ships would have had to pass through the English Channel first, and thus any German conflict with England, Holland, or France would have shut down communication with America. But fundamentally the problem was one of money and government. Most of the European nations that carved up the Americas did so as part of a nationally directed mission. The Spanish and Portuguese monarchies, for example, saw to the project firsthand. The English and Dutch set up "chartered companies" with heavy government subsidies. But the German Reich was in no position to order anybody to America, nor to fund them nor to provide the ships. And what would a German emperor have done with an American colony, anyway? *Whose* colony would it have been? The emperor's, personally? A Spanish king could claim Mexico as literally his own property, thus also meaning Spain's, but an elected German emperor had no such right. The only organization within the Reich that might have mounted voyages of discovery or conquest was the Hanse, but they represented not one ruler who could give commands, but rather dozens of free city-states, each of which wanted a stake in any joint venture.

The European conquest of the Americas affected the German lands in other ways. The sudden influx of gold and silver coins flooding the European economy caused German markets to boom and bust, just as they did everywhere else. New wealth meant new and sometimes dramatic rises and falls of new power centers and families. These were times of change, when conservative people had to rethink old superstitions about a flat earth, and new discoveries seemed to justify the controversial ideas of scientists. Intelligent people felt emboldened that old institutions could be changed and improved, and the printing press meant that ideas could travel across boundaries relatively easily and quickly.

The Roman Catholic Church had been fighting a losing battle against the unwelcome ideas of the Renaissance for much of the fifteenth century. The Church still commanded the loyalty of the huge majority of simple folk, who were rural, traditional, and usually illiterate. And it generally had the support of the aristocracy, who often filled many of the church positions. But the rise of a new middle class, a new economic system, and new science and philosophy was deeply troubling. And while it faced these theological challenges, Rome also faced an ongoing financial crisis. Although it had immense resources, the church was often short of cash. For at least three generations it had been selling church offices to anyone who could pay, a practice that offended those faithful who considered a church career out of true devotion. And, infamously, the church began hiring traveling preachers to frighten people into buying indulgences, which were icons or certificates that supposedly earned the purchaser a remittance on past sins, so as to lessen the soul's time in purgatory.

There were therefore people of strong faith, who had been educated in Renaissance Europe, who had many serious grievances against church practices. The most famous and arguably most important of these men was Martin Luther.

Luther came from a modest background of free peasants in a mining town in central Germany. His parents had high hopes for the career of their obviously extraordinary son, but instead of pursuing a law degree, Martin became a monk. He received his doctorate at the age of twenty-nine and became well known among religious scholars in the city of Wittenberg, where he was employed by the university and sponsored by the Elector of Saxony, Prince Frederick. Wittenberg was not only a center for religious study, but also a center for pilgrimage, since the Elector Frederick had put together, at great expense, a collection of relics from the Holy Land. These ranged from the highly improbable (bits of the cradle and clothes of the Baby Jesus) to the impossible (mother's milk from the Virgin Mary) to the macabre (remnants of boys killed by King Herod).

Martin Luther's lectures in Wittenberg were often controversial, and he seems to have been a person whose strong and trenchant opinions always sparked debate. It was in that spirit of debate and controversy in April 1517 that he wrote *The Ninety-Five Theses*, a very strongly worded list of grievances against Catholic church practices and corruption. According to legend, he nailed them to the church door in Wittenberg, calling for a public discussion.

The *Theses* spoke out explicitly against indulgences, which would not have been extremely controversial by itself, given that so many people felt the same way. Luther was also motivated by the more immediate offense of the sale of Church offices. In one well-known case, Prince Albert of Brandenburg, who was already a bishop in two different places, was trying to buy himself a third bishopric in Mainz with an outrageously large bribe to the pope. Though Luther criticized obvious corruption and malfeasance, what made the *Theses* shocking was the frankly angry and disrespectful tone he used against many elements of Catholic dogma and against the pope himself. At best, he was telling the pope how to do his job. At worst, he was a flagrant heretic.

Luther printed his *Ninety-Five Theses* in Latin because he wanted to attract fellow scholars. But it was soon translated into German and circulated and began to attract people of all walks of life. Over the next three years, Luther emphasized that his desire was to reform the church, not to divide it, but of course the debate he had started was proving extremely divisive. Many people, even those who agreed with his grievances, simply could not abide the disrespectful tone of his writing. And Luther made no effort to conciliate; he continued to write and publish in the same vein. The Elector Frederick of Saxony, although himself a devout Catholic, was nonetheless determined to protect Luther, and advised him not to answer the papal demands to come to Rome and recant his heresies.

In 1521 the pope excommunicated Martin Luther. The young Holy Roman Emperor, Charles V, decided to assert imperial authority by summoning an Imperial Diet (a special meeting of the Reichstag in which the emperor himself presided over the agenda) in the city of Worms. Luther, summoned to appear at Worms before the emperor, knew that he had reached the point of no return. He apologized for any offense his harsh tone had caused, but famously refused to recant his beliefs, and according to tradition concluded with: "Here I stand. I can't do otherwise. God help me. Amen."

It is very likely that the emperor would have authorized Luther's arrest and execution (probably by burning at the stake, the fate of many other famous religious martyrs in the previous century and in the decades to come). But imperial procedure called for deliberation, and Charles—a young and very new emperor—was concerned not to appear rash even though he had probably already made his decision. The evening after his famous speech, Luther departed for Wittenberg. As he traveled, he was kidnapped by men who revealed that they were sent by the Elector Frederick, Luther's protector, to take him into hiding.

Emperor Charles V condemned Luther to death as an outlaw, ordered the burning of all his writings, and promised execution to anyone who sheltered him. Charles, whose realm included not only the German Reich, but Spain, Burgundy, and much of Italy as well as the rapidly expanding empire in the New World, had concluded that Luther represented an existential threat not only to the unity of the Reich, but to his personal authority as a ruler over a huge swathe of Christendom. The Protestant Reformation had begun.

The New German

Frederick's men took Luther to the Wartburg castle, an immense fortress on a mountaintop overlooking the city of Eisenach. There, in a suite of rooms in the upper floors of the castle, Luther spent a year in almost constant work. He wrote a collection of hymns, many of which are part of Protestant Christian services to this day. He wrote essays and smuggled out instructions to friends across the Reich. And most crucially, he had decided to write a new translation of the Holy Bible.

It is impossible to exaggerate the importance of this act. Not only was the concept of a Bible for common people a revolutionary change in itself, but Luther had decided to break with eleven centuries of Catholic practice by rendering the entire text in German. He chose a very simple and clear construction that made the scripture accessible to people in any region of Germany. Luther's Bible did more than any other book by any author in history to create the modern German language.

Unlike English, which tends to use the simple past perfect tense for speech (I made, you ran, she carried, etc.), German and other continental European languages tend to prefer the compound past progressive tense (I have made, you have run, she has carried, etc.) for speech, particularly among educated people. Luther, however, often rendered the words of God and the scripture as dramatically simple and direct speech.

> *Am Anfang schuf Gott Himmel und Erde*
> *Und die Erde war wüst und Leer*
> *und es war finster auf der Tiefe*
> *Und der Geist Gottes schwebte auf dem Wasser*
> *Und Gott sprach: Es werde Licht!*
> *Und es war Licht.*

> In the beginning God created heaven and earth
> And the Earth was barren and empty
> and there was darkness upon the deep
> And the spirit of God moved across the water
> And God spoke: There shall be Light!
> And there was light.

The Lutheran Bible was ultimately the work of a half dozen collaborators close to Luther, who helped him with the Hebrew text of the Old Testament (the New Testament is almost totally Luther's work alone). Luther remained a sort of editor in chief of the project for more than twenty years, making several important decisions about inclusion or exclusion of certain texts, different from the Catholic Vulgate.

The style in which he wrote, the constructions he chose for famous passages, and the simple fact that this was a Bible meant to be read and recited by common people in their own language meant that the Luther Bible shaped the German language in a way that no one could have imagined. It eventually came into every Protestant German home, and eventually even a number of Catholic homes as well, for although Catholics continued to hold Mass in Latin, many nonetheless wanted to read the scriptures for themselves in their own language.

When Luther emerged from the Wartburg in the spring of 1522, he found that events had already accelerated beyond his control. Local preachers across Germany were building upon his message, with or without invoking his name, and starting movements of protest against the Catholic church and its officials and practices. In many communities this meant violence as people settled scores with neighbors or acted upon rumors of impending punishments or arrest. Some groups believed that the Second Coming of Christ was at hand, and that the time had come for a complete upheaval of all social norms and laws.

The movement we think of as the Protestant Reformation was launched by Martin Luther, but often not directed by him, despite his repeated efforts to do so. He preached sermons on tolerance, but those sermons could only be heard by a small audience. He wrote pamphlets on theology and Christian behavior, but those pamphlets initially reached only the small percentage of the population that could buy and read them. Luther managed to restore order in his own community in Wittenberg, but the "Peasants' War" soon broke out in southwestern Germany as radical Protestants attacked churches and monasteries and rejected the authority of their rulers. It became obvious to Luther that he could no longer control a reform movement of the Catholic church. He would have to create his own church.

Less than a decade after he nailed up his *Ninety-Five Theses*, Martin Luther had founded a new branch of Christianity. In some ways, it was obviously derived from Catholicism: the use of a Mass, with the Eucharist, a catechism, and the ritual of baptism. All these things convinced many Protestants that Luther had not gone far enough, and new movements emerged in the Reich and elsewhere, under new leaders. In other ways, however, Luther's changes were radical departures: a married clergy, a Bible in the local language that people could read and study, the freedom of churches to modify the rituals as they saw fit, and the absence of the administrative superstructure that had characterized Catholicism.

Luther was very fortunate that the Holy Roman Emperor, Charles V, saw the Reich as only one of his many realms and thus could not devote his full attention to it. Indeed, Charles's attention was most immediately drawn to the war against the Ottoman Empire, whose brilliant sultan, Suleiman the Magnificent, had laid siege to Vienna and was directly threatening Charles's homeland of Austria. The war against the Turks was a distraction that may have saved Luther's life, and certainly allowed him to thrive (although it didn't soften his opinions against Muslims). Several German princes converted to the new Protestant faith, seeing their opportunity to break free from the direct control (and taxation) of Rome and of the emperor, who was too busy to stop them. Some princes also saw an opportunity to "secularize" (i.e., confiscate) church lands and add this wealth to their lands.

Because of the tremendous influence of his work and the fact that he had three decades, virtually uninterrupted, in which to preach, write, and organize, historians have examined Luther's fingerprints on virtually every aspect of German history. His impact on Christianity and the German language is undeniable and massive. Historians debate his impact in other areas. The problem is that Luther wrote so much that it is often possible to find him on every side of a question. His views on women, for example, strongly reinforced the perception that they were morally and spiritually weaker than men, as well as less intelligent. Yet he also believed in a woman's right to obtain a divorce and keep her own property. His views on Jews were unambiguously hostile, yet have probably been taken out of context because they were reprinted ad nauseam by the Nazis. Luther may have been an anti-Semite who advocated the conversion of Jews, but he made no effort to do so, arguing that it was "the work of God alone," and he criticized the history of Catholic persecution of the Jews in Medieval Europe. As he grew older, his views against Judaism progressively hardened, but then so did his views against many other people and movements. Near the end of his life, he strongly advised Protestant rulers to expel all Jews who refused to convert to Christianity. This was done in some regions, although inconsistently. It is probably accurate to say that Luther's anti-Semitic writings had more influence after his death, among more dedicated anti-Semites who looked to him for inspiration and justification of their actions against Jews.

Martin Luther was born into a German empire that was intricately subdivided along family and political lines, with religious administration running throughout in complex ways. When he died in 1546, Luther had complicated the Reich in a completely new and hitherto unexpected way: the German empire was now the fault line of western Christianity. A little more than one-third of Germans had converted to either the Lutheran faith or some other Protestant sect.

Germans call Protestantism collectively Evangelical (*Evangelisch*) Christianity, which often, but not always, means Lutheran. Most Protestants were in the north and east, although there were some Protestant regions, like Württemberg and Baden, in the southwest, and other islands of Protestantism in Bohemia (present-day Czech Republic). Most Germans remained Catholic, concentrated in the south, in places like Bavaria, and in the west, in the Rhineland. But in fact Protestant and Catholic communities were intermixed all over Germany. There were several regions (Luther's own Saxony being one of them) where the ruling family remained one religion and the majority of people the other. Some German cities now had Protestant and Catholic cathedrals within a stone's throw of each other. And indeed, stone-throwing was the least of the problems that were brewing. In an era when people believed in witchcraft and the power of evil to kill them in their sleep, having neighbors of an antireligion was not simply unpleasant, it was a direct threat to one's very soul.

The Protestant Reformation stretched the Holy Roman Empire to the breaking point. A Catholic emperor now presided over a number of Protestant states, and in some cases Protestant electors, who had the dubious power to vote for an emperor in the service of what they believed to be the Antichrist (the pope). A Protestant elector might have to bring a case before an imperial court where he found all the judges to be Catholics and thus biased against him from the outset. It was an unsustainable arrangement, yet it hobbled on precisely because the Reich was fundamentally weak and disorganized. Unlike in France and Spain, where a powerful Catholic monarchy could crush Protestantism with systematic murder and torture, or in England, where a Protestant monarchy could witch-hunt Catholics, the diffused nature of the Reich meant that the problem lingered, unresolved. It affected every aspect of Reich governance. For example, when most of the Catholic regions of Germany switched to the Gregorian calendar in 1582, Catholics and Protestants had yet another fundamental argument to divide them. For the next 120 years a merchant in Hannover was eleven days behind a merchant in Cologne. A letter sent from Bavaria on October 20 might arrive in Brandenburg on October 16. To outside observers it was simply another example of the bizarrely complex and confused state of the German empire.

Breakdown

Throughout his long reign as Holy Roman Emperor, Charles V made a few limited attempts to reconcile with the Protestants, most notably in 1540 when he summoned a new Imperial Diet to Regensburg for the purpose of working out a compromise. But the Catholic princes were willing to offer very little, and Luther responded with counterdemands he knew they would not accept. Charles came away from the experience realizing the extent to which rulers were using Protestantism as a way of avoiding their obligations to him and the Reich, and his attitude hardened. Shortly after Luther died, a brief war broke out in the Reich, in which the imperial (Catholic) forces actually captured Wittenberg and forced reconversion on a number of other German cities and towns. It was an ominous sign of things to come.

By the 1540s the Reich was fractured into divergent *confessions* (i.e., faiths). Compromises kept a shaky peace for most of three generations. The Diet of Speyer in 1526 decided to allow each German state to determine its own confession in keeping with its constitutional duty to the Reich. The choice, however, was left to each ruler, and some states thus had princes of one confession and a population of the other. The Peace of Augsburg in 1555 established that Lutherans and Catholics were equal before the law in imperial courts, and that people who did not conform to the confession of their ruler were free to leave and resettle elsewhere.

In 1583 the question of a ruler's confession came to the forefront in an unexpected way. The archbishop of Cologne, ruler of the largest and most important electorate in the Rhineland, converted to Calvinism, a Protestant sect that was not covered under the Augsburg treaty. He then refused to give up his position as a prince and elector. War loomed as first German states, and then even foreign states, on both sides of the Protestant/Catholic divide threatened to become involved. When the war finally came, it was a stalemate until the Catholic side was heavily reinforced by Spanish armies. The Catholic forces gradually overcame Protestant resistance, laying siege and capturing one town after another and finally placing a Bavarian prince in charge of Cologne.

The Cologne War of the 1580s demonstrated two new and unfortunate developments. First, that the German religious conflict was increasingly becoming a pan-European conflict, increasing its scale, duration, and violence. (When the Elector of Brandenburg converted to Protestantism in 1613, for example, he welcomed the foreign support from England and Holland.) Second and more alarmingly, the conflict was becoming gruesome. During the fighting over Cologne, both sides committed atrocities against civilians and prisoners, and each side justified further atrocities by the rumors of the other side's atrocities. The discipline of soldiers was proving difficult to maintain when the enemy was regarded as anti-Christian.

In the decade after the war, a general economic downturn, coupled with ongoing cold weather and bad harvests, created a miserable period of poverty and starvation in which desperate people moved from place to place looking for work, food, and shelter. Large segments of the population were vulnerable as wages in many places fell below the minimum needed to survive. It is likely that people, in their desperation and anger, became very hard-hearted about the suffering of others. And to find sympathy and compassion for people of the opposite faith must have required an extraordinary moral strength that most people probably lacked. Thus religious conflicts, the increasing scale of violence, the political ambitions of princes and states, and the hard times for average people created the conditions for a terrible explosion.

Armageddon and Reprieve: The Thirty Years' War

In the early years of the seventeenth century, the Reich seemed to be collapsing as every attempt to transact normal business broke down along some sort of religiously motivated split. The event that triggered war finally came almost precisely one century after Luther had launched the Reformation. In the spring of 1618 a dispute arose over the succession of the next king of Bohemia. Here the majority of the nobility was Protestant, and they protested the new emperor's move to place a Catholic on the throne. The result was a Protestant revolt that quickly drew supporters and opponents from many regions.

It is easy for us in retrospect to note the developments throughout the sixteenth century that had made this conflict not only possible, but likely, not to mention prolonged and agonizing. But at the time it began, no one could have predicted a war that would last three decades and would engulf nearly all of central Europe, with more than a dozen major states and hundreds of smaller ones involved. Although the Thirty Years' War sprawled across Europe from Spain to Ukraine and from Sweden to the Balkans, the main areas of fighting were the German lands. For the sake of simplicity, we will refer to the two sides as Protestant and Catholic, although the Protestant states received help from some Catholic rulers (notably France), and in Germany the Catholics would have thought of themselves not just as fighting a "Catholic" war, but as fighting on the side of the legitimate emperor, and thus on the "imperial" side. Essentially, the Reich was at war with a third of its own people, and both sides eagerly sought the assistance of other powers.

The Thirty Years' War saw dramatic swings of fortune for both sides. Early Protestant victories were negated after Catholic forces rallied under Spanish and imperial leadership and came very close to crushing the Protestants, who were then saved by the intervention of the brilliant King Gustav Adolf of Sweden, and the war swung toward the Protestants again. When Gustav

Adolf died in battle, the Catholics again surged, and it looked as though the Protestants would have to sign a humiliating peace treaty that surrendered much of their southern and western German compatriots over to Catholic control. But then France—a Catholic power—entered the war on the Protestant side because it feared the outcome of a Spanish/imperial victory, and thus the fighting continued for another decade.

By the time the peace finally came in 1648, many parts of the Reich were a wasteland of destruction, famine, disease, and death. Hundreds of towns, and even a few medium-sized cities, had been utterly destroyed. The population of the Reich decreased by as much as a third. Commanders on both sides, in order to save money, relied upon mercenary soldiers who were promised—instead of regular pay—all the plunder they could capture from the civilians in areas through which they passed. Armies rarely took much care to plunder only the people on the enemy's side. Soon the passage of soldiers became a sort of plague. They devoured every bit of food they could find, took all farm animals and everything of value, raped women and girls, murdered men, and invented sadistic tortures for little reason other than their own amusement. For centuries afterwards, Germans remembered this era in common expressions and idioms. As recently as the twentieth century, if someone wanted to describe a terrible war or a period of famine or suffering, she or he would compare it to the Thirty Years' War.

How Many Germans Died in the Thirty Years' War?

Estimates vary, of course, and some areas suffered massive depopulation while others didn't. But considering the normally very high rate of population *growth* of an early modern society over the course of thirty years, the fact that the population instead *dropped* by at least 20 percent, and probably more, is staggering. It means that at least one out of every five Germans died in the war.

The war served as the inspiration for one of the earliest popular novels in the German language: Hans Jakob von Grimmelshausen's *The Adventures of a Simpleton* (*Der abenteuerliche Simplicissimus Teutsch*). This sprawling dark comedy follows a boy through various adventures and crises, which he usually manages to escape with miraculous luck, despite witnessing the cruelties inflicted on almost everyone else. The story is an almost relentless condemnation of German authority figures: commanders, nobles, and especially churchmen, who are usually depicted as shortsighted, brutal, and cowardly.

It depicts a society that had clearly lost faith in its institutions, and yet was engaged in an annihilating war precisely because of faith.

The scale of the war was so vast, and previous peace attempts so unsuccessful, that the French chief minister suggested a peace conference of all the participants: a new concept in diplomacy. The north German cities of Münster and Osnabrück were chosen and were guaranteed as demilitarized, and delegates from the warring states were granted safe passage. Discussions lasted more than four years, with over a hundred states represented, although never all at once. The treaties that came from these deliberations are collectively known as the Peace of Westphalia. It is one of the most important settlements in European history, and a decisive moment for Germany.

As a result of the peace treaties, the German emperor lost much of his remaining power to compel states to obey him. In a sense, this was a victory for the Bohemian rebels who had begun the war in the first place, more than a generation before. Protestants and Catholics were confirmed as equal before the law, the number and composition of the electors was altered, and the emperor, now formally at the mercy of Protestant electors, had lost what little power he once had to control the foreign policy of German states.

The Peace of Westphalia is one of the early foundational documents of the principle of religious tolerance. The German states had to declare themselves Protestant or Catholic, but people of a minority religion were protected in their right to worship, within certain restrictions. This did not end religious discrimination in the Reich, but in fact the war had been so brutal that very few "mixed" communities remained; it was relatively easy now to sort out Catholic from Protestant because most minorities had fled or been killed. That, and the fact that the war had so utterly exhausted Germans, meant that this basic tenet of the treaty was, for the most part, upheld.

One of the unexpected side effects of the Peace of Westphalia was that it legitimized an early idea of separating church from state. This was not the intent. Rather, the peacemakers hoped that the treaty would encourage each ruler to be the defender of his specific faith, and thus people of that faith could look to their ruler for a guarantee of protection. But—again due largely to the horror and devastation of the long religious war—some rulers adopted the then-radical concept of the state being the protector of *religious choice*, instead. This was the course taken by the up-and-coming small state of Brandenburg-Prussia, whose motto was *Suum Cuique*, or essentially, "to each his own." Initially, many people regarded this attitude as a cop-out by a ruler who wasn't living up to his responsibilities. But in time it came to be seen as forward-looking and progressive, and Prussia's indifference to religion proved to be a distinct asset as it grew and developed into a major German power.

It is very difficult to say who "won" the Thirty Years' War. Almost every state that participated in it ended bankrupt or near-bankrupt. The Protestants survived without losing any of their major states, which had seemed unlikely at several points in the war, and thus one could argue that this constituted a victory of sorts. But the majority of Reich states, and the position of the emperor, remained firmly in Catholic hands, and Germans were well aware that had it not been for the interventions of French Catholics and Muslim Turks, Protestant power might well have been crushed or reduced to a few besieged regions protected by a peace treaty, as had happened in France a generation earlier.

France, indeed, may have been the only real winner, if we take a long-term view of the war's outcome. Dozens of borders changed as German territories were adjusted by the final peace settlements. However, France not only grew substantially but came away from the peace with two crucial victories. The first was that the power of the great Habsburg family that had once surrounded France with its territories in Spain, Germany, and the Netherlands was greatly reduced, and indeed its imperial power was broken in western Europe. The Habsburgs held onto their Austrian, Italian, and eastern European lands, and to the crown of the German Reich, but the role of the German emperor was so diminished as to be a mere ornament to their power. That was the second great French victory: the Germans appeared permanently divided. The war meant that no great, unified German empire would exist to threaten France, and that instead the French would dominate the western German lands that they now touched on their expanded eastern borders. The indirect French domination of the Rhineland, in particular, meant that those Catholic regions of the Reich were economically and culturally as close to Paris as they were to Vienna. No one at the time knew it, but the Germans were entering a long period in the shadow of France.

It is perhaps unfair to lay the responsibility for all of this at the feet of Martin Luther, although it is hard to imagine any of these outcomes without his crucial actions in the early sixteenth century. He remains, undeniably, one of the most important Germans ever to have lived: a transformational figure in the history of the German people. In the centuries to come, Protestant Germans in particular regarded him as a sort of new Arminius: the earthy, simple Germanic hero who resisted the power of Rome (in this case, the role of Rome played by the Catholic Church). Catholics could just as easily identify him as the assassin who fatally wounded the Reich and condemned Germans to decades of brutal war and suffering that they only escaped by signing away a good deal of their political independence to foreign powers like France and Sweden.

As different as these two narratives are, however, there is something subtle that they have in common. Either extreme position, or anywhere in between, acknowledges an undeniable development: Germans were beginning to think of themselves as a nationality.

Suggested Reading

Bainton, Roland. *Here I Stand: A Life of Martin Luther.* New York: Penguin, 1995.
Eisenstein, Elizabeth. *The Printing Revolution in Early Modern Europe.* Cambridge: Cambridge University Press, 1983.
MacCulloch, Diarmaid. *The Reformation.* New York: Penguin, 2005.
Wedgwood, C. V. *The Thirty Years War.* New York: NYRB Classics, 2005.
Wilson, Peter H. *The Thirty Years' War: Europe's Tragedy.* Boston: Belknap, 2009.
Luther's collected works are available in a fifty-five-volume English translation, also published on CD-ROM, Concordia Publishing, 2002.

CHAPTER FOUR

~

What Is Enlightenment?

Even a casual observer of German history must notice the recurring and deep influence of France upon the course of German affairs. Because the French formed a unified and powerful nation-state long before the Germans did, their relationship to the Reich was often that of the superior, more developed power exerting influence or force upon the large, but disunified or underdeveloped, German lands. The zenith of French power upon and within the German lands stretches across two hundred years, from the mid-seventeenth to the mid-nineteenth century. Most historians date it from the ascendancy of the extraordinarily powerful French king Louis XIV, whose long reign (1643–1715) is traditionally seen as the best example of *absolutism*, a style of government that came to dominate much of Europe.

Over the course of several decades Louis created a political and cultural environment that placed himself not only at the center of the state, but placed him as the *embodiment* of the state itself. Historians have debated whether the absolute monarchy was really such a departure from previous styles, or was simply a logical evolution over time. There is more agreement, however, on what it entailed.[1] Absolute monarchs kept a large standing army that gave them a hierarchical, top-down institution reliably loyal to the regime. They reversed the old bottom-up style bureaucracy, in which local lords had taken responsibility for their regions and then pledged loyalty to the king, and instead the monarch sent *intendants* to administer the provinces for him. The monarch concentrated the social and political life of the kingdom at his home, the palace, where anyone who wanted to get anything done needed to have access. Thus the court became a huge institution, with constant and lavish entertainment to keep the nobles busy while the king played their ambitions off against each other and they in turn competed amongst themselves for influence with him. Absolutist monarchs tended to spend heavily on public construction projects, as well as on culture and the arts, as a way of showcasing the success of the regime and its intended legacy. It was a status symbol to attract the most famous scientists and scholars to come work at one's court (as well as a good way of keeping them under control!). The court was intended to be the center of the kingdom's artistic, fashion, musical, and literary life. Absolute monarchy was, of course, an astronomically expensive system.

France ended the Thirty Years' War in a position of greatly enhanced power and influence over many regions, including the German lands. This influence was not simply political or military. By the late seventeenth cen-

Figure 4.1. Saxon Baroque: The Zwinger Palace: A portion of the beautiful Zwinger Palace in Dresden, capital of Saxony, built in the early years of the eighteenth century, directly inspired by the Elector Augustus's visit to France. Much smaller than Versailles, the Zwinger nonetheless maintained an impressive collection of art and scientific instruments, and a large, attractive interior courtyard for performances and concerts. The baroque style is evident from the proliferation of sculptures and statuettes adorning the walls.

tury, educated Germans were increasingly using French as their preferred language of culture, philosophy, and scholarship. Every German prince who could afford to do so—and many who couldn't, but did anyway—copied Louis XIV's extravagant style and built miniature Versailles for their new residences. By the early eighteenth century, German statesmen routinely wrote to each other in French, and in several courts French had become the preferred language of daily business and conversation. Wealthy families who wanted to show their good taste hired French cooks to impress their dinner guests. Wealthy men and women dressed in the latest French styles. And educated Germans read and discussed the plays, novels, and essays of French Enlightenment writers.

In the northern Hanse ports like Bremen and Hamburg, this Francophilia was less noticeable, but only because the northern Germans tended to prefer an Anglophilia instead. In the Hanse, where so much trade was done with British and Dutch merchants, the bourgeois citizens of these free cities with their republican governments often had more in common with their colleagues in Amsterdam and London than they did with other Germans in Munich or Berlin. They read French journals, but also British and Dutch ones, and ideas from Britain, such as Freemasonry, arrived at this time and became popular among the north German intelligentsia.

Freemasons and Illuminati

Freemasonry began in Britain and entered Germany in the early eighteenth century. Semisecret brotherhoods of Masons were often viewed with suspicion, especially by the churches. In Germany the lodges were originally a way to share Enlightenment ideas without fear of censorship, and their intellectualism appealed to a large number of prominent men, such as Goethe, Herder, Kant, Mozart, and Bach.

The Illuminati movement originated in Germany as an alternative to the Masonic lodges, although often with the same purposes and membership. The brotherhood's alleged plans to place its members in positions of power across Germany led to fear and eventually repression, culminating in a witch hunt of Masons and Illuminati across much of Germany at the end of the eighteenth century. Many brothers were jailed or expelled.

As the eighteenth century unfolded, Germans felt increasingly tied to the larger intellectual, cultural, and economic life of Europe as a whole, but to western Europe in particular. This connection to the wider world played out against the backdrop of a great dynastic rivalry between two powerful families.

Habsburg vs. Hohenzollern

By the eighteenth century the power of the German emperor had declined so much that the Reich served mainly to represent the interests of the smallest states and free cities. The larger states—Saxony, Hannover, Bavaria, Württemberg, Brandenburg-Prussia, and many others—were more or less completely free to chart their own foreign and domestic policies. They only came up against imperial power when they made some sudden or dramatic move to upset the status quo.

For most of the past three hundred years the Habsburgs, one of the great aristocratic dynasties of European history, had held the imperial title. From their capital in Vienna, they ruled a variety of far-flung European lands. By the eighteenth century the Habsburgs were not the superpower they had once been in the reign of Emperor Charles V, the man who confronted Martin Luther at Worms. In those days they ruled Spain and Portugal (and all their American, Asian, and African conquests) as well as land in Poland, Italy, present-day Holland and Belgium, Bohemia (the present-day Czech Republic), much of the Balkans, and of course Austria. They had claims on a good portion of the German lands as well as having held the imperial crown for generations.

Since then the family inheritance had split, and the Spanish line had died out, being replaced (after a grueling war) by the Bourbons, a branch of the French royal family. By the 1700s, the Habsburgs were usually associated with Austria, their native provinces, but also ruled much of northern Italy, Hungary, Bohemia, Silesia, Belgium, Slovakia, Slovenia, and Croatia. They were the most powerful Catholic power in the Reich, and although they spoke German, and considered themselves German, and ruled from a German city (Vienna), and although they held the throne of the Reich, only a relatively small portion of their empire was in fact German.

Early in the eighteenth century the House of Habsburg faced an impending crisis. The emperor Charles VI was aging and had no sons, only a pair of daughters. As in many Catholic powers, the medieval Salic law prohibited a woman from inheriting any sort of fief, including an entire kingdom. Charles held out hope for a son, but nonetheless tried to pave the way for his younger daughter Maria Theresa to succeed him. Even before she was born, he had proposed a "Pragmatic Sanction" that would allow for a daughter to inherit all the Habsburg lands, making her Archduchess of Austria, Queen of Hungary, and so on. But since a woman could not be German emperor (as that theoretically implied a potential for military command), her future husband, whoever that might be, would hold that title instead. As Maria Theresa grew, her father walked a fine line between trying to preserve his dynasty by passing it on to her and still keeping up the pretense that he might one day have a male heir. For that reason, he took no steps to train or prepare her for her future role. She received a fine multilingual education and was well versed in the arts and literature. But training her in administration would have sent the signal that her father had given up hope of having a son.

Needless to say, this arrangement required a tremendous amount of political persuasion on Charles's part. It set off a heated debate and negotiations for Maria Theresa's marriage, which finally concluded with marriage to Francis Stephen of Lorraine when she was eighteen: somewhat late for a girl in her position at that time. And it inspired various schemes in European capitals, where rivals of the Habsburgs sensed a moment of weakness. The biggest and most dangerous opponent was France, where the Bourbons planned to attack the Reich as soon as Charles was dead. The French had prepared a veritable ring of enemies that would overwhelm Maria Theresa and force her to surrender. A Bavarian would rule the Reich instead, and would do so on behalf of French interests. It was a cynical plan that was partially inspired by the contempt that many European rulers had for the idea of a female monarch. None of them expected that she would rise to the occasion and demonstrate more intelligence, determination, and grace under pressure than her enemies. Although she had never been prepared for leading a major European power in the midst of an existential crisis, Maria Theresa emerged as a formidable ruler in her own right.

Maria or Maria Theresa? Queen or Empress?

It was a tradition in the Habsburg family that all women had the first name Maria followed by a second name. Thus, for example, Maria Theresa's daughter Maria Antoinette, the future queen of France, was known simply as "Antoinette." Maria Theresa herself was often simply "Theresa."

During the eighteenth century the Habsburg family usually held the position of Holy Roman Emperor. This means that a Habsburg ruler was an "emperor." Many people mistakenly refer to Maria Theresa as the Empress of Austria, but in fact she never held that role. Austria was not yet an "empire." Rather, Maria Theresa had a different title for each land she ruled (Duchess of Lorraine, Grand Duchess of Tuscany, Queen of Hungary, etc.). Because her husband Francis Stephen was the Holy Roman Emperor, she was also known as the "Queen of Germany."

As part of the great scheme of surrounding Austria with enemies, the French had concluded an agreement with the kingdom of Brandenburg-Prussia. This midsized north German state had kept a relatively low profile to this point. It was neither large in population nor wealthy, but the French considered it a useful ally in the coming struggle against Austria. When the emperor Charles VI died in 1740, and his twenty-three-year-old daughter Maria Theresa succeeded him, the eight-year-long War of the Austrian Succession touched off, among other things, the great rivalry between the Habsburgs and Prussia's ruling family, the House of Hohenzollern.

The Rise of Brandenburg-Prussia

In the twelfth century a prince/warlord named Albert the Bear led one of the many German campaigns to conquer and Christianize the Slavic and pagan tribes to the east of the Reich. Albert's brutal campaign was typical of this period: he slaughtered pagans who refused to take baptism and forced survivors to speak his dialect of German. The land he conquered was poor and cold, with sandy soil and few resources except plentiful water and pine trees. It became the Mark Brandenburg. (A mark was a frontier province, conquered and then ruled by its conqueror in the emperor's name.) Albert's coat of arms—the red bear—ultimately became the symbol for one of the small towns he founded on the river Spree: Berlin.

Brandenburg became an electorate of the Reich, but after Albert's family died out, it became the pawn of different emperors and princes. Effectively, the mark deteriorated into a wild and lawless frontier region again. In the early fifteenth century the emperor Sigismund wanted to restore order to it, and he owed a favor to one of the nobles who had helped him become emperor. That man was Albrecht von Hohenzollern, who became the *Markgraf* (margrave) of Brandenburg in the early 1500s.

The Hohenzollerns originally came from the southwest of Germany, where their mountaintop castle monitored a pass and forced travelers to stop and pay a hefty toll. It thus acquired the name "high tolls" (*Hohen-Zollern*). Through wars, service to the Empire, marriages, and negotiations, they had inherited lands and were co-owners of lands scattered all over the Reich. At about the same time that Albrecht von Hohenzollern became the ruler of Brandenburg, his cousin Albert was elected grand master of the Teutonic Knights.

The Teutonic Knights were one of those medieval orders that emerged from the Crusades as a powerful military and political force. In the thirteenth century the German emperor granted them permission to conquer and settle a land far to the northeast of the Reich: a place full of warlike pagan tribes whom the Germans called Prussians. The knights, supported by thousands of other Germans, carried out yet another brutal crusade and conquest. The campaign was so violent that German settlers had to be brought in, because so many of the native people had been killed. Ultimately the Teutonic Knights ruled over this land and called it Prussia.

The Knights were celibate. They recruited new knights from all over the Reich, because none of them owned the land as traditional lords who could pass it on to a son. Instead they elected a grand master. Thus in the early 1500s—as Martin Luther was beginning to make a stir in Saxony—the Hohenzollern family ruled over both Brandenburg (Albrecht's inheritance) and Prussia (due to Albert's election as grand master of the Knights), as well as bits of land elsewhere. Wanting to free Prussia from the domination of the much larger Kingdom of Poland that surrounded it, the Grand Master Albert von Hohenzollern converted to the new Lutheran faith, got married, made himself Duke of Prussia, and used the Protestant Reformation as his chance to break away from the Catholic Poles.

Within two generations the Hohenzollerns in Brandenburg and the Hohenzollerns in Prussia began a long process of inheritances, intermarriage, and alliance that ultimately resulted in the lands being joined under a single ruler in 1618. The new electorate of Brandenburg-Prussia was an interesting anomaly in the Reich. Its ruler, in Berlin, was an elector of the empire. But only Brandenburg was in the Reich; Prussia wasn't. So the elector had a number of political options. He could exercise his power within the Reich, if he desired, as Elector of Brandenburg. Or he could demur from his responsibilities to the Reich, if he desired, as Duke of Prussia.

In 1640, in the midst of the Thirty Years' War, a new elector came to power, Frederick William, soon to be known as "the Great Elector." Dismayed by the helplessness of his realm, Frederick William resolved to build a powerful army. It availed him little during the war itself, but when peace finally came in 1648, Frederick William began a comprehensive restructuring of his state with the aim of centralizing his authority and backing it up with military force.

Fortunately for Frederick William, although Brandenburg had been devastated by the war, Prussia remained unspoiled. He was thus able to use the resources of one region to help the other. To do this, however, he had to deal with the local Prussian aristocracy. These families, known as *Junkers* (derived from *Jung-Herr*, or "young lord"), traced their ancestry back to the original German conquest of Prussia. They were almost all owners of large farms and estates, and they counted among their possessions hundreds, sometimes thousands, of serfs. In order to get anything done in Prussia, Frederick William had to reach some consensus with them.

The Great Elector was only able to raise the money for his new army by granting considerable local autonomy to the Junkers. They would remain the absolute lords on their land, with the rights to make and enforce justice and manage their own local economies. The elector did not interfere in their social or economic privileges; indeed, he even expanded them. At first glance this looks like the very opposite of absolutism: the monarch devolving power to his nobles instead of bringing them to heel, as Louis XIV was doing in France. But given his options, Frederick William made a logical choice. By granting the Junkers this autonomy, he was able to build a powerful army—small compared to the great forces of France, Russia, Austria, or Spain, but abnormally large for a little state like Brandenburg-Prussia. And of course the Junkers were the officer caste of the army. It was the duty and prerogative of an aristocrat to serve in the military, and thus Frederick William bound his Junkers closely to his service after all. He might not have been able to control what they did on their farms, but he was able to command their loyalty when it mattered most: when the state was at war.

Frederick William became the "Great" Elector mainly because of his leadership in several wars, against usually vastly superior foes. Commanding the army in person, he scored a number of upset victories during his long reign, and when he died in 1688 he left a strengthened Brandenburg-Prussia, now considered one of the important states in the Reich, certainly a respectable small power for its diminutive population of less than 3 million inhabitants (France, by contrast, had over 20 million).

Remembering who was who in the Hohenzollern dynasty can be challenging, since for more than two centuries the family displayed a remarkable consistency in naming heirs to the throne. Every one was either a Frederick, a William, or a Frederick William. There was also an odd pattern in the personalities and policies of the Hohenzollern monarchs for much of this time, in which a strict, authoritarian leader was followed by a more liberal, aesthetic- and cultural-minded ruler, followed by a strict authoritarian, and so on. This is admittedly a great generalization, and one could find exceptions in many cases, but it does present a general pattern of development in Prussia: a duality that ultimately had an impact upon the broader course of German history.

Prussia was poor. The land was relatively unproductive, the population sparse, the weather cold, and the only plentiful natural resource was timber. There were several good harbors, but they were all in the Baltic, at the mercy of much more powerful navies like those of Sweden, Denmark, or Russia. As

Figure 4.2.   Equestrian Statue of the Great Elector: Commissioned by his son Frederick I, in the entrance of the Bode Museum in Berlin.

THE HOUSE OF HOHENZOLLERN

FREDERICK WILLIAM
"THE GREAT ELECTOR" 1640-88

FREDERICK I
"KING IN PRUSSIA" 1688-1713

FREDERICK WILLIAM I
"THE SOLDIER-KING" 1713-40

FREDERICK II
"THE GREAT" 1740-86

FREDERICK WILLIAM II
1786-1797

FREDERICK WILLIAM III
1797-1840

FREDERICK WILLIAM IV
1840-61

WILLIAM I
(GERMAN KAISER) 1861-88

FREDERICK III
(GERMAN KAISER) 1888

WILLIAM II
(GERMAN KAISER) 1888-1918

Figure 4.3. The Hohenzollern Dynasty

a matter of simple necessity, since the days of the Great Elector, the Prussian government had to be extremely parsimonious in spending, and extremely efficient in tax collection, to squeeze every last penny and to afford their outsized army. There was little margin for error or waste. Tax inspectors inspected tax inspectors. There were bonuses for finding corruption, bonuses for catching a cheater or embezzler, and penalties for letting one get by. The bureaucracy was notoriously efficient, cheap, and honest. King Frederick William I even hired spies to bribe his own officials, to check whether they reported the attempted bribery to him.

Contrast this political culture with the lavish waste of Bourbon France, which had a population eight times the size and an economy twenty times the size of Prussia's. The French regime was notorious for immense expenditure on luxuries, for nightly balls and dinners. One might say that wasting money was a symbol of prestige and wealth in France, as in many other European courts. In Prussia, by contrast, by the time of Frederick the Great in the eighteenth century, guests were encouraged to bring their own wine when they visited the palace, because the king only served cheap table wine!

The Prussians ultimately took a sort of perverse pride in their own stinginess. It became a badge of status; they considered themselves sober, serious, efficient, and incorruptible. This (obviously flattering) self-image ultimately became something of a self-fulfilling prophecy. What began as simple necessity evolved as a way to set themselves apart from their rich, powerful rivals, including the Habsburgs of Austria. And as time passed, it became impossible to separate the stereotype from the ideals of behavior.

Many nationalities have a collection of sacred stereotypes; things which any intelligent person knows to be gross oversimplifications and full of exceptions, yet which leaders do not dare to contradict in their public utterances, and thus they get repeated generation after generation. Many of the stereotypes the world holds about Germans come from the ego-boosting self-image of eighteenth and nineteenth-century Prussia: the precise, meticulous, ruthlessly efficient technocrats with a humorless devotion to order and discipline. That was the Prussia that many Prussians wanted to believe in, and the image they promoted.

As with many cultural stereotypes, this was, in fact, one part of the larger picture. There was another Prussia developing in the eighteenth century, one of art galleries and concerts, of well-manicured gardens and immense libraries full of scholars working in the various schools and academies. This world began with the ascent of Prussia's first real king, Frederick I, the son of the Great Elector.

The new elector was a very different man from his father. He was determined to raise the profile of Brandenburg-Prussia and to bring culture to this dreary little military state. In this, Frederick was assisted immensely by his second wife, Sophie Charlotte. Brilliant and witty, fluent in several languages, fascinated by the arts and science, Sophie Charlotte was, like her husband, an intellectual who wanted to be surrounded by intellectuals. Royal grants established the Prussian Academy of Arts and the Prussian Academy of Sciences, the latter ultimately including some of the most famous scientists of the nineteenth and twentieth centuries, such as Max Planck and Albert Einstein. The royal couple hired artists and architects from across Europe to transform their small provincial capital, Berlin, into a major European city. A visitor to the city today, taking in the famous structures, sees the outcome of the city center that Frederick began or expanded: the immense structure of the armory (now the Museum of German History), the great central boulevard Unter den Linden ("under the linden trees"), the German Cathedral, and (soon to be restored) the king's residence in the Stadtschloss. Under the

Figure 4.4. Charlottenburg Palace: It began as Frederick's gift to his wife: a house beyond the suburbs in the pleasant lake country west of Berlin. By the time of their grandson, Frederick II, it had become the main residence and working space of the Prussian monarchy. Expanded several times and then badly damaged in the Second World War, Charlottenburg is now a museum and park in western Berlin where people can relax and stroll in the gardens and along the wooded paths.

leadership of Frederick I and Sophie Charlotte, a small and well-organized military state became a respectable German kingdom with a modest contribution to the European Enlightenment.

Frederick's plan to raise the profile of Prussia included raising his own status. In 1700, he persuaded the Reich to recognize him as a king in his territory of Prussia (which was outside the Reich), although he remained Elector of Brandenburg (which was inside the Reich). He was careful to style his new title "King *in* Prussia," rather than King *of* Prussia, since only the German emperor could certify a German ruler as King *of* something, and there were usually no kings in the Reich other than the emperor himself. But in fact, Frederick was simply entering kingship via the back door. By the end of his life people were in fact referring to him as the King of Prussia, meaning Brandenburg-Prussia and all the other small lands he owned, and shortly after he died, the title became formalized in a treaty. Prussia had become a kingdom.

In 1713 the new kingdom passed to his son, Frederick William I, and again the Hohenzollern dynasty shifted from its liberal/aesthetic side to its military/autocratic side as a son seemed determined to be as unlike his father as possible. The new king was uninterested in what he considered the excessive and ostentatious displays of culture at his father's court. He was a notoriously stingy man, determined to wring every penny out of the tax laws (which he rewrote several times), and to cut expenses wherever possible. His personal life was a model of frugality: Frederick William I's only indulgence was an excessive fondness for tobacco, which he chewed and spat while playing cards late into the night with a handful of close friends and associates, after which the king could often be seen patrolling the palace to make sure candles had been extinguished and excess food saved for tomorrow.

Although he tolerated no waste in his civil administration, Frederick William I rarely denied anything to his army. In fact, the goal of his savings elsewhere was to afford the best and largest military that little Prussia could possibly sustain. Nicknamed "the Soldier-King," Frederick William could spend hours studying military uniforms or watching his infantry on the drill ground. His interest was both personal fetish (as when he sent recruiters across Europe to find the tallest men in every land for a special parade unit of "giants") and practical application. Under his guidance the Prussian army developed a number of new innovations that seem minor, such as a cadenced march step or the use of metal ramrods. But when taken all together with the incessant discipline and drill that the king demanded, the Prussian army evolved into something new and different from any possible competitors; it could march and maneuver much faster than other European armies, and its soldiers could shoot more than twice as fast as the soldiers of other nations, thus laying down a storm of firepower that more than compensated for their small numbers.

And yet the Soldier-King was determined not to squander this army in war. The military was also an instrument of his domestic administration. By strengthening Prussia's military and thus its position in Europe, the king was in turn able to solidify his control over his aristocrats. He helped create a culture within the Prussian aristocracy of service to the state and a unity of purpose for the monarchy. The monarch was in a position to reward aristo-cratic service with more service.[2] (The better you serve the king, the more likely you are to get promoted, with more responsibility and access, and thus more prestige and power for your family.) This helps to explain why genera-tions of Prussian aristocrats offered up their sons to the battlefields of the Prussian kings, particularly the Soldier-King's son, Frederick II.

Once again the Hohenzollern family demonstrated its strange genera-tional oscillation. The father, Frederick William I, was stocky, gruff, uninter-ested in culture, overtly masculine, and short-tempered to the point of being abusive and violent. His oldest son, Frederick, was small and thin, sensitive, intellectual, and fascinated by the arts, philosophy, poetry, and especially music. He spoke and wrote in elegant French, keeping up a correspondence with French Enlightenment figures such as Voltaire. In short, he reminded Frederick William of his own father, which troubled him profoundly.

It is hard to imagine the childhood and adolescence of the young Freder-ick II as anything other than recurring misery. The father was increasingly horrified by his son's development, likely suspected Frederick of being ho-mosexual, and tried with increasingly brutal means to correct him and make a "real man" out of him. When the teenaged Frederick tried to escape to England with the help of his close friend and tutor, the king had him hauled back to Prussia, forced him to stand and watch as his friend was beheaded, and then court-martialed Frederick and threw him in a military prison. He emerged only upon an oath of loyalty to obey the king. Thus Frederick II was forced to live in two worlds simultaneously. In his father's world, he learned to lead soldiers and became a stern disciplinarian. In his private world, he played the flute and harpsichord, discussed the ideas of the Enlightenment, read great literature in several languages, and indulged his formidable intel-ligence in a huge variety of fields.

By the final years of his father's reign, Prince Frederick had developed many of the fascinating and contradictory traits that characterized his long reign and his immense impact upon German history. He was well known throughout intellectual and scholarly circles, and many prominent Euro-pean thinkers were looking forward to the day that he became king, so that they could move to Berlin and work for what they imagined to be a perfect enlightened kingdom. Yet he had also developed that famously cold and occasionally vindictive spirit that would lead him to destroy people's careers if they disappointed him even slightly. And his contempt for women was legendary. It is likely that Frederick was gay, which in his time and position meant that he was emotionally and sexually frustrated. But he actively disliked women to the point of making extraordinary efforts to exclude them from his company, and he effectively banished his own unhappy wife (whom his father had forced him to marry) to a sort of luxurious house arrest at her own estate, rarely seeing her, much less speaking to her. There is no evidence that they ever slept together, indeed that he ever had a sexual or romantic relationship with any woman.

Frederick presents us with perhaps the best portrait of that idealized "enlightened despot" that philosophers hoped for so fervently, and which so many rulers claimed themselves to be. Fundamentally, of course, he was an absolute ruler with no intention of giving up any of his power to an elected body or even to a written constitution. And as we shall soon see, he rarely hesitated to use deadly force to resolve a problem to his advantage, and could be quite cold-blooded in doing so. He led the Prussian army in person, like his ancestor the Great Elector, and he was undeniably a brilliant and ruthless commander.

On the other hand, he was deeply impressed by the ideas of the Enlightenment, and all his life thought about how or whether they could be implemented by someone with absolute power. For Frederick, this meant being a patron of the arts and sciences, creating an environment in which great thinkers could work and write. It also meant that the monarch did what he could to liberate the consciences and bodies of his subjects: granting religious freedom, allowing some degree of social mobility, and encouraging the development of capital.

Frederick the Great and Religion

Like many of the Enlightenment thinkers he admired, the king thought that religious freedom was an important basic human right, yet he had very little respect for religion itself and at times seemed agnostic. He chuckled at Voltaire's *Candide* and its many crass jokes about the hypocrisy and corruption of religious authorities. Inspecting his army on the morning before the battle of Torgau, Frederick noticed that one regiment was singing a Lutheran hymn.

"I don't like that," he muttered to a companion. "It means my buggers are scared."

Of course, the very expression "enlightened despot" is an oxymoron, and its contradictions were often on display in Frederick's regime. He abolished torture, for example, yet had no objection to whipping soldiers for various military offenses. He found slavery to be abhorrent, yet generally did not interfere with the privileges of his Junkers over their serfs. He celebrated the American Revolution as the right of enlightened democratic people to choose their own government, yet he blithely helped himself to slices of a helpless Kingdom of Poland (which was arguably more democratic than Prussia) because the Russians and Austrians were also doing so, and he didn't want Prussia to be left out of the landgrab. The contradictions seemed literally to be embodied in the man himself. While on the move with his army, in the midst of tens of thousands of soldiers and preparing for battle, Frederick could often be found playing his flute, or writing poetry, or corresponding with a philosopher on some metaphysical question such as the meaning of beauty.

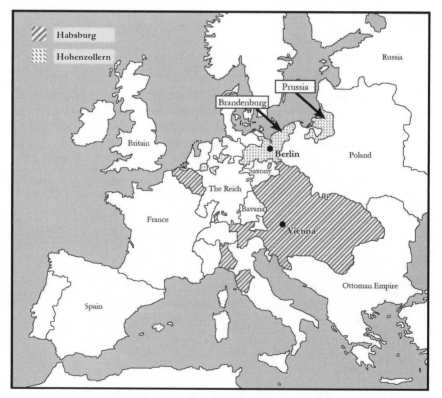

Figure 4.5. Europe in 1740 (Simplified): The realms of the Hohenzollerns and Habsburgs. Note the "sprawl" of both states, whose lands are often not contiguous.

Old Fritz

In 1740 the German-speaking world reached a critical juncture. When both their fathers died within five months of each other, Frederick II became king of Prussia and Maria Theresa became the Habsburg ruler. The great crisis of the Pragmatic Sanction finally came to pass, as the French-inspired alliance prepared for war to defeat the Habsburgs and place the Holy Roman Empire in the hands of a pro-French Bavarian dynasty. A small but important element of that larger plan was the role of Prussia. The French had agreed to recognize Frederick's rather flimsy claim on the rich Austrian province of Silesia, a hilly landscape of prosperous towns, farms, and textile mills. Prussian involvement on this far side of the war, the French leadership believed, would be a useful distraction to confuse and trouble the Austrians while the major campaigns unfolded in Italy and the west German lands.

Frederick was a problematic ally who played by his own rules. He moved suddenly and unpredictably. In the eighteenth century armies rarely moved or fought in cold weather, since it caused disease and fatigue and it was difficult to find food for the troops and horses. But Frederick launched his invasion of Silesia in late autumn 1740, wrapping it up in two months, to the astonishment of friend and foe alike. The Prussians marched faster than anyone thought possible and in the subsequent fighting revealed that they maneuvered and fought with startling superiority.

The War of the Austrian Succession raged for eight years. Maria Theresa's regime was surrounded by enemies, supported only by a handful of European states (most importantly by Britain, who provided desperately needed cash). Yet the Habsburgs managed to hold their own and ultimately took the initiative and drove back the French, Spanish, and Bavarian attacks. They did not, however, know what to do about Prussia, whose young king was soon being called "Frederick the Great" for his amazing string of victories. Fortunately for Maria Theresa, Frederick was a faithless ally who was more than happy to negotiate his own peace and bow out of the war when it seemed convenient. He made peace in 1742, reentered the war in 1744, and made peace again a year later. These separate conflicts between Prussia and Austria, in the midst of the larger war, are also known as the first and second Silesian Wars. Maria Theresa had to stomach the loss of Silesia, but at least Frederick left her free to deal with her larger enemies.

When a general peace finally came in 1748, Maria Theresa should have felt lucky to have survived at all, much less to have done as well as she did. Her realm remained intact, and her husband Francis Stephen retained the title of Holy Roman Emperor. She had also mastered the skills of eighteenth-century absolutist politics. Her enemies had assumed that their attack would topple a shaky female monarch from her throne. But in fact she emerged stronger than before, having cultivated an image as a steady and reassuring mother figure for the empire and its peoples. For the rest of her long life, Maria Theresa was a popular and even beloved ruler.

But the loss of Silesia smarted. As Austria licked its wounds, her government quietly pursued a diplomatic path over the next decade that would realign much of Europe against Frederick the Great. She ultimately secured alliances with Russia, Sweden, Saxony, and France. Her intent was to attack Prussia from so many angles with such overwhelming numbers that he would have no choice but to make peace on her terms, and thus she would retrieve Silesia and finally avenge herself against the godless philosopher king from the north.

Frederick anticipated the plan and moved to preempt it. In 1756 his forces invaded Saxony to prevent the Saxon army from mobilizing against him and to prevent the Austrians from using Saxony as a launching platform for their own offensive. His initial campaign was successful, but it brought on the general European war that Maria Theresa intended. Within a few months, Frederick found himself surrounded by enemies. Although the British provided him with financial support and eventually a small army, Prussia was desperately outnumbered. The nations allied against him had a combined population of nearly 100 million. Prussia's population was a little less than 4 million.

The period from 1756 to 1763 is known as the Seven Years' War. It displayed Frederick at the height of his extraordinary military skill as the Prussians bounced from one front to the next, fighting continuously to hold back the closing ring of enemy armies. There were Prussian defeats, and Frederick exposed himself personally to great danger on several occasions, but he won about two-thirds of the major battles, and his enemies' fear of his skill made them more cautious than they probably had to be. By the end of 1762, with all the participating states exhausted physically and financially, with the Russian tsarina Elizabeth dead and the new tsar Peter declaring his support for Frederick instead, it was clear that the war had ended in stalemate. At the peace negotiations, central Europe remained virtually unchanged from the status quo ante bellum. Frederick, and Prussia, had survived.[3]

Frederick the Great and Maria Theresa remained enemies for decades, and their rivalry shaped the course of European history. She referred to him as "that evil man." Frederick reserved for her probably the worst insult his mind could conceive, calling her "that *woman*." But in fact, they came to feel a grudging respect for each other. Despite their very different personalities and styles of monarchy, both were superb, hands-on leaders. Both were undeniably committed to important concepts of the Enlightenment: tolerance for different religious affiliations; establishing a legal system that protected basic human rights and dignity; a reformed, secular civil service; and sponsoring education, the arts, and culture. At the end of her life, in 1780, Maria Theresa's son Joseph II became emperor, determined not only to improve relations with Prussia, but to effect a sweeping modernization and secularization of the

Figure 4.6.   Maria Theresa at Age Forty-Two. Portrait by Martin Meytens. Digital copy in public domain.

Figure 4.7.   Equestrian Statue of Frederick the Great: On Unter den Linden, Berlin's great central boulevard.

empire. Joseph was truly a child of the Enlightenment. At the end of Frederick's life in 1786, he had already become something of a demigod throughout much of the German-speaking world. His reputation extended abroad, even across the Atlantic to America, where Benjamin Franklin wrote a celebratory play in his honor, New Yorkers and Bostonians named streets and inns after him, and King of Prussia, Pennsylvania, appeared on the outskirts of Philadelphia. The stern image of "Old Fritz" (as Frederick was called by his soldiers) became immortalized as a symbol of Prussian values, and eventually as a pan-German icon and hero, which he remains, arguably, to this day.

Of course, had Maria Theresa succeeded in her larger plans for the Seven Years' War, it would not have simply meant the return of Silesia to her realm; her allies would have carved up Prussia extensively, leaving it probably beyond hope of recovery as a major power. The history of Germany and Europe would have been altered in dramatic, unforeseeable ways, and it is impossible even to imagine when, how, or if a nation-state called Germany would have emerged on the map. Because Frederick survived the onslaught, Prussia remained the most powerful north German state and the most powerful Protestant state on the Continent, and of course was eventually the force that drove German unification. For good or ill—and there are strong cases to be made either way—Frederick's success laid the foundation for modern Germany.

Germany in the Eighteenth Century: A Journey

Imagine that you are a traveler in the Reich in the midst of the eighteenth century. Starting where present-day France and Germany meet, you cross the Rhine into Baden and Württemberg. There are no bridges here, so a ferry boat takes you across, which of course requires a toll. Indeed, this is something that you will encounter over and over again on this trip. The roads in much of Germany are miserably bad, but river ferries are everywhere, and represent the best means of transportation. Unfortunately, the rivers pass through so many different regions, each one requiring a toll, that you are constantly reaching into your purse.

Most places in the German empire use the same basic unit of currency now. As long as you stay in the Reich, you can produce a Reichsthaler (everyone calls it a "thaler"—it rhymes with the English word *dollar*) and people will accept it as legal tender. A thaler in those days was a good amount of cash, similar to using a one-hundred-dollar bill today. On this trip you will experience some confusion and probably get into arguments as you make change. In one place they break the thaler into *Groβchen* (called

Kaisergroßchen in some places), but in another place they break it into marks, instead. A mark is worth a lot more than a Großchen . . . but how much more, exactly, depends on where you are. That mark breaks down into schillings . . . sometimes. Here in the south, you still find people using the old silver *Gulden*. And you might be able to change your thaler for a purse full of little *Kreutzer* in some places, but not in other places where they use *Gröschel* instead (which of course aren't worth exactly the same amount as Kreutzer). Don't forget that there's a difference between the *Kaiserkreutzer* and the *Gute Kreutzer*, and bear in mind that your thaler isn't worth as much in the next place along the route because there they use "specie" thaler, which are pegged to a silver value, and are actually one thaler plus one Großchen . . . sometimes.

Here in the southwest you would hardly know that there's a major European war. Most of the townsfolk are Protestants, and openly admire Frederick the Great, despite the fact that their princes have declared war on Prussia due to their obligations as part of the Reich. (The Holy Roman Emperor, after all, is Maria Theresa's husband, Francis Stephen.) But the nasty religious conflicts of the Thirty Years' War are just stories now that people tell to frighten children into behaving themselves. Protestant Württemberg is close to Catholic Bavaria, and even though the Reich is in the midst of a war, trade goes on peacefully between them.

The people here are farmers and small-town shop owners. Many of them can read and write, at least a little. The shopkeeper and his wife can both read the Bible, and can keep their shop records in order. They are religious people, who have heard about the ideas of the Enlightenment, but don't have many occasions in their daily lives to worry much about it. The pastor in their church has preached several sermons about the evils of godlessness, republicanism, and "reason." It is known that the local duke has thrown some writers in prison for having expressed forbidden ideas, but nobody in town can say exactly what those ideas were. The people have taken this in and concluded that there are more pressing concerns. The population seems to be growing, the town is getting more crowded, and the increase in unskilled laborers coming looking for work has driven wages down. This is good for a few wealthy farm owners and the people who own the big mill on the river, but generally not so good for most other people.

You stay in the town long enough to hear about some of the local political issues. A butcher is pursuing a lawsuit because he feels he has been cheated by the butchers' guild. They charged him twenty-four gulden—a lot of money—to enter the guild and practice his trade in the town. After he paid, he learned that he should have been charged only eight gulden. The guild claims that the higher amount is the correct entrance fee for a foreigner. This man was born in Rottweil, about forty miles to the east, which as a free city does not have an associative relationship to this guild. But the butcher argues that his wife is from this local principality, and thus he isn't a foreigner at all, because the marriage law of 1740 permits a person to marry into local citizenship, which the guilds should then recognize. Do the guilds have the right to make their own decisions about who is a "foreigner"? Or do they have to accept the local laws in each town? After a year of deliberation, the court has avoided angering either the town authorities or the guilds and has submitted the case for a legal opinion from the professors at the University of Tübingen. Their decision is expected within the next month. Meanwhile, next week the town council will meet to discuss something that they've been arguing about for years: tearing down a large section of the town wall to build more streets and houses for the growing population. It's an issue that has become touchy because both church lands and the lands of a local imperial knight are involved. But you need to move on.

Head north through the forests and hills of the Hessian duchies and your trip takes you down one river and up another, crossing overland through hundreds of tiny dorfs, each with an old church and a cluster of houses in the midst of farmland. Your boat ride down the Werra River now indeed takes you into a theater of war. But it is not nearly as bad as you feared. It is still spring, and the armies have not yet moved out from their cantonments for the summer campaigning.

You have to pay to be issued a pass through the lines of the French and imperial army. This force is under the command of a French marshal, but includes a large contingent of German troops from the small states across the Reich. The imperial soldiers wear dozens of different, often brilliantly colorful uniforms, and present more the appearance of an acting company than an army. Getting the pass takes longer than you expected, because so many of the officers are still at home in France, having not returned from the winter break, and many of the rest are being hosted at the castle of a local German prince, who has prepared a weeklong series of events for them, including banquets, dances, plays, and a tour of the extensive grounds. The local merchants are excited, but grumble that the French try to pay on credit and are notorious for leaving their bills unpaid for months, even years. Nonetheless, business is good, and admission to these parties is the most prestigious social honor for miles around.

You finally get your pass and cross over to the "Prussian" side of the battle lines. Here the British, Prussian, and other German forces are under the command of the Duke of Brunswick. This gentleman is famous for his courtesy and personal honor. For example, the (enemy) French commander recently requested that the Duke of Brunswick release a young French nobleman who had been taken prisoner in last autumn's battle, because the young man needed to return to France to get married. If he missed the marriage date, it would cost his family an immense amount of money and possibly jeopardize the marriage contract altogether. The Duke agreed without hesitation and issued a pass for the young Frenchman. Now he has just returned, a happily married man, to resume his captivity.[4] This is a gentleman's war.

It is only a few days' ride to the famous university town of Göttingen. The German lands are covered with universities, many of which trace their roots back to the Middle Ages. Göttingen is a new arrival on the scene, having been established only in the eighteenth century by a grant from the British king (in his dual role as Elector of Hanover). Although it is new, Göttingen is already recognized as one of the most prestigious and important schools, particularly for its law program. A growing number of the bureaucrats and civil servants across the Reich, including many young men who will soon hold powerful ministerial posts, have law degrees from the University of Göttingen. Here you are surprised to find that the sharp class distinctions have broken down. Within the academic community, students from very humble families mix freely and form friendships with young men from some of the oldest aristocratic families in the land. The origins of the professors are likewise diverse, in part because German professors have a tendency to migrate from campus to campus, depending upon where they can get the best offer.

The University of Göttingen

Although it began as a new Enlightenment institution for the humanities and law, within a few generations Göttingen became equally famous for its math and science programs. At the time of this writing it has produced or employed forty-five Nobel Prize winners, more than any other German university. Some Americans refer to it as "the Harvard of Germany."

A German university campus—especially a liberal one like Göttingen—gives you a glimpse of the Enlightenment in full bloom. Even though everyone still studies the classics, everyone also discusses the new and controversial ideas about politics, religion, and society. Yes, some schools feel the heavy hand of regulation and censorship from the state, but most don't. The trouble usually comes from the fraternities. German students are devoted to their many fraternities, and new ones keep appearing based on various sorts of allegiances: sometimes segregated by class, region, or religion, but more likely by political beliefs. The professors likewise tend to have their associations, called "circles," of like-minded intellectuals. But it's the fraternities that can sometimes get violent, as the excited and/or intoxicated young men challenge each other to duels for the usual reasons: politics, personal insults, or girls.

After having spent time in the more conservative south, you are surprised to see so many open signs of membership in "forbidden" organizations like the Freemasons and Illuminati. In fact, many of the most prestigious scholars only seem to go through the motions of keeping it secret, but in fact are well-known participants in these associations. You have the chance to chat with some of the students. One young man, a member of a conservative, Lutheran-oriented fraternity, disapproves of the Freemasons, but has no complaints about his situation here. The son of a middle-class pastor, he feels very lucky to move in these circles at this prestigious university. Not only does it provide him with an array of future career choices that he wouldn't have had in his small town, where almost every decent job is regulated by a guild, but more importantly, being in college has kept him out of the army! He is studying law, French, and classics, and hopes for a civil service job in some important German state. At the very least, though, he knows he can make ends meet by working for a few years as the tutor for the children of an aristocratic family, where he might make some useful connections.

When not in classes, the young minister's son spends his time back at home, helping his family. Life is easier for the many aristocratic boys at Göttingen. Several of them leave for weeks on end, visiting their parents, relatives, or family friends at the nearby resort of Bad Pyrmont. Here the high and mighty set aside their political differences and "take the waters" at the many spas, stroll the gardens, and enjoy the fine cuisine and wine. The guests often include kings and queens, famous celebrities, and a few lucky professors who have managed to get themselves invited to provide stimulating (but not controversial!) conversation.

Alas, such luxury is not permitted by your itinerary or budget. Instead you board another boat and continue north along the Leine and Weser rivers to the port city of Bremen. In this old Hanseatic free state, business continues much as before, with the ships docking along the banks of the Weser. Although Bremen is part of the Reich, and the Reich is technically at war with Frederick the Great, the city claims neutrality even while collecting fees for the use of its port to supply the British and Hanoverian troops on the

Prussian side. You have to get out of the way as a regiment of British cavalry passes on the narrow street, having disembarked from ships and now heading south toward the army. The wealthy merchants are grumbling that the war has cut off the supply of French wine, but British and Dutch goods still flow freely and Portuguese and Italian wines are still available.

It is time to relax after your long journey, in one of Bremen's many coffee-houses. Unlike the so-called coffeehouses of London or Paris, which are often simply fronts for prostitution, in Bremen a coffeehouse is truly a coffeehouse. The Bremers are exceptionally fond of this beverage, but it is considered a man's drink, too strong for women. Ladies have their own tea houses in the fashionable part of the old city center. Whether it's tea or coffee, however, these are clubs where people can read from the huge assortment of journals and newspapers in a variety of languages. They bring them in and take them out, like books from a lending library. The men usually read about business and commerce, although the more cerebral among them scan the many scientific journals or philosophical magazines discussing history and religion. The ladies do even more reading than the gentlemen. Journals for young women arrive from across Europe, often written in French or English, and any girl whose family has enough money to give her an education will jump at the opportunity to read about the latest fashions and scandals from Paris, the controversial new novels from England, or—if her mother is watching—books about Christian morality and feminine behavior.

Near the window, overlooking the many ships tied up at the docks, you see a group of businessmen discussing the possibility of Spain entering the war, and what that might do to the price of coffee, rum, and other products from the Spanish colonies in the Americas. The politics here are very different from what you found in the south. There is a large, well-read middle class, and they are fluent in the ideas of the Enlightenment. They also have a sort of haughty pride and the superior attitude that comes from prosperity and the belief that they are more liberated and free than most men anywhere in the world.

Take a ship from Bremen and transit the cold, gray North Sea around Denmark and into the Baltic. On your way, you get into an argument with the captain. He refuses your request to go to Stralsund. Although it is an old German-speaking Hanse port city on the Baltic coast, Stralsund belongs to Sweden. And the Swedes have been at war with Frederick the Great. Prussian forces have come near one too many times, and your captain is no hero. He takes you instead to Kolberg, another old Hanse port city on the Pomeranian coast.

How different from Bremen this place is! Kolberg is a small town of only about five thousand people, many of whom speak Polish. Your captain points out that it is one of the few remaining harbors open to Prussia, since the Russian and Swedish fleets have blockaded the Baltic coast. You arrive a few weeks after the Russians have departed. They tried in vain to capture this place, and the town shows the damage from the siege. The little hamlets and farm communities on the outskirts of town have all been leveled; the enemy took everything. The city is crowded with refugees and soldiers, and nobody seems happy to see you. It will be a while before business returns to normal. Even if the Russians don't return—and it is rumored that they soon will—Kolberg's economy won't be restored until peace comes and the ships can once again freely trade with the other Baltic ports.

And so you set off across Pomerania, heading west toward Berlin. It is a troubling and unpleasant journey. The war here is very much unlike the orderly, low-intensity conflict that you saw in the west, and here it has clearly touched people. After the Russian victory at the battle of Kunersdorf, many villages were plundered. Farms were stripped of most of their food and livestock. Frederick the Great has taken many of the able-bodied men into his army, making it that much harder for the farming families to eke out a living in the sandy soil. The people seem poor and depressed. The local aristocrats don't seem to be doing much better. Here in the east one doesn't find the fancy balls and parties, with the pleasant entertainments hosted by enemy officers. The sons of these noble families are in the army, dying by the dozen on King Frederick's battlefields. It is an honor and a tradition to serve the King of Prussia; there is no other path for these young men whose proud ancestors have worn the famous blue coat since the days of the Great Elector. But the war keeps dragging on, and some families have lost entire generations as boys as young as twelve start their careers as officer cadets on active duty. In the elite Guards regiment, by this midpoint of the conflict, more than two-thirds of the officers who began the war are now dead.

When you reach the fortress town of Prenzlau, you are amazed at the inflated prices for horses. The army has bought all the good ones, the dealer tells you. As you consider whether or not to buy one, a platoon of Prussian soldiers passes, escorting a ragged, stinking column of men whose wrists are in iron cuffs, and who are chained together in a long line like convicts. The soldiers halt the column here for a rest, and the men fairly collapse on the ground. When the soldiers announce that they are staying here for the night, some local washerwomen take pity on the prisoners and set up an impromptu laundry on the spot to wash their filthy clothes. A middle-class woman, the wife of a Lutheran pastor, has brought bread out to them, and the soldiers tip their hats to her, and then look the other way as she distributes the food.

These men are deserters. Under normal circumstances they'd have been shot, or perhaps whipped nearly to death, but the Prussian army is desperate for manpower now. Most of these men aren't Prussians at all. They were Saxon soldiers when Frederick invaded at the start of the war. He captured their army intact and forced the men into his regiments. Many of them deserted, but were subsequently caught and punished. Aside from these Saxons, the deserters include men from across northern Europe. One young man was "recruited" when he took his father's wagon into town to sell the potatoes from the family farm. He foolishly stopped for a beer at a tavern, and there met a Prussian sergeant and some soldiers who bought the next round for him . . . and the next. He can't remember exactly what happened after that, but he found himself kidnapped and dragged off to a fortress to begin his military training. Believing that it was all a case of mistaken identity, he simply deserted and tried to come home. Now he has been caught. Within a few weeks he will probably be back in the army.

After an exhausting week struggling along the poor, sandy roads, you finally reach Berlin. It is surprising to find a city this big without a wall or any fortifications, but the capital's recent growth forced the Berliners to tear down all the old medieval boundaries. The city is four times the size of Bremen, and yet it seems less busy. There are fewer people engaged in commerce, and much of the traffic is official or military in nature. Evidence of the war is everywhere to be seen; Berlin has already been occupied briefly by the enemy, but fortunately not for long, and the occupation forces generally behaved themselves. The king, of course, is not here; he is more than a hundred miles to the south, with his army in the field. But the government cranks on without his physical presence as a steady tempo of couriers and military men transit between the nodes of the administration.

There is, however, some time for culture. In the buttoned-down military atmosphere of Prussia, Berlin is a welcome oasis of music, theater, and the arts. One of the interesting facets of the Prussian Enlightenment is the *Haskalah*, or Jewish Enlightenment, that has been flourishing in Berlin for more than a decade. Frederick the Great is known to personally dislike Jews, but his liberal ideas about religious and intellectual freedom have resulted in the Prussian capital becoming a center for Jewish culture and learning. The philosopher Moses Mendelssohn, considered by many people to be the founder of Reform Judaism, translated the Torah and other Hebrew scriptures into German, thus bringing Jewish philosophy into the mainstream of German Enlightenment thought. Mendelssohn's children included the famous composer Felix Mendelssohn and Henriette Mendelssohn Herz, who went on to create one of Berlin's most important salons. Mendelssohn's friendship with the great playwright Gotthold Ephraim Lessing inspired that author to write the controversial play *Nathan the Wise*, which was set during the Crusades but was in fact a parable about the limits of religious tolerance in Enlightenment Europe. A visit to one of Berlin's salons, coffeehouses, or debating clubs will almost certainly introduce you to both Jewish and Christian thinkers of the Enlightenment in a way that you wouldn't encounter in a French or English city.

What Was a Salon?

In the late eighteenth and early nineteenth centuries, intellectual women, usually from the upper classes, created "salons." These were essentially clubs by invitation, where people had dinner and drinks and then discussed important new ideas in science, literature, the arts, religion, politics, and other matters. Most salons met once a week, usually on a weekday evening. Often the woman who hosted the salon invited some important thinker, writer, or scientist as a guest of honor. The guest might give a brief lecture, and then salon members would discuss his or her ideas. Unlike most social gatherings of the day, salons mixed people from different classes and ages, and men and women interacted socially and intellectually.

Salons became popular in France but soon spread across Enlightenment Europe. In Berlin the two most famous and influential *salonnieuses* were Jewish women who had been born during the Haskalah: Rachel Lewin and Henriette Herz, the daughter of Moses Mendelssohn. Many of the intellectual and political leaders of Prussia knew them and attended their salons.

During your evening at the salon, you were surprised to hear people openly criticizing some of the policies of King Frederick, even though there were members of the Hohenzollern family in the room. While chatting with the publisher Christoph Nicolai, you realize that he has friends in the same Masonic lodge as you, and with a few words of introduction, you manage to obtain a seat at tomorrow night's concert conducted by Carl Philipp Emanuel Bach, son of the great Johann Sebastian and one of king Frederick's favorite composers. He has been living in the capital for years, richly rewarded to keep him (and his prestige and talent) from leaving to work elsewhere. Berlin has several auditoriums and halls, and in fact several high-profile composers, but a seat for C. P. E. Bach is a stroke of luck indeed.

The performance opens with his Sinfonia no. 5 in B Minor, a beautiful, exciting piece of music characterized by dramatic shifts of tempo and volume, yet always returning to a lovely, subtle interplay between the strings, as if they are chasing each other around the harpsichord at the center. You close your eyes and allow the music to flow around and through you as you contemplate this vast nation, full of so much wealth and poverty, peace and conflict, Enlightenment and misery.

Three Germanies?

In the eighteenth century, the rise of Prussia and its rivalry with Austria created a new, bipolar German politics. However, as we have seen, not all Protestant Germans sided with Prussia and not all Catholic Germans sided with Austria. This was not a religious division, like in the previous century. By the middle of the eighteenth century people were using the expression "Third Germany" to describe the many small states, cities, and principalities who wanted to remain loyal to the Reich, and who looked to the Reich for their protection and political rights, yet didn't want to take a side in the Austro-Prussian conflict. Third Germany was an old expression that had meant different things in the past, but it had always represented the "little guy" in German affairs.

The eighteenth century was a time of frequent war, and yet most Germans, in most parts of the Reich, managed to avoid the worst of it. The campaigning was limited to about three relatively contained theaters. War touched other places in other ways. Several small German states made handsome money by leasing their soldiers to Great Britain to fight in America against the colonial rebels, a practice which deeply offended a number of Enlightenment thinkers.

But most Germans lived through a time of peace, if not always a time of prosperity. With a growing population, many people were on the move. Tired of scraping out a living on their small, expensive plots of land, tens of thousands of families, especially from the southwest, traveled north to the Hanse ports and boarded ships for America.

It is generally less known that tens of thousands of Germans also resettled in Poland, Hungary, Romania, and elsewhere in the east. Pockets of German settlers—in some cases very large numbers of people—appeared in these eastern lands after Prussia and Austria had carved up the old Polish kingdom and annexed it, and after Austria had taken much of the Balkan lands from the Ottoman Empire. Both regimes wanted to settle loyal, German-speaking subjects in these far-flung provinces. In some cases the colonization worked as intended, but in other places it created communities that were considered ethnically German (*Volksdeutsch*), but that often assimilated to the local cultures and spoke the local languages.

Farming communities did not see the era as a prosperous one. But for people who dealt in cash, the eighteenth century was a boom time. Many merchant and banking families became rich and powerful. Regional fairs developed across the land (some, like the Leipzig Fair, drew buyers and sellers from as far away as Italy and France). Shippers built up fleets of merchant vessels and riverboats as business increased in volume and breadth. Much of northern and western Germany took important steps toward a cash-based capitalist economy in the eighteenth century.

For those with the time, money, and inclination, the eighteenth century offered a range of new cultural opportunities and entertainment. Every German court that could afford to do so tried to employ the most prestigious writers, musicians, and artists. The competition among the many German rulers resulted in many opportunities for the creation of high culture. The German lands produced the most famous and successful composers in Europe, from the prolific Bach family to Telemann, Händel, Gluck, Haydn, and of course Mozart.

And what of the Enlightenment? Historians have exhaustively debated the meaning of the Enlightenment in Germany. Since 1945 this debate has included questions about whether Germans really "got" the basic concepts of personal and political liberty that the Enlightenment promised for Americans, Britons, the French, and others. It has become customary to cite the famous essay "What Is Enlightenment?" by the great Prussian philosopher Immanuel Kant, who praised his king for allowing the people to "reason all you want, and about what you want; but obey!" Later developments in German history seem to indicate that unlike the other peoples of enlightened Europe, Germans thought of Enlightenment as something internal, having to do with one's own individual spiritual and intellectual growth, not as a system of political ideas and principles that one could put into practice, and certainly not as a revolutionary ideology.

Kant's short essay answers the question in its title by arguing that the German lands are in an "age of Enlightenment" but are not yet fully "enlightened." This was admittedly a safe position for him to take in 1784, since the old king Frederick effectively controlled Kant's career and income and wouldn't have received strong criticism on this, of all subjects, with a generous spirit. Kant walks a fine line, admitting that enlightened men in the service of the state have to respect authority and hierarchy, but that the authorities shouldn't expect to be free from criticism by enlightened people who have the right to discuss affairs of state.

In all fairness, we could probably debate the degree to which anybody really implemented Enlightenment ideals in the revolutionary era. The Americans practiced slavery and continued ethnic cleansing against Indian tribes. The British placed religious, ethnic, and class-based restrictions upon political participation (and practiced slavery). And the French created a dystopian republic that spent as much effort terrifying its own citizens as it did fighting foreign enemies and which was ultimately overthrown by a military dictator.

Seen in this light, the conservative and inward-looking German Enlightenment appears to be not a bad option. Literacy increased dramatically, publishing flourished across the German lands, and the growing middle class sought the best academic preparation they could afford for their children. But compared with England and France, the German states came somewhat late and slowly to embrace the new inquiry, philosophy, and secular sciences. There were notable exceptions, like the great scientist Gottfried Leibniz or the philosopher Christian Wolff. (And of course German rulers invited foreign scholars to their courts, most famously exemplified by Frederick the Great's tempestuous friendship with his erstwhile houseguest Voltaire.) By and large, the names we associate with the German Enlightenment are known for their work at the end of the century, a period of tremendous intellectual ferment in the German lands. In the last decades of the eighteenth century, as revolution transformed North America, then France, and finally most of Europe, Germans produced a golden age of literature, music, and scholarship.

Suggested Reading

Blanning, T. C. W. *Joseph II*. Essex, UK: Longman, 1994.

Browning, Reed. *The War of the Austrian Succession*. New York: St. Martin's, 1993.

Clark, Christopher. *Iron Kingdom: The Rise and Downfall of Prussia, 1600–1947*. Cambridge, MA: Belknap, 2009.

Duffy, Christopher. *The Military Life of Frederick the Great*. New York: Atheneum, 1986.

Epstein, Klaus. *The Genesis of German Conservatism*. Princeton, NJ: Princeton University Press, 1966.

Fichtner, Paula Sutter, *The Habsburg Monarchy 1490–1848: Attributes of Empire*. New York: Palgrave MacMillan, 2003.

Fraser, David. *Frederick the Great*. New York: Fromm, 2000.

Hertz, Deborah. *How Jews Became Germans, the History of Conversion and Assimilation in Berlin*. New Haven, CT: Yale University Press, 2007.

Holborn, Hajo. *A History of Modern Germany, 1648–1840*. Princeton, NJ: Princeton University Press, 1964.

Ingrao, Charles. *The Habsburg Monarchy, 1618–1815*. Cambridge: Cambridge University Press, 2000.

Ritter, Gerhard. *Frederick the Great*. Berkeley: University of California Press, 1968.

Roider, Karl, ed. *Maria Theresa: Great Lives Observed*. Englewood Cliffs, NJ: Prentice-Hall, 1973. An excellent collection of contemporary writing by and about the empress.

Walker, Mack. *German Home Towns: Community, State, and General Estate, 1648–1817*. Ithaca, NY: Cornell University Press, 1971.

CHAPTER FIVE

~

Imagining a Nation

If you had been a regular theatergoer in the imperial free city of Frankfurt in the summer of 1771, you might have encountered a brilliant and emotional young attorney who seemed utterly ill-suited for the profession of law. Johann Wolfgang Goethe was twenty-three years old, from a well-connected and wealthy bourgeois family who had provided him with an excellent education. But thus far the young man had failed to make much of an impression. He was high-strung, often sick, passionate, and constantly falling in love with young women who didn't know what to do with the poems and long romantic letters he sent to them. He had exasperated his father by seeming unable to focus upon the dry memorization required of legal scholars. Instead young Goethe traveled, dabbled in painting, and wrote poetry, short stories, and plays. He spent much of his free time and money in the theater, which was considered distasteful by his superiors, and he finally got himself fired for mishandling a trial and lecturing his peers once too often about human rights and the corruption of the legal system. In short, he seemed to be a spoiled young man who had wasted his talents and education.

This is the person who became the most important writer in the German language, the creator of a gigantic body of work including several globally recognized masterpieces. Goethe is to German what Shakespeare is to English, except that in addition to writing great poetry and fiction, he also wrote extensively on the law and administration, art and science, religion, and philosophy. In a period of extraordinary creativity and cultural accomplishment in the German lands, a golden age of German literature abundant with great writers and thinkers, Goethe is usually recognized as the greatest of the masters.

Romantics

Toward the end of the eighteenth century, a tension emerged within Enlightenment thought. On one hand, the purpose of Enlightenment was to use one's reason to sweep away old prejudices and superstitions and to develop the intellect. But was it possible to be enlightened while also being passionate, emotional, or religious? Was there, after all, room for feelings alongside reason? And if there was, what was the ideal balance? If one believed in God, or Fate, or the power of love, or patriotism, then was one no longer using one's reason? The trend toward a more passionate and sentimental style in art, music, and literature went by many names at the time, but later came to be called romanticism. In many European countries, the Enlightenment came first, followed by romanticism later existing alongside it and gradually replacing it. In the German-speaking world, arguably, they happened at the same time. Most of the greatest works of the German Enlightenment were also romantic, and many of Germany's greatest enlightened thinkers and writers were clearly fascinated by romanticism. This was compounded by the fact that the German Enlightenment began somewhat slowly and relatively late, and soon after it did, the French Revolution and the wars of Napoleon swept across Europe, engulfing the German lands in conflict and causing tremendous stress and change. The majority of the great German Enlightenment writers lived through that period, and thus their works have come to be known as the *Sturm und Drang* movement.

What does Sturm und Drang mean?

The word *Sturm* means "storm," but *Drang* is difficult to translate. It comes from the verb *dringen*, meaning "to insist upon" something and is related to the adjective *dringend*, which means "urgent" or "desperate." So although *Sturm und Drang* has usually been translated as "storm and stress," a better translation might be "storms and urgency." Many of the Sturm und Drang novels, plays, and poems emphasized young people, often full of passion and with conflicted feelings about their future.

When he was twenty-five years old, Johann Wolfgang Goethe wrote one of the great early works of Strum und Drang, a novella written in epistolary form: *The Sorrows of Young Werther*. (An epistolary novel is one that is presented as a series of letters.) The narrator, Werther, suffers as the young woman he adores wants only to be friends. The story is full of the profound and often witty insights into love and human nature that made Goethe such a beloved author. It ends with the shocking suicide of the young hero, who sends one final letter and then shoots himself. Within a year *The Sorrows of Young Werther* was read across the German-speaking world. It was soon translated into half a dozen other languages, and Goethe became a literary sensation. His fame and popularity were enhanced when several German rulers banned the book because it had supposedly inspired copycat suicides by other young men who had been rejected by young women.

Shortly after his (probably unexpected) success, Goethe moved to Weimar to take a job as an advisor to the new duke, who was even younger than he was. He remained a resident there, in a handsome large house on one of the central marketplaces, for the rest of his long and productive life. The city of Weimar has ever since been something of a living monument to Goethe and his work.

Goethe's work embraces a tremendous range of subjects. Aside from his philosophical and scientific essays, he was considered one of the great legal theorists of his day, often on controversial topics. For example, he condemned the sending of German mercenary soldiers to help Britain fight the American rebels, because many of those men had been sent to the army as part of a punishment for some misdemeanor or just for debt, and thus their "sentence" on a battlefield might end up being death. Like many Enlightenment thinkers, he was agnostic and generally nonreligious, yet personally fascinated with religion as an historical and moral phenomenon. The best example of this is available in his magnum opus, the work he spent most of his life writing and revising: the great two-part epic play *Faust*.

Goethe began working on *Faust* in his twenties and was still revising part two when he died at the age of eighty-two. It was an old legend that had been addressed by many authors in many countries, but Goethe saw it as a universal story. Professor Faust is a classic enlightened man: frustrated by the limitations of his humanity and desperate to know more, to have power and control over the mysteries of the universe. He sells his soul to Mephisto in return for a period of supernatural power on earth, but gradually realizes that it brings only sorrow and frustration to him and others around him. And yet he was warned all along by Mephisto that it would be so. In one of the most famous lines ever written in German, Faust is told: " *Du bist am Ende was du bist*" ("In the end, you are what you are").

In 1799 Weimar became the home of another famous and successful writer. Friedrich Schiller had made a name for himself as a playwright and poet, as well as a historian and philosopher. His work on aesthetics and the concept of beauty was widely discussed by scholars and intellectuals, but his plays were pitched to common people and were hugely popular. They featured larger-than-life characters, often taken from history, grappling with ter-

Figure 5.1. Goethe (left) and Schiller (right): The statues stand in front of the National Theatre in Weimar. Digital photograph in public domain

rible moral dilemmas, with plenty of action, romance, and adventure. Schiller and Goethe collaborated on several projects and ended up living within a few blocks of each other in Weimar, creating for a few years a sort of nexus of German intellectual and cultural life in the small Thuringian city. They jointly sponsored the creation of what became the National Theatre, and their statues stand, arm-in-arm, in front of the famous building to this day.

Schiller kept returning to the theme of heroism: the courage to stand up against the odds. His greatest plays feature lonely heroes who lead by example. In *William Tell*, his last major work before his premature death from tuberculosis in 1805, the hero leads a rebellion of Swiss townsfolk against the oppressive fifteenth-century Habsburg overlords. By this point, with Napoleonic France spreading its power across the German lands and with millions of Germans already under French rule, it was obvious to many people that the Swiss in the play represented the German people; could they find a new hero to unify them against the foreign imperial ruler? A few years later the playwright Heinrich von Kleist explored the same themes in his plays *Michael Kohlhaas, Hermannsschlacht,* and *Prince Friedrich von Homburg.* In all three cases, using stories of long-ago Germans rising up against oppression or unifying against a foreign enemy, Kleist managed to avoid the censors by not specifically pointing out Napoleon or the French by name. Beethoven's music for Goethe's play *Egmont* celebrated a Dutch rebel who rose up against the Spanish overlords, another not-so-oblique reference to the Napoleonic empire.

With the arrival of the French invaders, German romanticism took on a new, sharply political tone.

The New Prometheus

In the late 1780s the Bourbon monarchy of France began to disintegrate. What began as a crisis over a hopeless debt situation evolved into a liberal convention to create a constitutional monarchy, and then turned violent as the radical Jacobin party came to power. By the early 1790s France was a republic, intent on tearing down all traces of the old regime and spreading revolution across Europe. The area most directly and immediately affected by the aggressive new policies was the German Rhineland.

The German powers were unsure how best to deal with the French Republic. Some, who were nowhere near France, mustered little enthusiasm for intervention. But French *émigrés* (aristocrats who had fled the revolution and were now living in exile) told horrifying stories of peasant revolts and beheadings, and a number of German aristocrats had reason to fear that if the

Jacobin spirit took root in German lands, their own heads might roll next. The aristocrats did have some reasons for concern: there were a few German Jacobins, particularly in the Rhineland, who supported many of the ideas of the French Revolution, including secularizing the society and separating church from state.

But what to do? The Prussian and Austrian governments were more interested in carving up Poland, and neither entirely trusted the other's motives. It was also hard to muster enthusiasm for what promised to be an expensive war with no immediate gain. While they considered their options, the French struck first, declaring war upon Austria. The Reich mobilized halfheartedly. In 1792 the allied German armies moved cautiously into France, but a Prussian-led army suffered a setback at the battle of Valmy that September. That was enough for the reluctant Prussians, who decided to withdraw. Their lack of resolve only emboldened the French revolutionaries, who recruited huge new armies. The war spread to the low countries, northern Italy, Spain, and the Rhineland.

By 1794 much of the German Rhineland was under French occupation and indeed in the process of annexation to France. Revolutionary armies reached as far into the German interior as Mainz and Mannheim. By this point many Germans who had initially supported the revolution had become disillusioned by its violence, by the reign of terror and the execution of the king and queen, and by the hard realities of war and occupation.

Prussia withdrew from the war in 1795, but the Austrians fought on, supported by Britain and other allied states. The armies passed back and forth across the Rhineland, causing tremendous damage to the rich towns and farmlands and dislocating hundreds of thousands of people. In the city of Strasbourg, for instance, on the French side of the Rhine, revolutionary leaders carried out an ethnic cleansing against the German-speaking majority of the population, killing hundreds and driving away thousands.

The political disruption to the Reich was also significant. Hundreds of free imperial knights lost their estates under French occupation, and dozens of German states lost some or all of their land. Peace came, briefly, in 1797 because the Austrian armies had been so badly beaten by the new rising star of the French revolutionary army, General Napoleon Bonaparte, who led French forces in northern Italy. The fighting resumed in 1799 and again armies traversed the Rhineland and the French penetrated deeper into the German lands. Napoleon took control of France later that year and became, effectively, its dictator. Under his leadership the French were again victorious, and again the Austrians were forced to make peace. By 1802 the Reich had to accept the obvious: millions of Germans were now citizens of the French Republic.

Various plans for a reorganization of the Reich had been discussed as early as 1799, but the Habsburg emperor Francis, who was also Holy Roman Emperor, was understandably reluctant to make changes. His capital, Vienna, was overpopulated with displaced German nobility who lobbied the Habsburgs and the Reich either for restitution of some sort or for more zealous efforts against Napoleonic France to recover their lost lands. The Catholic church was similarly horrified by the forced secularization carried out by the French administration in the Rhineland, with the land and wealth of dozens of monasteries and abbeys confiscated and thousands of church employees now superfluous and unemployed. If the emperor cut a deal with Napoleon too easily, or pushed the Reich to accept a settlement that acknowledged French conquests, then it would not only be an obviously massive defeat for the emperor personally, but would betray the hopes of many of his prime constituents.

But defeated yet again by Napoleon, the Austrians were forced to concede massive changes in the Reich. In early 1803 the Reichstag passed the *Reichsdeputationshauptschluß* (loosely translated as "final imperial settlement"). It compensated a number of noble families with land or wealth, ignored the claims of others, and annexed huge numbers of estates, free cities, and church lands to their surrounding or neighboring states. For example: the two counties of Bentheim, dating from the eleventh century, were annexed to Prussia and Berg. Or consider the Leiningen family, whose branches had ruled small slices of lands across western and southern Germany since the twelfth century. Most of their territory had already been conquered and annexed by France. The remaining bits were annexed to Bavaria and Baden, for which the family was handsomely compensated. In all, over a hundred political entities completely vanished.

The delegates who concluded the imperial settlement of 1803 may or may not have sensed that the end of the Reich was at hand. They knew they were living in a tumultuous age, and Napoleon was a figure who excited strong passions in people, both positive and negative. On one hand, he seemed to be a kind of Prometheus who would sweep away the old regime and make anything possible. Many German intellectuals were initially enthusiastic about him (Beethoven is a famous example), at least until he became dictator for life. On the other hand, he was a disruptive figure who placed the security of his regime first, the prosperity of France second, and the "liberation" of Europe a very distant third. In any case, it was clear that Napoleonic

France was now as much a player in German affairs as Prussia or Austria. In 1804 Napoleon had himself crowed emperor, which only hardened the resolve of his enemies to bring him down.

It was expedient for some German rulers to side with Napoleon. Bavaria, for example, was an early Napoleonic ally, and the French ruler rewarded the Wittelsbach dynasty's loyalty by elevating the elector to a king and by adding large new tracts of conquered territory to Bavaria after his victorious campaigns. Napoleon did the same for Württemberg, and later for Saxony. Baden, Berg, and a few other German regimes similarly benefitted from the Napoleonic alliance. Napoleon expected, in return, that these German rulers would provide armies to augment his own for his ongoing wars. And of course he expected absolute political loyalty, because if Napoleon had the power to rearrange the map at will, then he certainly could take as well as give, and the ruler of a small German state would have to be very brave or very foolish to stand against him.

In 1805 a coalition of Britain, Austria, and Russia again went to war against France and its ally, Spain. Napoleon demonstrated his customary speed and skill, capturing one Austrian army intact and driving the remaining Austrian forces back across the Habsburg empire before finally catching and destroying a Russo-Austrian army at Austerlitz that December. Again, the Habsburgs signed a humiliating peace treaty that gave up more land to Napoleonic France. By signing the Treaty of Pressburg, Francis II gave up his claim to the Holy Roman Empire, which Napoleon intended to dissolve. In 1806 the Reich, which had endured for nine centuries, died with a whimper.

Napoleon created a new "Confederation of the Rhine" with himself in the role of "protector." The Confederation was a French-controlled military alliance of sixteen German states, all of which had to contribute soldiers to Napoleon's armies. Its creation worried the Prussians, who had spent the last decade dithering, trying to preserve their neutrality while opportunistically trying to take advantage of whichever side in the ongoing wars seemed to be winning. In 1806, prodded by his Russian ally, his generals, his wife, and likely by his own conscience, Prussia's King Frederick William III finally declared war on France. Unfortunately for the Prussians, their military muscles had atrophied since the days of Frederick the Great and they were in no way prepared to take on the new, highly mobile forces led by Napoleon.

The result was another stunning Napoleonic victory, as the French struck the plodding Prussian army and destroyed it in a single day's work in October 1806. Napoleon's forces chased down the Prussian remnants and occupied more than 90 percent of the country. French power now stretched from the Atlantic to the frontier of Russia. As he passed in triumphant parade through

Berlin, Napoleon made a detour to pay his respects at the tomb of Frederick the Great. He supposedly stood in silence for a minute, finally saying, "If you were still alive, I wouldn't be standing here." He then took the old king's sword as a personal trophy and moved on.

In the summer of 1807 Napoleon came to terms with Russia's Tsar Alexander and signed the Peace of Tilsit. The settlement was disastrously harsh for Prussia, although it might well have been worse; Napoleon had considered removing the kingdom from the map altogether. He settled instead for taking Prussia's recently acquired Polish provinces to create a new Polish state and by stripping away all of Prussia's west German lands. Prussia was saddled with huge reparations, with French garrisons it had to feed, and left with a severely truncated army. Finally, Napoleon created a new Kingdom of Westphalia from Saxon and Hessian duchies, as well as portions of Prussia, Hanover, and Brunswick. He gave this realm to his twenty-three-year-old brother, Jerome, who was hastily married to a Württemberg princess, but who never managed to learn German.

Thus, as the year 1807 closed, all the German-speaking lands were either under Napoleon's direct control, or under the control of a German vassal loyal to Napoleon, or part of a state conquered by or surrendered to Napoleon. Millions of Germans were now "French" citizens. Millions were under military occupation. Every German harbor was blockaded by Britain and/or occupied by the French military and customs officials. The Habsburgs and Hohenzollerns had both been humiliated and beaten. The Third Germany was locked in a military alliance with Napoleon.

If ever there was a time to consider what it meant to be German, and whether Germany was a place, or if it ever had been, this was surely the time. It is not surprising, then, that these years of the French Revolution and Napoleon were not simply an era of tremendous political upheaval and change, but also a remarkable period of German literature, scholarship, artistic activity, and social change.

Addresses to the German Nation

Not everyone in the German Enlightenment was eager to demonstrate their culture and education by speaking or writing in French. As early as the 1770s, Johann Gottfried Herder urged his readers to speak their native German tongue. Along with his contemporary the legal scholar Justus Möser, he argued that Germans lacked a political nation but nonetheless constituted a "cultural nation." In other words, there was something innately German about all the people of the common fatherland, more important and powerful than the political or regional differences that separated them, and thus it was possible to feel a pan-German identity and patriotism.

That was a concept that had never been very popular among German rulers, who were worried about any loyalty people might feel to anything other than their own regimes. But with the passing of a generation and the arrival of Napoleon, pan-German identity gained ground among intellectuals. If the German rulers were either powerless in the face of French power or were willing to collude with it, then who was left to speak for the Germans and what it meant to be German?

In Prussia in particular, where the proud aristocracy had been humiliated by their total defeat, men from the civil and military authorities formed secret and semisecret societies in which they plotted and planned for a Germanic resurgence against France. It is striking that although they were all Prussian patriots who longed for the restoration of *Prussian* power first and foremost, for the first time many of them were thinking and speaking in terms of German unification, or at least hoping to find some common purpose among all the German states and peoples to rise up against Napoleon. The most prominent of these organizations was the Tugendbund (literally "League of Virtue"), which was a veritable who's who of the younger generation of Prussian leaders. They believed that Prussia had to reshape itself as a new, reformed, modern state, and embrace pan-German identity, in order to lead all the other Germans out of Napoleon's embrace, or out from under his domination. They wrote in terms that were almost unheard of for Prussian aristocrats, such as *freedom* and *the German fatherland* and *liberation*.

The beginning of this movement is often linked to a series of lectures called *Addresses to the German Nation*, given in French-occupied Berlin by the professor Johann Gottlieb Fichte. Fichte was an example of the enlightened/romantic intellectual who had discovered a new pan-German patriotism after the defeats of 1805–1806. He argued that the defeated Prussians, and Germans in general, could no longer resist French power with weapons, but had to defend their culture and identity and nourish the things that made them German. His thinking was in many ways a logical extension of the ideas of Herder, Möser, and the other German romantics who had rejected the radical anti-Christian and antimonarchist Jacobin ideas from France. Germans, in their view, did not need a violent revolution, but rather a reformed state: a ruler more organically united with his people through culture and identity, and hopefully through some sort of democratic representation or institutions.

The Prussian reform movement was connected to various anti-Bonapartist movements in other German states, particularly in Austria, but also in Westphalia, where Jerome Bonaparte's new regime was on fairly shaky ground. The activists wanted to coordinate the work of writers producing patriotic novels, plays, and poetry with the work of civilian authorities, creating new reformed and expanded school systems to train young men from all the classes in a common school environment that would bind them together more tightly and give them a sense of common patriotic purpose. They persuaded Prussia's King Frederick William III to abolish serfdom, to grant full social equality to Jews and other minority groups, and to flatten the tax code and remove most class-based exemptions. None of these reforms would have been possible without the existential crisis into which Napoleon had thrust Prussia. In fact, many of these reforms were playing catch-up with the social reforms that had already been introduced by the French revolutionaries a decade earlier.

The dramatically shrunken Prussian military restructured itself, introducing conscription and relying upon a new system of reservists. These men were given some training and rudimentary equipment and then returned to civilian life so that another group could be called up in their place. In this way the Prussians did not obviously violate Napoleon's limitations on the size of their military, but they did create a relatively large pool of manpower that had at least some military preparation. The military high command was less impressed with the various pan-German identity projects, as their naturally conservative inclination was to serve and support the Prussian monarchy. But several of their leading thinkers, such as Scharnhorst, Gneisenau, and Grolman, did see the utility of the Germanic propaganda as a motivating tool for recruiters.

Historians have debated whether the Prussian reforms were a serious movement or just the idle dreaming of a few hundred frustrated activists. In the case of the Tugendbund, for example, the leaders were mainly bourgeois intellectuals and military officers, but the inscription rolls of the many chapters in towns and cities across northern Germany reveal that the organization reached both deeply and broadly in German society. Men who signed their names to these documents (an act that could cost them their lives if Napoleon's police caught them in suspicious activity) listed a variety of working-class trades and middle-class professions. That does not mean that their plans and schemes were effective; in fact, they usually were not. But it does indicate that in many regions the Prussian patriotic propaganda had the desired effect, or at least that the anti-French patriots were preaching to the converted.

But did Germans really want to be "liberated" from Napoleonic rule? Was being ruled by the French that much different for the average person than being ruled by the Duke of Hessen-Kassel or the Duke of Brunswick? Would a Rhineland Catholic have preferred to be ruled by the Protestant king of Prussia, rather than by the religiously neutral French empire? Many educated Germans had admired Napoleon in the early days of his career, before he became emperor. And many, like Goethe, admired him in retrospect, once French troops were no longer marching through German towns and cities. But at the time, their views were more conflicted.

The arrival of the French was often unpleasant. Villages were looted. Women were raped. Crops and animals were taken, leaving farming communities destitute. Museums and palaces were plundered, their art taken back to Paris. Churches were cleaned out, down to the coins in the collection boxes. In the port cities, commerce came to a virtual standstill due to the British blockade and Napoleon's "Continental System" embargo. In most German cities poverty, begging, and prostitution rose dramatically. People did their best to cheat the system, smuggling and finding ways to avoid conscription. It was more difficult to cheat the taxman; Napoleonic administration was notoriously efficient at tax collection. The average resident paid more than double the rates under the old regime. Napoleon also demanded "contributions" to France to cover the expenses of the French occupation troops in these regions; this was administered by the local mayors and prefects as special requisitions, usually on the upper classes. Troops were often quartered upon the local people at their own additional expense. The town of Schmalkalden, for example, with a population of about 5,300, had to quarter over 128,000 imperial troops during the seven years of French overlordship.[1]

Of course, what was misery for some was opportunity for others. The secularization of society under Napoleonic rule opened public service jobs, for example, to Jews and other minorities that had formerly been excluded. The abolition of guilds shook up the tradesmen and allowed more flexibility in employment. Offices that had been restricted to church-appointed administrators were eliminated, and new departments were created that needed educated local people who were willing to work under the new system. In the Rhineland, where French rule lasted twenty years, people began to adjust to the changes and the new system began to take root. In most of the German lands, however, Napoleonic rule didn't last that long.

The changes were undoubtedly jarring for many people. The French brought new weights and measures, a new calendar, new currency, and of course a new language. Names of people and places had to be changed to their French spellings in order to use the postal system ("Heinrich" became "Henri," the city of Lübeck became Loubeq, and so on). Testimony in a court of law could only be entered in French. All official proclamations and communications had to offer a French version (in part because they were monitored by Napoleon's ubiquitous censors).

Napoleonic rule in the German lands lacked an obvious constituency to support it. German aristocrats were horrified by the confiscation of their land, the annulment of their titles, and the creation of new French nobility in their place. German peasants faced uncertain employment because of the economic blockade, the threat of poverty, and the ravenous demands of the Napoleonic armies for ever more conscripted manpower. German bourgeoisie, who should have been the logical supporters of the new system, resented the censorship and shutting down of their newspapers and journals, and more so the crushing taxation and the failures of so many of their businesses due to the blockades and the embargo. All classes feared the arbitrary arrests, with men often taken far away to France, tried, and imprisoned in secret. Many people might have eventually benefited from the changes in the long term, if a lasting peace had ever come. The Napoleonic system did offer some enticements, but was generally imposed with force, through military occupation or the use of puppet states, which inevitably caused resentment.

Liberation or Restoration?

In 1812 Napoleon invaded Russia with the largest land army yet assembled in Europe. It included forces from virtually every continental state, including a grudging Prussia. Although he took Moscow, Napoleon was unable to force a negotiated peace, and in late autumn began a disastrous retreat that resulted in the near-total destruction of his main army and the death of hundreds of thousands of men. He abandoned the remnants and rushed back to France to begin building a new army, while excited Prussian nationalists realized that their opportunity for revolt had finally come. They were frustrated, however, by the chronic fearfulness and hesitation of King Frederick William III, who believed that if he drew his sword against Napoleon again, and lost again, it would mean the total extinction of Prussia.

Prussian commanders began to take matters into their own hands. Officers and regional administrators in East Prussia began calling up the militia (known in German as the *Landwehr*). General Yorck, who had commanded a corps supporting the French in Russia, signed his own cease-fire with the Russians, signaling his desire to cooperate with them. Angry and nervous, but realizing that he had been presented with a fait accompli, the king finally declared war on Napoleon at the end of February 1813.

The so-called "War of Liberation" has been the subject of much historical controversy. For most of the nineteenth and twentieth centuries, German writers exaggerated the events into a great patriotic legend in which all the people spontaneously rose up against the French and drove them out, led by the heroes of the Prussian army and its patriot-reformers. The legend was under construction from the moment the war began, as the Prussians especially amplified the propaganda that they had been circulating for six years and called upon all Germans to rise up.

There were in fact many enthusiastic volunteers in the new Prussian army. Officers in particular were motivated by a desire to avenge the humiliation of defeat and occupation. In some regions, especially East Prussia, towns did indeed send the Landwehr off with parades and cheering crowds, as depicted in all those patriotic pictures of later years. In several northern towns and cities local civilians and hastily organized militias rebelled against their French garrisons. Their revolts were usually put down by French troops, but in some cases they generated stories that became pan-German legends. In the little town of Lüneburg, for example, where the townsfolk fought alongside Prussian troops against imperial forces, a young woman named Johanna Stegen became famous for courageously bringing ammunition up to the firing line. For more than a century thereafter she remained a sort of German Joan of Arc figure, with her brave behavior celebrated in children's books and school texts, popular art and songs.

Men often took note of the contributions of women, who made ammunition, sewed uniforms, worked in field hospitals, and ran a number of charities to collect money for Prussia's desperately poor army. Indeed the government sanctioned a women's edition of the Iron Cross, the medal given to common soldiers, to recognize women who excelled in their contributions to the war effort. A woman like Johanna Stegen, who put herself in the path of bullets, was exceptional, but there is plenty of evidence that civilians of both sexes were directly involved in the revolts against the French in early 1813.

Other regions were less enthusiastic. Men simply had to be conscripted, and typically during this period that caused resentment and resistance. For most of northern Germany the spring of 1813 was just another war in the midst of many wars, with all the grim, inevitable suffering that implied. The Prussians did not experience significant trouble mobilizing their militia; the trouble was finding the money and equipment for them. But neither did the German people really "rise up" against Napoleon, except in certain high-profile cases. Indeed, it is worth noting that half of the troops fighting *for* Napoleon in that little battle at Lüneburg, where Johanna Stegen became so famous, were Saxons. Most German soldiers remained grudgingly loyal to Napoleon until the autumn of 1813, when their officers and civilian leaders began to switch sides.

"You Bold Lützow Jägers"

Adolf von Lützow was a young Prussian officer who believed in the patriotic, pan-German mission of the War of Liberation. He formed a Freikorps (a "free corps"—an irregular, all-volunteer unit) that attracted an abnormally highly educated and motivated group of men. The Lützowers are one of the few military units in history more famous for their songs and poems than for their battles. They became a sort of traveling propaganda machine. One of their most famous volunteers, the young poet Theodor Körner, wrote the famous poem that became a motto for the Prussian volunteers in the War of Liberation, including the verses:

> The people arise
> The storm is breaking loose!

The black-red-gold banner of the Lützowers became the emblem of the German reform movement in the nineteenth century and the basis for the German flag today.

Fighting raged in central Europe all through 1813, with the largest battles fought in Saxony. Austria joined the allied war effort in midsummer. At the climactic battle of Leipzig in October, the huge allied force finally inflicted a decisive defeat upon Napoleon, whose battered army fell back into France. His German allies by this point had abandoned him and switched sides. He was pursued by the allies, including vengeful Prussian forces who wrecked havoc upon French civilians. Napoleon abdicated in April 1814 and was banished to the island of Elba. As the allies began the process of negotiation and restoration, however, he escaped, returned to France, again took power, and raised a new army. He was finally defeated by the British, Dutch, and Prussian armies at Waterloo in June 1815.

At the Congress of Vienna, representatives of all the belligerents worked through the difficult questions of trying to restore the old order after twenty years of revolution, war, and Napoleonic empire. The boundaries of German states were particularly messy and contentious, not least because some of them had designs upon each other. (Prussia, for example, demanded all of Saxony as compensation for land lost elsewhere.) The Austrian chief minister, Prince Clemens von Metternich, emerged as the most effective orchestrator of the negotiations, and is generally credited or blamed (depending upon one's view) for the settlement that resulted.

Metternich was principally worried about preserving the status quo and balance of power. He was a conservative aristocrat from the Rhineland who had seen the result of the French Revolution and who feared that without the legitimacy of strong hereditary monarchy, Europe would be in a constant state of war and revolution, class against class and ethnic group against ethnic group. Metternich knew that the entire French Revolution could not simply be erased, but that any settlement would have to contain the most dangerous or threatening ideas that came from that period, if monarchy and stability were to prevail. Thus, in addition to settling the boundaries as carefully as possible, the Congress of Vienna had to find some superstructure for the German states that could replace the Reich.

The German Confederation that resulted from these negotiations had basically the same boundaries as the old Reich, but a completely different and streamlined composition reflecting the massive changes wrought by Napoleon. From over 360 German states before the French Revolution, there were now only 38. Only four free cities remained. The most striking difference was the total lack of an executive. There was no more emperor, imperial courts, or Reichstag, only a deliberative body that could be used to express the views of its member states. Among those members, Prussia and Austria were obviously dominant.

An important part of the conservative restoration was the tamping down of all those patriotic pan-German movements that had motivated many people to fight Napoleon. Now that the French had been expelled, German rulers did not want to deal with any charismatic leaders or movements that challenged their dynasties. The Prussian Tugendbund, for example, was banned by the king, and several of its leaders were imprisoned when they tried to continue despite the royal bans. Patriotic student fraternities at German universities came under close government supervision, and many members were arrested. Several liberal laws that had been enacted during the reform period were rescinded after 1815. Over the next five years censorship gradually returned, until it was as tight as it had been under Napoleon. Many former volunteers felt angry and betrayed that the German rulers had cynically used their patriotic enthusiasm and then discarded it as soon as Napoleon was gone. Urged by Metternich, Prussia and Austria joined Russia in a "Holy Alliance," specifically with the intent of cooperating to prevent liberal political uprisings and protect hereditary monarchy. Their officially stated goals to "protect religion, peace, and justice" were correctly understood as a bulwark against liberalism.[2]

The German-speaking world after Napoleon was a very different place than before. Many old regime institutions and privileges were gone forever, particularly with regard to the power of the churches. Several German states became constitutional monarchies shortly after the wars. The concept of citizenship had evolved, and people now expected an increased role in their government. When they didn't get it, they often protested. Thus festivals which began as celebrations of victory over Napoleon often turned rancorous, as veterans increasingly came to agree with the students of the *Burschenschaften* (politically active student societies) who demonstrated against reactionary states and in favor of a liberal, unified Germany. At the Wartburg festival in 1817 students mixed with veterans of Lützow's free corps, waving their black-red-gold battle flags while they demanded a constitution and bill of rights. At Leipzig the next year—ostensibly a celebration of the fifth anniversary of the great victory, but also a charitable event for recent victims of a crop failure—students and veterans signed petitions against oppression and sang patriotic songs. By the time of the Hambach festival in 1832, Germans were obviously more politically conscious than their parents' generation. Twenty-five thousand attendees—both men and women from all classes and many regions—cheered the recent spate of constitutions in Brunswick, Saxony, and Hessen-Kassel; the refugees from the failed Polish rebellion against Russia; and the fall of absolute monarchy in France two years earlier.

After the French Revolution it was easy to frighten aristocrats with images of popular uprisings. In 1819, after more student agitation had been linked to the murder of a conservative writer and political figure, Metternich persuaded the leaders of the German Confederation to ratify a set of laws that became known as the Karlsbad Decrees. These regulations outlawed most campus political clubs and societies, imposed draconian new censorship on the press, and placed limitations on the freedom of assembly. They also created a supra-national commission to monitor political activism throughout the German lands, which was deeply resented by liberals. Metternich was aware that these moves were unpopular, but he correctly gambled upon the ability of the governments to control the most outspoken individuals and groups.

If any one political figure dominates this era, it is surely that of Prince Metternich. Because the Habsburg throne was occupied by a series of mediocre (at best) emperors, Metternich remained the real power in government for decades. By playing upon the fears of conservative monarchs across the German lands, he parlayed his power in Vienna into trans-German power, but generally only in a repressive sense. In his self-appointed unofficial role as central Europe's chief of police, Metternich had the ability to prevent things from happening, but he had far less power to make things happen. This was probably an arrangement that suited him, however, since he prized stability and order above all.

No one did opinion polling in the early nineteenth century, but historians have generally assumed that German governments were broadly unpopular for a variety of reasons, some of which were beyond their control. Abnormally cold weather and the lingering damage from twenty years of war resulted in crop failures and widespread hunger until at least 1818. The German economies remained in recession for several more years thereafter. The lifting of the wartime embargoes and blockades resulted in a wave of cheap British goods being dumped on continental markets, depressing prices and making it very hard for German manufacturers to compete. A fierce debate began between the northern Germans, especially in the merchant-dominated Hanse cities, who promoted free trade, and the middle and southern Germans, who wanted protectionist high tariffs on imports to help local manufacturing and farming. The latter position represented many more people (and governments, who saw an opportunity to raise tax revenues through the tariffs), thus most Germans began to favor various plans for protectionism, including customs unions. At a conference on German economic union in 1820, southern German representatives angrily accused the Hanse of "selfishness" and "lack of interest in the whole of German economic life."[3]

The Prussian government read the protectionist mood as an opportunity to strengthen the state and raise revenues. Prussia was also anxious to do something about the problem of their large western (Rhineland) provinces being cut off from the Prussian heartland in the east. Every product that moved from western Prussia to eastern Prussia and vice versa passed through at least two other German states. As early as 1818, Prussia had been proposing a *Zollverein* (customs union): a league of German states who would agree to set the same tolls and tariffs and thus trade with each other on equal terms, but jointly protect themselves from cheap foreign imports. Goods, money, and people could move freely inside the Zollverein. Such a union would have to be regulated, obviously, and Prussia being by far the biggest state in the union was proposing itself as the leader and standard setter. German governments gradually began to see the benefit of hitching themselves to northern Germany's largest economy, and of course of the chance to sell their goods to millions of Prussian customers without tariffs. The Prussian-based Zollverein came into effect in 1834.

It has been traditional to assume that the Zollverein marks the beginning of Prussia's efforts to unify all of Germany under their control. But there is no indication that Prussian leaders at the time wanted to do anything other than strengthen and enrich Prussia. If other, smaller German states in the north came along for the ride, so much the better. When Prussian leaders proposed that the next logical steps would involve currency unification and a common banking system, they were still thinking in terms of using German unity to strengthen and unify Prussia, not vice versa. Nonetheless, the eventual result of these developments was that Berlin gradually became the center of northern Germany's economic policy, and thus inevitably also much of its political momentum. The normally perceptive Metternich completely missed the signals. He dismissed the Prussian Zollverein as insignificant, and Austria opted to remain outside. It was the first of several steps that the Habsburgs began to take, mostly unwittingly, away from their centuries-old position of leadership in the German lands, as Prussia gradually spread its influence.

Almost a Nation?

German economic activity picked up in the late 1820s and into the 1830s, but prosperity was unevenly spread. Rural people, particularly in the south, continued to suffer and found it increasingly difficult to make a living on the land. More families and individuals were willing to take the risks and sign contracts of indentured servitude to emigrate to America. Middle-class people were also tempted to leave. There were so many fees and taxes, compounded by the unpleasant politics and the difficult economic environment, that it was actually cheaper and easier to uproot one's life, take a ship to America, and start a new business there than it was to try to found a new business in a German town or city.[4] By the 1840s the German emigration to the United States had become a flood, with hundreds of thousands in transit.[5]

In the lands of the German Confederation, the period between the end of the Napoleonic Wars in 1815 and the great revolutions of 1848 was characterized by the steady transfer of people, wealth, and power from the countryside to the cities. Farm prices remained depressed, even when the rest of the economy began to prosper. Poor working people fled the country for the cities, where the first industries were appearing. Because in many places the farmland was still owned by aristocrats (in eastern Prussia, over 80 percent of it was), the noble class saw a steady loss of their wealth and power. Meanwhile governments began to centralize many functions that had once been done at the provincial level in the capital. Police departments, for example, were controlled by a central ministry in the capital, often staffed by men from middle- or even lower-class backgrounds, rather than keeping the administration in the provinces under control of the nobles. Aristocrats clung to the few places where they still had privilege and power, particularly the high command of the military. In short, it was a time of upheaval for people at the very bottom and people at the very top.

Many historians have referred to the nineteenth century as the "bourgeois century." If any group benefited, it was surely those with a good education and some cash, usually city dwellers. The conventional wisdom is that middle-class people, deprived of the right to any political activity or freedom of expression, turned instead to a shallow consumerism, filling their homes with the new mass-produced goods that were starting to appear by the end of the 1820s. The period takes its name from a style of inexpensive home furnishings and decoration that began in Vienna after the Napoleonic Wars and soon spread throughout the German lands: *Biedermeier* (the word *bieder* means "simple," "honest," or "unpretentious"). By the 1840s millions of German homes featured Biedermeier-style furniture, carpets, decoration, tableware, and so on. Naturally, aristocrats and others of old wealth turned up their noses at the mass-produced simulations of elegance, and in fact the word Biedermeier came to mean "philistine" or "lowbrow." But it satisfied the growing German middle class as the nation recovered from the wars at last, and they began to prosper. For many writers, the entire period from 1815 to 1848 has become known as the Biedermeier Era.

A typical middle-class German home in the mid-nineteenth century was also full of images. People purchased illustrated calendars and almanacs, prints, statuettes, and even tableware such as cups, dishes, and placemats that featured images, usually of heroic scenes from the German past, real or imagined. The Prussian heroes of the Napoleonic Wars were ubiquitous decorations, but so were folk heroes from the more distant past and images from German mythology stretching back to pre-Christian times. In the midst of the Biedermeier Era, Germans were simultaneously discovering a love of romantic folklore. This development was tied to the nationalism that emerged from the War of Liberation against Napoleon, which was heavy on patriotic songs, poems, novels, and plays. Its current did not dry up after the wars; if anything it swelled. The anti-French sentiment of the wars resulted in a rejection of the French styles and language that had so impressed Germans in the Enlightenment. Intellectuals rediscovered their own language and began to study its history and traditions, and average people circulated old Germanic tales and published memoirs of their adventures and exploits in the wars against Napoleon.

In 1812 the brothers Jakob and Wilhelm Grimm published a volume of old folktales that they had collected over a decade of research with friends and colleagues. The collection grew steadily in popularity and soon became a cottage industry for the Grimms as they kept expanding, adding new editions, and selling tens of thousands of copies. Originally, the Grimms had not considered any national identification with their work; they collected stories from across Europe in half a dozen languages. (As a linguist, Jakob Grimm was fascinated with etymology and culture.) As the tales grew in popularity, however, the Grimms moved with the times, including more old Germanic tales and "Germanizing" many of the others by changing words or names to more Germanic spellings. By the 1850s people across Europe now associated many of these stories with German history and folklore, whether they had been thus associated originally, or not.

Jakob Grimm became one of the most important and successful publishers in German history, with a huge body of work either written, compiled, or edited throughout his long life. His career was full of irony. He was a committed political liberal and activist, often in trouble for arguing against the repressive monarchical systems of his time. Yet Grimm was beloved by people for promoting an essentially conservative, patriotic, and traditional genre: German language and mythology. His success lay in creating works that people found indispensable in their middle-class Biedermeier homes. In addition to the tales, he published a guide to German mythology and an immensely influential history of the German language, in which he traced the roots of German words and grammar back to pre-Roman times, which in turn excited the nationalist mood, reawakening interest in the story of Arminius and the concept of an ancient "pure" Germanic people. Grimm's German dictionary became a standard in schools, libraries, and homes.

By the 1840s most German children had access to public education and learned to read and write. The German educational system was highly regarded and studied as a model by foreigners such as Horace Mann, one of the founders of American public education. From kindergarten (created in this period by the early-education pioneer Friedrich Fröbel) through graduate degrees in universities, Germans had access to arguably the best educational system in the Western world. It was, however, a dramatically nationalistic and patriotic education. This was in fact one obvious goal of the creators of the system: teaching young people to be patriotic Germans. Never before in German history had the pan-German idea been promoted across so many different German states. The heroic tales of the Napoleonic Wars often filled more than half the pages of school history texts, with battles against the French described in minute day-by-day detail for children to memorize. By this point, the Prussian version of the Napoleonic story was obviously dominant. Saxon and Bavarian school officials, for example, did not want children learning that their ancestors had fought on the "wrong" side of the great German national struggle, and thus adopted essentially the Prussian tales, whitewashing their own participation as Napoleonic allies. A generation of German children was emerging by the 1840s, fed on romantic, patriotic mythology that was often specifically anti-French and unificationist in tone.

In 1840 a diplomatic blunder by the French prime minister, in which he discussed the idea of extending France to the Rhine, caused a wave of anger throughout the German-speaking world and an outpouring of patriotic fervor about "Father Rhine." By the mid-1840s there were so many patriotic popular songs and volumes of patriotic poetry that some humorists joked about a "Rhine song epidemic" that was sweeping the German lands. In this atmosphere the poet A. H. Hoffmann von Fallersleben composed three verses of lyrics for an old Haydn tune that he called simply "Song of the Germans," but which came to be known by the lyrics in its first stanza, "Deutschland über Alles."

> *Deutschland, Deutschland über alles*
> *Über alles in der Welt*
> *Wenn es stets zu Schutz und Trutze*
> *Brüderlich zusammenhält*
> *Von der Maas bis an die Memel*
> *Von der Etsch bis an den Belt*
> *Deutschland, Deutschland über alles*
> *Über alles in der Welt.*

> Germany, Germany above everything
> Above all else in the world
> If it comes to protection and defense,
> [We] will stand together in brotherhood
> From the Meuse to the Memel
> From the Adige to the Belt,
> Germany, Germany above everything
> Above all else in the world.

This song has meant many things to many people. Hoffmann's specific reference to the four rivers bordering the German-speaking lands on the west, east, south, and north (as well as his call for "unity" in the third stanza) indicates that he meant it as an anthem of German unification. His declaration "Germany above all [else] in the world" was a call for Germans to place their nationality above their politics and to think first of their ethnic identity, not their regional states. In subsequent years, as the song became the national anthem, it was used to call for the return of lands lost in the First World War, and then by the Nazis to justify their conquests and the expansion of their "Greater German Empire." Today, the modern Federal Republic of Germany uses only the third stanza, considerably less controversial, as the national anthem.

Einigkeit und Recht und Freiheit
für das deutsche Vaterland
Danach lasst uns alle streben
Brüderlich mit Herz und Hand
Einigkeit und Recht und Freiheit
sind des Glückes Unterpfand
Blüh im Glanze dieses Glückens
blühe, deutsches Vaterland!

Unity, Justice, and Freedom
for the German fatherland
And so let us all strive
in brotherhood, with hearts and hands
Unity, Justice, and Freedom
Are the pledge of happiness
Flourish in the brilliance of this happiness
Flourish, German fatherland!

German romanticism was a complex phenomenon that attracted both liberals and conservatives. People like Hoffmann, or the poet Heinrich Heine, or Jakob Grimm, were certainly part of the romantic trend of the times, yet saw pan-German patriotism and identity as the social current that would bring the German people together to create a new, liberal German state, preferably a republic. For their troubles, many of them were banned or placed under surveillance by the conservative aristocrats who still ran nearly all the German states. But conservatives also embraced the romantic movement because they identified it as a traditional return to German folk roots, shaking loose the influence of the French, English, and other foreigners who had dominated German thought and culture for so long.

As it turned out, however, Germany's great social and political crisis did indeed hinge upon its connectedness to France and the rest of European politics and ideas.

Suggested Reading

Brose, Eric Dorn. *German History 1789–1871*. Providence, RI: Berghahn, 1997.

Craig, Gordon. *The Politics of the Prussian Army, 1640–1945*. Oxford: Oxford University Press, 1955.

Godsey, William. *Nobles and Nation in Central Europe: Free Imperial Knights in the Age of Revolution, 1750–1850*. Cambridge: Cambridge University Press, 2004.

Gooch, G. P. *Germany and the French Revolution*. New York: Russell & Russell, 1966.

Hamerow, Theodore. *Restoration, Revolution, Reaction: Economics and Politics in Germany, 1815–1871*. Princeton, NJ: Princeton University Press, 1958.

Johnston, Otto. *The Myth of a Nation: Literature and Politics in Prussia under Napoleon*. Columbia, SC: Camden House, 1989.

Levinger, Matthew. *Enlightened Nationalism: The Transformation of Prussian Political Culture, 1806–1848*. Oxford: Oxford University Press, 2000.

Meinecke, Friedrich. *The Age of German Liberation*. Berkeley: University of California Press, 1977.

Rowe, Michael. *From Reich to State: The Rhineland in the Revolutionary Era*. Cambridge: Cambridge University Press, 2003.

Simms, Brendan. *The Impact of Napoleon: Prussian High Politics, Foreign Policy, and the Crisis of the Executive, 1797–1806*. Cambridge: Cambridge University Press, 2002.

Simms, Brendan. *The Struggle for Mastery in Germany, 1779–1850*. New York: St. Martin's, 1998.

CHAPTER SIX

~

An Empire of Monuments

Once again, an explosion in France sent shockwaves through Germany. In 1830 the reactionary Bourbon dynasty had been brought down by a brief uprising that resulted in a new king, Louis-Philippe, who pledged to rule under a more liberal constitution. But by the 1840s Louis-Philippe had disappointed many of his initial supporters due to the corruption of his regime and his ongoing attempts to stifle opposition politics. French society was bubbling with new political movements and social frustrations that finally exploded in early 1848. As the French monarchy collapsed in revolution, excitement spread throughout Europe as liberals believed their time had finally come and the end of hereditary monarchy was at hand.

1848: The Revolution that Wasn't

The latest wave of uprising reached a Germany that was profoundly different from Germany at the time of the last French revolution in 1789. By 1848, the German population was booming, particularly in the cities. In just one generation, for example, Berlin's population had more than doubled, Munich's had nearly tripled, and Leipzig's had more than tripled. Industrialization was underway in several regions. Railways were spreading across the country. New steamship lines and even an entirely new port city (Bremerhaven, on the North Sea) were created for the exploding commercial activity. All of the social problems that people had observed in the industrial slums of Britain were beginning to appear in German cities. Birthrates, for example, were very high, but so were death rates and infant mortality. As in Britain and France, the numbers of illegitimate children increased dramatically, and thousands of infants were abandoned to churches and charities.

Despite the best efforts of Metternich and the conservative monarchies, the German Confederation was, like France and other parts of Europe, a fertile ground for new political ideas. Liberalism was by this time no longer revolutionary. It was increasingly mainstream for people to speak of creating democratic republics, particularly now that millions of Germans had relatives in the United States who wrote of the religious and political freedoms they enjoyed. Middle-class urban people, especially businesspeople or those with higher education, had grown very impatient with the glacial pace of social change in the German lands. Meanwhile new political movements were arising on the left. Early socialist and anarchist thinkers in France and elsewhere proposed a radical restructuring of society to liberate the working people from their miserable slums and allow them to write their own futures and run their own affairs.

On the other hand, rural areas were still very conservative. Churches and aristocrats retained both formal and informal powers, and peasants generally mistrusted the city folk and their ways. Roughly three-quarters of the population lived in rural areas or small towns. These people were the backbone of most German regimes in 1848, because aristocrats still held most of the highest ministerial ranks and because peasants made up most of the army. Things like censorship laws, which were considered intolerably oppressive among educated bourgeoisie in the cities, were often irrelevant on the farm. Nonetheless, the rural folk had many reasons to be unhappy. While much of the economy had prospered in the 1830s, the farming regions had been stagnant or in decline. In the 1840s the agricultural economy suffered a series of catastrophes, resulting in some uprisings. Hungry people ignored laws designed to keep them off state or aristocratic hunting lands, mobs broke into granaries and mills, even grape-growers in the wine regions of the Rhineland rose up against what they regarded as unfair taxes and restrictions. Rural Germans might have been conservative and obedient under normal circumstances, but by the mid-1840s poverty had made many people restless and even lawless.

The Prussian king Frederick William IV had come to the throne in 1840 after the very long reign of his father, and was initially very popular for his apparent willingness to embrace change and liberal ideas. It soon became apparent, however, that he was much less of a liberal than people had hoped. When weavers in Silesia rose in revolt in 1844, the king sent the army to restore order, with the result that troops fired upon and killed demonstrators. Many small-town people began to doubt that anything important had changed at the top in Prussia.

Because the revolutions began in March 1848, the period of several years leading up to them has been labeled in retrospect the "Pre-March" (*Vormärz*). There was no single event or chain of events that led to the uprisings. Many constituencies in many German lands had good reason to resent their existing governments or to want them deposed. What is striking is the speed with which the regimes toppled. In less than two weeks governments fell across most of the German Confederation, to a combination of violent street revolts and protests. Several German states had some form of limited assembly or diet—usually not a parliament or senate (the Hanse cities were a notable exception). In many cases the delegates in these bodies were liberal bourgeoisie who sensed a chance to discard the old constitution and create a new one, and they began that process immediately in a series of declarations of their autonomy. Many rulers left their capital cities in haste, taking refuge in exile or in the safety of some rural palace protected by their army. Metternich bundled out of Vienna unceremoniously on March 14, heading for London.

Rulers who dared to stay behind tried to appease the crowds with proclamations of sweeping new reforms. Ludwig I in Bavaria, for instance, wasted no time promising a new constitution with broad new civil liberties. It availed him nothing; the revolutionaries were done with promulgated constitutions handed down from a prince. They intended to draft their own. Within two weeks the king had abdicated in favor of his son Maximilian, who promised to fill his government with new liberal ministers.

In Berlin Prussia's King Frederick William IV seemed unable to grasp the gravity of the situation. He initially tried to offer a new parliament, but then bungled the crowd control, which resulted in soldiers firing into a mob of protestors. Events quickly spun out of control as mobs threatened the safety of the government. While his generals urged him to flee the capital and relocate in Potsdam, the king was convinced that his people loved him and wanted him on their side. Facing demands that he pull the soldiers out of the city, the king draped his royal carriage with the black-red-gold colors that had become the symbol of the revolutionaries and led a procession through the capital in an attempt to restore order. This only encouraged people to demand that the king swear an oath of loyalty to limit his powers under a new constitution. Deeply humiliated, Frederick William finally agreed. With the army gone, he became effectively a prisoner of his own capital, defended by a civil guard that represented the revolutionary interests, not those of the Hohenzollern monarchy.

In the spring of 1848 new provisional governments ruled in many German states, promising comprehensive reforms. As dramatic as that had been, however, it was now overshadowed by the promise of an even larger and more fundamental change: German unification. Of course, this debate posed huge fundamental questions. If, for example, Austria were to join a new unified Germany, what would happen to all the non-German peoples ruled by the Habsburgs, such as the Hungarians, Czechs, Poles, Romanians, Croats, and so on? Many of these nationalities were in full revolt in 1848, and it was unknown whether they would remain under Habsburg control. The proposal for simply bringing the entire empire into a new Germany came to be called *Grossdeutschland*, or Greater Germany. By implication, Austria would play the leading role in such an entity. On the other hand, many Prussian liberals and other northerners often spoke of a *Kleindeutschland*, or Smaller Germany, that would not include Austria at all, or perhaps only its German-speaking regions. In such an arrangement, Prussia would obviously be the dominant power. Still others suggested that perhaps both Austria and Prussia could be left out, and only the Third Germany would unify, thus creating a balance to the traditional Habsburg-Hohenzollern rivalry. This debate was immensely complicated, and not just because it involved the rivalry of power politics. There were religious issues; a Kleindeutschland would be mostly Protestant, for instance, while a Grossdeutschland would be mostly Catholic. There were cultural and linguistic issues between north and south. And what about those German-speaking lands ruled by non-German states? Some people were concerned that certain combinations would result in a war with France, Denmark, or other states, while others actually hoped for such a war, as a way of unifying all Germans against a foreign foe.

In the earliest days of the revolution liberals began calling for a national German parliament. A "preparliament" met first at Heidelberg in March, and by April had invited nearly six hundred delegates to meet in Frankfurt for the first-ever German national assembly. The number of delegates was the subject of fierce debate, and ultimately grew to over eight hundred. The composition of this body overwhelmingly reflected the liberal, urban tone of the revolutions. Educated professionals dominated, with a disproportionately high number of professors, writers, and lawyers (although, admittedly, not as high a percentage of lawyers as in the American Constitutional Convention or Congress). There were very few delegates from small-town, rural areas, and only a handful of aristocrats.

Although they represented a relatively narrow slice of German society, the delegates at the Frankfurt Parliament brought a huge array of political views and visions for a new Germany. Not surprisingly, the proceedings were

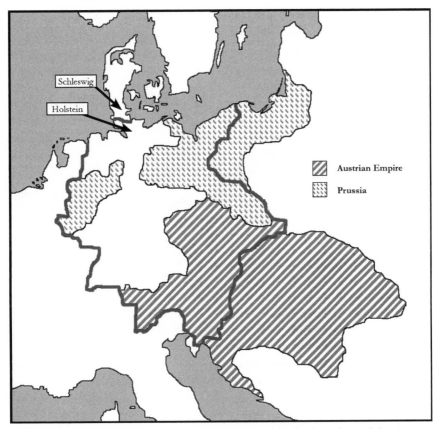

Figure 6.1. Germany in 1848: The thick gray line marks the boundary of the German Confederation in 1848. Note that the Confederation encompasses all of the "Third Germany," but only part of Prussia and Austria.

fitful and difficult. Media coverage of the event was intense, and the highly literate German population followed the debates with increasing frustration. Average people, with no experience of the democratic or legislative process, often found it all laughable and pathetic and began to lose faith that it would amount to much.

The revolutionary activity didn't stop when the Frankfurt Parliament convened. Unrest continued across the German Confederation, often linked to the practical needs of common people. Small-town peasants wanted better prices for their farm produce. Factory workers wanted labor laws and unions. The remaining guilds of craftsmen rebelled when they suspected that the liberals were planning on doing away with the last vestiges of the guilds and their protectionist systems. Many churches fomented dissent against godless republicanism. The bottom line was simply that the Frankfurt Parliament was not a true governing body; it could not solve the practical problems about which the majority of Germans were concerned.

In June 1848 tensions rose over the fate of Schleswig-Holstein, a north German region ruled by the Kingdom of Denmark. Denmark had also convulsed during the 1848 revolutions and during that early chaotic period the local people of Schleswig-Holstein had risen up and declared their independence. The Frankfurt Parliament seemed to be moving to declare it part of a united Germany. This rallied the Danes, who responded by blockading German harbors. The Parliament tried to create a German navy, but of course had to ask the major German states to donate their ships and/or to build new ones, which made it obvious that the old regimes and their militaries still held important assets. Not only had the regimes in exile been spared, but their militaries, for the most part, were still loyal to them. When the Parliament asked the Prussian army to help in the war against Denmark, people all over the German Confederation cheered King Frederick William IV and the Prussian aristocrats who—in the space of only six months—had been transformed from evil old regime relics who needed to be deposed into pan-German patriots and heroes. Even though the Schleswig War ended in diplomatic stalemate and frustration, the mood of many Germans had shifted back decisively in favor of the traditional states and the military.

Thus in the autumn of 1848 the old regimes and their armies began to counterattack and reasserted themselves. In Vienna the imperial family had returned over the summer, but fled again in October during a fresh uprising. This time the Habsburg army laid siege to Vienna and decisively retook the city in late October. By 1849 the revolutionaries had been defeated in most German states, and only a few liberal regimes still held out (Baden was one of the last). In March 1849, a year after the tumult had begun, the Frankfurt Parliament finally completed its draft constitution for a German empire, and offered the position of emperor (*Kaiser*) to the Prussian king. Although he officially offered his thanks, Frederick William IV didn't wait a week to consider it. Knowing that he was well on his way to reestablishing total control over Prussia, he rejected the offer out of hand, disdainfully adding later that he would never pick a crown up "out of the gutter." The parliamentarians began to leave Frankfurt. By June only about 150 of them remained, relocated to Württemberg where they finally disbanded.

The old regimes were back, although there were changes. The Habsburgs emerged dramatically weakened, having had to reconquer not only their own Austrian subjects, but also the Hungarians, Czechs, and Italians. The new system evolved into a complex "Dual Monarchy" that increasingly tied Vienna to the concerns of south-central Europe and its Balkan peoples, rather than to German affairs. Prussia, on the other hand, actually seemed strengthened by the experience of revolution and counterrevolution. The army had reasserted itself as the primary instrument of the state in both foreign and domestic affairs. In 1850 the king approved a new constitution with a bicameral legislature, but it was carefully constructed so that the voting was divided by "class," and thus the seats chosen by most of the people never amounted to a majority in the lower house, which didn't have very much power, anyway. What little legislative power the 1850 constitution did grant belonged to the House of Lords (*Herrenhaus*), which was dominated by the old land-owning East Prussian families who also ran the military.

It is easy in retrospect to see the Frankfurt Parliament as a hopeless fantasy. An assembly with no army, very little control over its budget, and only a very shaky claim to a constituency could not possibly hope to un-invent three dozen German regimes that had centuries of tradition behind them and replace them all, somehow, with a single unified state. In the decades since the failed revolution, many historians have attached greater significance to the event, arguing that 1848 was a decisive moment in German history: a missed opportunity to create a modern, liberal German republic that fell apart because of petty political bickering. This seems, at best, a great stretch. In all fairness to the parliamentarians in Frankfurt, they did complete an astonishingly complex task in only one year, less time than the American or French revolutionaries required to create their constitutions two generations earlier. And the German Confederation was hardly the only region of Europe to see failed liberal uprisings in 1848. In fact, the conservative regimes triumphed almost everywhere. Even in France, the new Second Republic lasted only three years, ultimately overtaken by Louis Bonaparte, nephew of Napoleon, who created a dictatorship and then an empire modeled upon that of his famous uncle.

The most fundamental point about 1848 is also the hardest to prove. For many historians, the failed 1848 revolution is the moment in which the German people had the chance to embrace liberal democracy but decided that they preferred authoritarian rule. Having had a glimpse of the perceived impotence of a deliberative body, especially in the face of a foreign war, Germans turned instead to the old traditional strength and patriotic values of the military men, who could defend the nation and who evoked the images of all those heroes the people had learned about in school, like Frederick the Great and the men of the War of Liberation against Napoleon. The autocrats, at least, could get things done. This argument is problematic for the simple reason that very few German people were ever given the choice in the first place. There is no way of knowing exactly how many people participated in the 1848 revolutions, but active participation was disproportionately limited to the urban population, who were a minority of the national body. Regardless of who participated, Germans did not think they had to choose between democratic freedoms and strong patriotism. Like most people in nineteenth-century Europe, they simply wanted both.

The Iron Chancellor

In 1847, the year before the great revolutionary outbreaks, King Frederick William IV of Prussia finally made good on a long-delayed promise from the days of his father and called a United Diet, a carefully limited body that represented the existing ruling classes of the provinces—certainly not a national legislature. But it seemed to be a tentative step toward granting a constitution, and as such generated some passionate arguments. One of the more conservative delegates elected to the Diet was a wealthy rural Junker named Otto von Bismarck.

Even among that conservative group, Bismarck stood out as reactionary in his views. He was an unapologetic monarchist who disdained the bourgeois intellectuals, whom, in the following year, he blamed for the 1848 revolutions. In fact, he was disturbed and disappointed that the king hadn't simply used the army to crush them immediately and end the disturbances earlier. After the revolutions, Bismarck initially rose quickly in the Prussian state service, becoming Prussia's main advocate in the restored German Confederation, where he kept a wary eye on Austria's ambitions. But after this initial ascent, and for more than a decade, Bismarck felt frustrated and diverted by his diplomatic career, which often kept him out of Germany altogether. His naturally hot temper boiled over on several occasions, including a celebrated duel with a liberal Prussian politician.

Because he ultimately became such a gigantic figure of German history, and the recognized architect of German unification, Bismarck's career has usually been simplified to a teleological story in which he planned all along to create a German empire, led by Prussia. And because that German empire ultimately became a fiercely patriotic and nationalistic entity, many people assumed that Bismarck, its creator, had held such views all along. But neither of these depictions is correct.

Bismarck was fixated upon building and protecting the strength of the Prussian state. For all the flexibility he displayed in his methods over the years, he remained single-minded and absolutely loyal to that goal. Thus the expansion of the Zollverein and the creation of a single north German economic zone was, in his view, a way of strengthening the Prussian economy, by making it dominant in central Europe. The policies he ultimately pursued that brought about German unification were, in his view, a way to strengthen and protect Prussia by creating a pan-German union in which Prussia would always be dominant. That strategy, in turn, would put Prussia in a position to minimize the power and influence of the Habsburgs. Bismarck was not a German nationalist; he was a Prussian patriot who believed that there could only be one great power in Germany, and he wanted to make sure it was Prussia. But he was more than willing to use German nationalism if he felt it would strengthen Prussia and enhance the loyalty people felt toward the monarchy.

By the 1850s the German population could be divided almost evenly into three groups: 50 million people with one-third each in Prussia, Austria, and the Third Germany. Outside the Habsburg empire, Protestants now outnumbered Catholics in the German lands. In economic activity Prussia was not only ahead, but was pulling ahead faster as it rapidly industrialized.[1] Prussian cities in places like Silesia, the Rhineland, and especially the Ruhr attracted waves of unskilled labor to the new factories, mines, and railroads. As the balance of Prussia's demographic and economic power shifted steadily toward the cities, the election results produced the inevitable deadlock between the rising liberals and the conservatives. By 1861 the Diet had become the political battleground testing whether the monarchy had the ability to expand the military (which required new funding), or whether this power rested in the hands of the legislators. The ailing Frederick William IV died in that year, replaced by his younger brother William I. Having decided to fight the Diet for his royal prerogatives, William wanted a powerful advocate. Thus in 1862 he chose Bismarck to serve as minister-president (effectively prime minister) of Prussia. Bismarck was simultaneously the foreign minister, and thus arguably the most powerful man in the most powerful state in Germany.

Long after both men were dead, it became customary to assume that Otto von Bismarck had really run Prussia, much as Metternich had manipulated the Austrian emperors in his day, and that King William I was little more than a rubber stamp for his policies. But in fact William was very much alert and active in his job. The king wisely insisted that he had to remain above politics altogether. He was broadly popular at the time. Already an old man when he became king, William represented a living link to the heroic age of the Napoleonic Wars (when he had been a young officer and had fought with distinction in several battles). He maintained a warm, grandfatherly image,

Figure 6.2. King William I (left) and Chancellor von Bismarck (right). Image of William excerpted from the photograph by Gustav Richter, digitally reproduced in the public domain by Bob Burkhardt. Image of Bismarck in the public domain.

combined with the stern self-discipline of a Prussian officer. William gave Bismarck great latitude in the day-to-day management of the government because the king did not want to get his hands dirty in party politics. But he reserved the right to be the final arbiter of any important decision. Bismarck was powerful, but William was still the king.

The Prussian government faced three fundamental questions in the 1860s. First, how to position Prussia within the German Confederation and whether and how to expand the state by taking direct control over other lands as opportunities arose to marginalize rivals like Austria or neighbors like Denmark and France. Second, how to expand the power of the military to achieve this aim without giving up royal power to the diet, whose liberal delegates now held at least some of the purse strings. And third, how to manage the shifting demographic and economic situation of Prussia, heading off revolutionary groups who demanded social change.

In each of these cases, Bismarck believed that the most useful approach was to unify people around patriotic causes. He was probably influenced by what had happened in the 1848 revolutions, when the king and aristocracy restored the people's faith in their legitimacy by leading the war against Denmark. By this point an entire generation of Germans had grown up in an atmosphere of intense patriotic nationalism and had passed through public schools that had reinforced that spirit and taught all children that Prussian heroes had rallied the German people and unified them in victory against Napoleon. Partly as a manipulator and partly as an opportunist, Bismarck planned to use foreign conflict to rally the Third Germany behind Prussia.

In 1864 the conflict with Denmark over Schleswig-Holstein erupted again. Prussia and Austria both sent forces to intervene, and despite some embarrassing defeats for the fledgling Prussian navy, Bismarck initially got the result he desired: angry Germans, unified in their desire to "liberate" the people of Schleswig-Holstein and proud to rally behind the cause. But the national mood turned against both Berlin and Vienna when people realized that the peace treaty had failed to bring the province into the German Confederation immediately. The settlement left Schleswig-Holstein in joint Austro-Prussian occupation and administration, a situation that was bound to cause friction between the two. Again, Bismarck took advantage of existing opportunities, but also manipulated events into a war with Austria two years later, in 1866.

In the years since the Napoleonic Wars, the Prussian military had conducted an intensive series of exercises, developed new tactics, and studied communications, logistics, and the new mobility options created by technologies like the railroad and telegraph. While the Austrians had been absorbed by internal conflicts, Prussia had honed its military forces to a remarkable level of efficiency. When William I came to the throne, this was enhanced by fact that the king himself had a military background and was actively interested in the army leadership and its policies. The Prussian army in the 1860s was probably the best-trained and most modern in the world.

The Austrians learned this to their dismay in the so-called Six Weeks' War of 1866. Although individual Austrian soldiers fought bravely, their leadership was totally overwhelmed by the speed of the Prussian attack, and Habsburg resistance collapsed after a few days' fighting in Bohemia. The Austrians were then surprised to find that Bismarck's peace terms were remarkably lenient, at least toward them. The Prussians annexed a few small German states and punished some of the others who had sided with Austria by occupying them and imposing martial law. True to his basic goals, Bismarck wanted to exclude Austria from the further influence in Germany, but was willing to offer them a separate alliance and guarantee of security. Bismarck's turn from ally to enemy to ally again, all in three years, is an excellent example of his practice of *realpolitik*.

What Is *Realpolitik?*

(pronounced: ray-AL-po-li-TEEK)

Although it was later associated with Bismarck, the expression first appeared in German when used by the liberal publisher Ludwig August Rochow during the 1848 revolutions. This word does not translate well into English, meaning essentially "practical politics." It refers to a nonideological approach to diplomacy and public policy, in which one does not take a rigid moral stand on any issue, nor hold grudges, nor hang on to loyalties, but rather keeps calculating the political merits of any decision on a day-by-day basis.

The objective is to remain in power and to manage the affairs of the state rationally and flexibly as circumstances change. An enemy today might be an ally tomorrow. A policy you oppose today might be a useful expedient next year, if it helps you to prevent something worse.

In the wake of the 1866 victory, most of the central and northern German states were now either allied to Prussia, intimidated by Prussia, or annexed by Prussia outright. After lengthy negotiations with several of the smaller states, Bismarck proposed a reform of the old German Confederation, creating something more closely resembling an actual, unified German state, at least in the northern two-thirds of Germany. The resulting North German Confederation was not quite a nation-state. It had its own currency and customs, a flag (the black-white-red stripes that became the imperial flag), and theoretically its own military. In another deft performance of realpolitik, Bismarck pushed for a national assembly (Reichstag) that would be elected by universal male suffrage. Why did he, of all people, want to saddle this new creation with a true legislature? For one thing, it would prevent the liberals from demanding one, and thus creating one of their own. And for another, it would make it more palatable for people to accept the rest of the government, which was anything but democratic. The tiny upper house of the parliament was appointed by the German rulers, the "president" of the Confederation was King William of Prussia, and Bismarck himself became chancellor, a new office with significant executive powers. Thus by offering a shiny new democratic facade, the Confederation actually strengthened Prussia's dominance and Bismarck's personal power. Most significantly for the immediate future, the North German Confederation was a military alliance in which all the member states put their armies under the unified command of the king of Prussia.

The unification of Germany is often told as a series of three wars engineered by Bismarck specifically for that result. This is an exaggeration; the chancellor was generally more a keen opportunist than a long-range schemer. He would have been happy to get what he wanted without war. But in the case of the 1870 conflict with France, he did indisputably work to ensure a conflict. His task was made considerably easier by the general mood of Germans, who had by this point absorbed two generations of passionate anti-French nationalist propaganda, and by the Prussian military chiefs, who were confident of their army and well prepared for war. King William I, however, was considerably less enthusiastic, and Bismarck almost overplayed his hand by pushing the king too hard. (Among other things, he was caught altering a diplomatic telegram to make it more inflammatory.) The ostensible cause of the war was a dispute over the succession to the throne of Spain and the possibility that a member of the Hohenzollern dynasty might become the Spanish king. Many historians also believe that the Prussian leadership, being Protestants, wanted to unify Germany's Protestant majority and intimidate German Catholics into obedience by systematically humiliating or defeating any major Catholic powers (Austria or France) that might rally German Catholics and keep Germany divided along religious lines. Effectively, the cause of the war was that Bismarck and the Prussian high command believed the timing was right, and a great many Germans simply wanted it.

In July 1870 France's emperor Napoleon III declared war. He, and most of the French army and people, were shocked by the speed with which the Prussian army cut through France, supported by smaller forces from the other German states. The main French armies were outmaneuvered and destroyed, with Napoleon himself captured by the Prussians. A French provisional government tried to fight on, and Paris held out under siege for months, ruled by a Socialist "commune," but the German forces simply starved them out. France sued for peace in 1871.

The Prussian high command favored a severe dismemberment of France, along the lines of what the first Napoleon had done to Prussia in 1807. Bismarck was satisfied that the victory had unified the German states behind Prussia, and he desired only to ensure that the status quo remained in Germany's favor. He settled, therefore, for a hefty bill of war reparations and annexation of two regions of the French Rhineland that could plausibly be considered at least partly German: Alsace and Lorraine. That annexation, however, guaranteed that there would be no realpolitik with France; the French remained furious about their lost provinces for decades and getting them back became a national obsession.

For Bismarck, the more important outcome of the war was the creation of a new German nation-state, an arrangement that had to be negotiated with the southern German regimes like Bavaria and Württemberg. Bismarck knew that he had a window of opportunity that would not last forever. Germans were euphoric over the victory. Celebrations expressed the idea that a cycle of historical justice had been completed. King William of Prussia, who was a child when Napoleon humiliated his parents and ruled over the Germans, had now led the Prussians in their crushing victory over the second French empire and another emperor named Napoleon. That generation of Germans, in Prussia and elsewhere, often referred to him as William the Great. Bismarck's own popularity and political capital had never been greater. He knew he would not have a better opportunity to shape German politics.

On January 18, 1871, as the last French armies were straggling toward surrender and the war was obviously won, King William I of Prussia stood upon a platform in the Hall of Mirrors at the palace of Versailles and received the

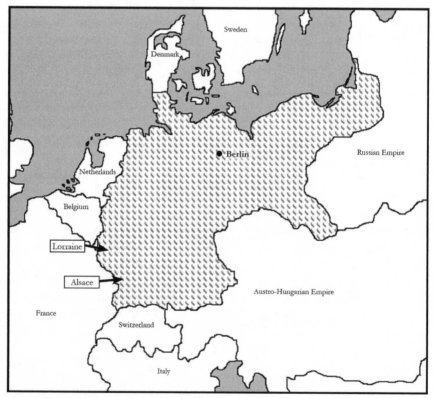

Figure 6.3. The Second Reich, 1871–1919

acclaim of his fellow German rulers. He was proclaimed emperor of a new German Reich. The choice of Versailles was an obvious declaration that the age of the French mastery in Europe had ended, and the age of the Germans had begun.

The Second Reich

At the time of its existence, Germans referred to their nation-state as simply the German Empire. In retrospect it has been called the Second Reich, or in the idiomatic German expression, the *Kaiserreich*. Bismarck received much of the credit for its creation then, as he still does today, but it was in a sense an idea whose time had come. Although the Second Reich endured only forty-seven years, it remained broadly popular, indeed even an object of passionate patriotism for the large majority of the German people. This demonstrates that although the structure of the imperial state itself was shallow—in some ways a collection of compromises and half measures—the *idea* of a German empire ran deep.

The Second Reich was a federal monarchy. The regional governments and their borders remained; the king of Bavaria was still king of Bavaria, for example. Prussia, by far the largest unit of the Reich, dominated but did not directly rule over many bread-and-butter issues. The public school systems, for instance, the judiciary, social services—all these and many other issues remained controlled by the states. Even the regional armies remained distinctive, although the Prussian high command became the imperial high command, and thus by default Prussians ran the combined German army. William, who remained king of Prussia, was now also German emperor (kaiser). He was supposedly not able to initiate legislation; that was the job of the upper house, or *Bundesrat*, with delegates chosen by the states. Prussia held such a strong plurality in the Bundesrat that it could effectively veto any initiatives, and Bismarck, as Reich chancellor, presided over this body, being directly appointed by the emperor. The lower house, or Reichstag, was directly elected by universal male suffrage, and became the scene of lively political debates and party politics, but its power was limited. It could only vote on bills that were put before it, having originated with the Bundesrat. It could not initiate new policies, nor choose any imperial officials. Its one meaningful power—which the members soon discovered and used—was its ability to block the passage of the budget.

The Second Reich included large minorities of non-Germans, particularly Poles, Danes, and French speakers. Protestants outnumbered Catholics, and many regions remained staunchly one or the other, with little mixing. And of course the federal structure was supposed to have preserved the regional distinctiveness of the German states, with their different histories, dialects, and traditions. But—apparently to Bismarck's surprise—the Second Reich began to develop a national character of its own, and a solidly *German* identity. Even if its institutions were not truly those of a unified nation-state, German political, social, and economic life increasingly took on a unified tone. In the 1880s the national government even began a project of cataloguing the major regional dialects of German, with the intent of creating a single "official" German language within two generations. Although Bismarck tried to swallow up Germany into Prussia, what actually happened more resembled Prussia being swallowed up into a unified Germany. Emperor William had recognized this from the beginning; Bismarck found him in tears on the evening before his coronation at Versailles, crying that he was "burying the Prussian kingdom."[2]

Two years after its creation, the German Empire was struck by the global depression of 1873. In the protectionist mood that followed, with the em-

Figure 6.4. The "William the Great" Monument: The moniker "the Great" never stuck to him, as it did to Frederick or Charlemagne, but one can see it inscribed in the many monuments and other patriotic memorabilia created in the late 1800s. This huge equestrian statue of William stands in the Rhineland city of Koblenz, where the Moselle and Rhine rivers meet, at the so-called German Corner (Deutsches Eck). The monument was damaged in the Second World War and then demolished by the Americans. It was reconstructed in the 1990s and is now a United Nations world cultural site.

phasis on saving German businesses and jobs, the Reich passed through a period not only of nationalism, but also of religious bigotry. This period came to be known as the *Kulturkampf* (cultural struggle). It featured anti-Semitic harangues and publications against Jewish bankers and merchants, who were accused of placing "foreign" interests above the good of working-class Germans. And it involved a political struggle between Protestant and Catholic Germans, again with the minority (the Catholics) being accused of "foreign" connections (in this case loyalty to the pope or to Catholic states like Austria-Hungary, Italy, or France), or being accused of supporting independence for ethnic minorities like the Poles in eastern Prussia. The mid-1870s saw Prussian legislation to illegalize certain Catholic groups like the Jesuits, shut down monasteries and Catholic schools, and remove Catholics from certain civil service positions. Bismarck himself fanned the flames, perhaps as a way of distracting those discontented with the slow pace of economic recovery after the depression. His motives were likely also political; the laws enabled the state to exert more control over activities that had been in the hands of churches (of all denominations). Finally, Bismarck was probably trying to draw battle lines in the Reichstag, where the Catholic Center Party was growing stronger. The episode lasted several years, and although it did damage to many people's lives and careers, it had little effect upon the patriotism of Catholic Germans. By the 1880s, Bismarck sensed that the most serious threat to the imperial status quo came not from liberals, Jews, or Catholics, but rather from a swelling new movement that had roots in Germany, but which was now a European phenomenon: socialism.

Karl Marx came from a bourgeois Jewish family in the Rhineland. At the University of Berlin he was particularly influenced by the great philosopher Friedrich Hegel, whose ideas about the pattern of historical development and the creation of ideas and systems shaped Marx's thinking. As a young professor and newspaper editor, Marx was frequently in trouble for his radical ideas and controversial essays and articles. By 1843 he was in self-imposed exile in Paris.

In Paris, Marx befriended another expatriate German, Friedrich Engels, who had already made a name for himself with his passionate exposés of the terrible poverty and suffering of working-class people in Britain. Engels had come to believe that only a complete revolutionary transformation could save these people from the dreadful exploitation inherent in capitalism. Together they worked on several projects, and scored an unexpected success with a little sixty-seven-page paperback called *The Communist Manifesto*. It was published in February 1848, just as all Europe seemed to be catching revolutionary fever. The booklet appeared and reappeared for decades, gradually reaching a huge audience in dozens of languages and becoming a sort of basic manual of instruction for working people interested in Communism. It remains one of the most widely read books in human history.

Marx always insisted that his ideas represented "Scientific Socialism," that is, an approach based upon comprehensive research into economics, politics, and history that demonstrated the inevitable changes in human production and employment. He believed that capitalism was leading inexorably to the degradation of humanity, turning people into mere resources to be consumed by the factories, destroying the middle class and dividing society into a small elite who owned all the capital and the large majority who worked for wages. He was convinced that eventually this system would be toppled by Socialist revolutionaries who would then lead the working class to the next stage of human development: Communism.

By the time of Marx's death in 1883, socialist parties were growing in nearly every European state. In his homeland of Germany, the Socialist Party (eventually the Social Democrats, or SPD) was an emerging force in the Reichstag. The great crash of 1873 had shaken many working people's faith in liberal policies, and the dramatic demographic changes in Germany gave the Socialists a new base of support.

As Germany emerged from the depression years of the early 1870s, population growth and economic activity dramatically accelerated. In the twenty years between 1871 and 1891, for instance, the populations of many German cities doubled again (Hamburg tripled), and the national population increased from 41 million to 65 million. This was largely an urban growth spurt; the population of industrial areas like the Ruhr nearly quadrupled as Germany's industrial output surpassed that of every other continental European state, and was coming close to that of Great Britain. The shift to an urban, industrialized population and the growing disparities between the few very rich and the many very poor in the industrial slums gave the Social Democrats a sympathetic audience.

Bismarck's counterattack against Socialism was two-pronged. On one hand, he passed a number of restrictive laws, blaming Socialists for public disturbances and even for plotting to assassinate the emperor. These laws only had the effect of making the Social Democratic leadership very careful in their public utterances, and willing to work within the parliamentary limitations of the Reichstag. The German Socialists became more evolutionary than revolutionary; a normal part of the political landscape. Bismarck's second tactic was another example of his realpolitik: he attempted to head off Socialist demands by introducing new state-run welfare programs. In the 1880s Germany developed the first socialized medical insurance, state-run pension systems, and workers' compensation programs. None of these developments, however, stemmed the red tide. With each Reichstag election they gained seats, until by 1912 the SPD received nearly 35 percent of the national vote and were the largest party in parliament. By that point they were arguably mainstreamed. Following the 1891 party congress in Erfurt, the SPD had officially distanced itself from Marx's goals of bringing down the capitalist system through revolution. The party pledged to work within the existing system to bring incremental change and improve the lives of working people.

The rapid growth of Socialism in Germany presents us with a fascinating dichotomy. On one hand the Second Reich was a fiercely nationalistic, religious, and conservative place, where people celebrated the heroes and battles of the past; loved patriotic poetry, novels, and plays; and seemed to live in the midst of a profusion of monuments, statues, and flags. On the other hand, it was the heartland of European Socialism, a political movement that celebrated the common working man and wanted to bring down national borders and get rid of aristocrats and churches. The contradictions give us some clue as to why Marx thought that a proletarian revolution would first occur in a place like Germany. Socialism seemed to be growing fastest and

Figure 6.5. The "Valhalla" Monument near Regensburg: A pantheon of German heroes going back to pre-Roman times. Image from the private collection of Markus Schirmer, used with permission.

Figure 6.6. The Arminius Monument near Detmold. Image from the private collection of Markus Schirmer, used with permission.

strongest in Europe's most vibrant industrial economy, where capitalist factory magnates and shipping tycoons marched in lockstep with conservative aristocrats in military uniforms.

Looking Ahead to the Past

Throughout its existence the Second Reich had a motif of historical vindication, often specifically anti-French in tone. From the coronation of the emperor in Versailles, to the ongoing celebrations for the centennials of the births or deaths of famous heroes from the Napoleonic Wars, to the great monuments that proliferated in both the cities and the countryside, imperial Germany reconstructed the German past as a unified and heroic story of a single German people. Germans seemed determined to transform the very landscape, as over 1,100 monuments were erected between 1871 and 1914, 600 of which were either for Emperor William I or for Bismarck.[3] Many of these were small, local endeavors celebrating some hero from a particular town or some event that had occurred there. Others were veritable monstrosities, obviously intended as punctuation for a national epic.

During the imperial era, Germans wrote thousands of novels, poems, operas, and songs celebrating real or imagined heroes of the distant and not-so-distant past. Klara Mundt (writing as Luise von Mühlbach) became Europe's most widely read female author, with dozens of historical novels, many of which injected romance and adventure into famous episodes of German history. The outsized operas of Richard Wagner mesmerized audiences (including a teenaged Austrian named Adolf Hitler) with their tales of Germanic gods and heroes. In a highly nationalistic age, imperial Germany was not out of step with the times, but seemed to many observers to be deafeningly jingoistic.

Figure 6.7.   The Victory Column in Berlin: Part of a circle of monuments to the German victory over France in 1871.

And yet for all its simplistic clichés and sentimentality, the Reich was also a place of remarkable intellectual accomplishment. By the 1880s the German university system was considered a model for most of the Western world. American students sought opportunities to study in Germany, and scholars across Europe followed the work of the Prussian Academy of Sciences. German graduate programs dominated European scientific accomplishment for the next several decades, as evidenced by the nationality of so many Nobel laureates in the early twentieth century.

German industry benefited directly from this work. By the 1890s German firms were world leaders in chemical engineering and the development of electronics, optics, and engines. German cities were among the first in the world to have modern electric lighting, subways, streetcars, and electric elevators. Gottlieb Daimler and Wilhelm Maybach produced one of the first internal combustion engines in 1883, which within two years powered the first motorcycle. At the same time their rival Karl Benz began building what became by 1900 the world's largest automobile factory. Germans were pioneers of aviation, particularly lighter-than-air craft, which soon began to be known by the name of the inventor, Count Ferdinand von Zeppelin.

In 1888, the "year of the three emperors," the elderly William I died at the age of ninety-one. He was succeeded by his son Frederick III, a kind and intelligent man in whom many liberals had placed hopes for a new, reformed constitutional monarchy. But Frederick was already dying of throat cancer, and expired only three months later, leaving the throne to his son, William II, aged twenty-nine. This unexpected transition dramatically illustrated the passage of power from the older generation to the younger.

William II was in many ways the living embodiment of the temperament of the Second Reich. He was a young ruler of a young nation—both politically and demographically. Unlike his predecessors, he had no personal experience of the great conflicts of the past, nor of the struggles for German unification. He represented his generation: fiercely patriotic, fed on mythologized history, and convinced that the German people's time had finally come to lead European civilization. His understanding of diplomacy and statecraft was a near-perfect opposite of Bismarck's; William believed in deep loyalties, based upon race and shared ancestry. Historians have long debated how much direct power William II held, and to what extent German policies were truly his own doing. The question is to some extent moot. The emperor's brash self-confidence reflected a national mood that Germany, as a late arrival among the great powers, might have to do some pushing and shoving to secure its deserved place.

Not surprisingly, Bismarck and William II clashed immediately and often. The old chancellor resigned in 1890, marking the end of an era for many Germans. Although the country in general celebrated his accomplishments, particularly in retrospect, few people despaired at his departure at the time. His immediate successor as chancellor, Leo von Caprivi, was initially very popular precisely because his promised new political course seemed a welcome change. Caprivi and Wilhelm hoped to navigate Germany's changing political landscape with policies that could appeal to broad segments of the Reichstag, rather than trying to work with a single party at a time. The empire introduced new social programs, asserted the rights of workers to arbitration in disputes with their employers, and relaxed the restrictive laws against certain political parties (notably the Socialists). It was a well-intended but futile effort. A fundamentally conservative, hereditary monarchy could never hope to win over the Socialists with a few handouts. As Bismarck had understood, the monarchy could only hope to hold the Socialists at bay by using the social programs to stake out a new political center thus forcing the Socialists further to the left, where they would have more narrow support. With his new policies, Caprivi's government only angered traditional conservatives. His chancellorship lasted only four years.

The Caprivi government, however, did oversee a period of dramatic change in Germany's foreign policy, a departure from Bismarck's careful juggling act of the past two decades. Almost from the moment the Second Reich was founded, Bismarck had repeatedly emphasized to diplomats that Germany was a "satisfied power," that it was finished with war and expansion. Knowing that France would remain an implacable foe, Bismarck worked instead to ensure that Germany maintained good relations with all other major European powers, "to be left in peace by France and to prevent her from finding allies if she should not wish to keep the peace."[4] This generally meant not injecting German interests into the Middle East or Africa, to avoid conflict with the British and Russians, nor into the Balkans, to avoid conflict with the Russians and Austrians. Indeed, Bismarck's major diplomatic efforts were focused upon conflict resolution, not German gain, such as the Berlin Treaty of 1878 that ended the Russo-Turkish War or the Berlin Conference of 1884–1885 that settled a number of imperial questions in Africa and elsewhere. Germany maintained solid alliances with Russia, Austria-Hungary, and Italy, along with cordial relations with Great Britain.

Under William II, however, Germany became an active competitor in the European power struggle. The effort to acquire colonies in Africa and Asia, which Bismarck had resisted and then pursued only reluctantly and halfheartedly, suddenly accelerated. Coming late, however, the result was primarily that Germany acquired very little of value, at the expense of making enemies in European capitals. (To this day, Caprivi's name is attached to a strip of desert in Namibia.) The German navy, which had long been insignificantly small and considered marginal, began to take shape—at tremendous expense and with furious political debate—as a first-class modern fleet, which alarmed the British and caused fear of German intentions as far away as America. Most seriously, William allowed the alliance with Russia to expire. The emperor had always preferred an alliance with Austria-Hungary and Britain, for reasons of ethnic similarity as well as political calculation. The British and Russians were embroiled in near-constant conflict over central Asia, and the Austrians and Russians were squabbling over a variety of incipient conflicts in the Balkans. Consequently, William assumed that he could do without the Russians and take the side of their rivals, instead. Despite the Russian government's repeated requests, Germany did not renew the treaty, which lapsed in 1890. Two years later, Russia and France signed an alliance. It was a decision that came to haunt Germany. France had finally obtained an ally, and a conveniently massive one that shared a long border with archenemy Germany.

William's personal diplomacy was generally disastrous. Although the emperor could not make or break treaties single-handedly, he nonetheless was a ubiquitous spokesman for the Reich, and could not resist the urge to speak his frequently uncensored mind in front of audiences and reporters. He casually and haughtily threatened small neighbors like Holland and Belgium, insulted the Russian tsar, and promoted a controversial railway project in the Ottoman Empire, which he boasted would be "a dagger aimed at the heart of [British] India." He injected Germany into various Anglo-French and Anglo-Russian colonial disputes, with the result that the disputants came away feeling that Germany was a threat to them both.

The emperor was often deaf to the worries of educated people or diplomats who had to clean up in the wake of his tactless interventions. He was, however, generally within the mainstream of the public mood. German people increasingly demanded a higher global profile. National pride swelled—as it did in other imperial nations—at the acquisition of colonies, at the building of a large battle fleet, or when the sparks flew in international disputes with rivals. In the early 1900s, under Chancellor Bernhard von Bülow, Germany made one last, unsuccessful attempt to craft an alliance with Great Britain. But by 1908 the German military high command had resigned themselves to the likelihood that any future war would find the Reich surrounded by powerful enemies.

Ever since the mid-nineteenth century and the days of the great Prussian general staff that had won the wars of unification, most European armies had learned to imitate the German system of meticulous staff planning, annual major exercises, timetables for the calling up of reserves, and a reliance upon an intricate schedule of mobilization. Depending upon the state, a large army could be mobilized for war and marched into action in anywhere from two to six weeks. Getting this period of mobilization to move as quickly and smoothly as possible was considered essential. The Germans, pioneers of this system, prided themselves on their efficiency and speed. Of course, the mobilization plans were entirely under the control of the military, who practiced them and refined them every year, and who awaited only the signal of their governments to begin the process. This meant that most of the European states had developed systems in which any potential warlike crisis could cause political leaders to call for military mobilization, which would then lead inevitably to full-blown war. The political leaders, once they gave the military their mobilization orders, would lose control of the situation.

Germany's generals knew by the early 1900s that they faced a war against Russia and France simultaneously, with their Italian allies wavering and uncertain, and Britain probably unfriendly at least. The growing power of Russia terrified German military leaders. Various legal and budgetary limits constrained the German army to a maximum peacetime size that could never match the combined strength of all their enemies. Consequently, their plans began to take on the attitude of "better sooner than later." By 1910, German generals believed that war might even be desirable in the near future, while Germany still had a mathematical chance of winning, rather than waiting until it was too late.[5] Consequently, the men whose opinions the emperor valued the most—the Prussian aristocrats who ran his army—encouraged his naturally aggressive temperament to respond to each new diplomatic crisis by threatening war, or at least seriously considering it. And German statesmen, finding it increasingly difficult to navigate the complex politics of a Reichstag dominated by unfriendly parties like the Socialists, recognized the political value of unifying the people against a foreign enemy, real or contrived.

The assassination of the Archduke Franz Ferdinand of Austria-Hungary by Serbian terrorists hit William at a personal level. Not only were all European monarchs understandably sensitive to questions of terrorism and assassination, but by June 1914, Austria-Hungary was in fact Germany's only remaining ally. When the Austrian government sought German support for a war against Serbia to punish the assassins, William did not hesitate to offer that support, even though he must have known that it would result in a war with Serbia's ally and sponsor, Russia. That, in turn, meant a war with

France. When he learned that Russia had ordered mobilization on July 29, 1914, Emperor William II ordered German mobilization the following day.

Suggested Reading

Berghahn, Volker. *Imperial Germany, 1871–1918: Economy, Society, Culture, and Politics*. Providence RI: Berghahn, 2005.

Blackbourn, David. *The Long Nineteenth Century: A History of Germany, 1780–1918*. Oxford: Oxford University Press, 1998.

Craig, Gordon. *The Politics of the Prussian Army, 1640–1945*. Oxford: Oxford University Press, 1955.

Hamerowe, Theodore. *Restoration, Revolution, Reaction: Economics and Politics in Germany, 1815–1871*. Princeton, NJ: Princeton University Press, 1958.

Herrmann, David. *The Arming of Europe and the Making of the First World War*. Princeton, NJ: Princeton University Press, 1996.

Wawro, Geoffrey. *The Austro-Prussian War: Austria's War with Prussia and Italy in 1866*. Cambridge: Cambridge University Press, 1996.

———. *The Franco-Prussian War: The German Conquest of France in 1870–1871*. Cambridge: Cambridge University Press, 2003.

CHAPTER SEVEN

Modernity and Its Discontents

German summers can be unpredictable, but the summer of 1914 was beautiful, hot, and sunny. As the war excitement built, crowds gathered in the warm city evenings, especially in Berlin, where news of the crisis was awaited with nervous tension. People mobbed newspaper delivery wagons to get the latest news. Chancellor Bethmann-Holweg worried that revolutionary chaos might ensue whether or not there was a war declaration. His fears were misplaced. When the announcement came that Serbia had rejected the Austrian ultimatum, thus making war virtually inevitable, tens of thousands of people filled the boulevard Unter den Linden as they headed toward the imperial palace, singing the national anthem. Other crowds gathered downtown deep into the night. Two days later, when the Kaiser and his sons returned to Berlin from their summer vacation, people mobbed their vehicles, cheering, singing patriotic songs, and calling for war.[1]

William II and his military high command have generally been held responsible by historians for pushing Germany toward an unnecessary war. But for millions of people in Germany in the summer of 1914—as in many places across Europe—the war seemed anything but unnecessary. As Germany hurtled toward war against the traditional French enemy once again, nobody could have guessed that the Reich had only a little more than four years left to live.

The "Civil Peace"

Historians disagree regarding the level of support people initially expressed for the war, in Germany or elsewhere. While scenes like the one described above occurred in many German cities, there were also some antiwar demonstrations, particularly among working-class people who presumably knew that they were most likely to be called up for the army. Two big antiwar demonstrations in Berlin in late July were even larger than the prowar demonstrations had been.[2] Several historians have suggested that the most ardent support for the war, across Europe in general, was among the urban middle classes, the affluent, and educated people, although historians have generally been unable to explain convincingly *why* that would be so, and it is possible that we simply know more about the feelings of these people because the educated classes were more likely to leave their thoughts in writing. Of course the huge majority of people never attended a demonstration, for war or against. It is clear that Germany, like most of the other belligerents, experienced a wave of enlistment. So many men rushed to volunteer in August that hundreds of thousands had to be turned away because the army couldn't take them all, and because entire sectors of the economy would be paralyzed if so many working men departed for the front.[3]

In many countries with parliamentary systems, the opposing parties declared that the war called for a special moratorium on normal politics, in the interest of common effort and patriotism. In Germany, this phenomenon became known as the *Burgfrieden*, or civil peace. The Kaiser famously tried to set the tone by addressing the Reichstag with the slogan: "I no longer recognize any parties; I know only Germans," which soon was mass-produced on posters, calendars, wall hangings, postcards, and household items.[4] Effectively, it meant that the traditional opposition parties like the Social Democrats shifted from their normal skepticism of the government to a loudly patriotic support for the war effort. Some Socialists remained opposed to the war on ideological grounds, and in fact they later ended up splitting from the SPD in the midst of the war to form what ultimately became the German Communist party. But in the early days of the war most Socialists were full-throated in their patriotism, many volunteered for the military, and in general it seemed that nationality had trumped class as a motivating factor.

This raises the question, obviously, of what Germans thought they were fighting *for*. It is striking that the event that sparked the war—the assassination of an Austrian archduke—seemed to be on nobody's mind in August 1914. In the popular media, people wrote of the allied plots to "encircle" Germany, or to crush the Reich, or to prevent Germany from having her rightful place in the world. People who left opinions in writing often spoke in vague terms about their level of excitement and the moral clarity of simple patriotism. In Germany, as in most European countries in 1914, the government enjoyed a period of general support simply because the nation appeared to be united in a common struggle.

In the autumn of 1914 the German offensive in France ground to a halt, and the opposing armies settled into long lines of increasingly elaborate trenches that came to define the Western Front. With some exceptions, the Germans shifted to a defensive posture in the west and devoted their energies instead to the Eastern Front, on which German forces began to score dramatic victories against the Russians. With their battered Austrian allies in tow, the German forces advanced deep into Russian territory by early 1915. The war continued to expand as Italy joined the Allies, opening a new front in the Alps; Bulgaria joined the Central Powers, opening a new front in the Balkans; and the Ottoman Empire joined the Central Powers, bringing the war to the Middle East.

The nature of the fighting in the First World War was shockingly different from anything experienced by past generations. On the Western Front, where German forces faced the British and French armies, both sides dug deep and elaborate systems of trenches, extending from the Swiss border all the way to the English Channel. Movement all but ceased as the opponents bombarded each other with high explosives and poison gas, and as infantrymen were expended in repeated and fruitless attacks across minefields and barbed wire and into entrenched defenses bristling with machine guns. The casualty rates were astronomical, and since generals could not measure success in miles on a map, they measured it in the numbers of enemy killed and disabled.

Fighting on the Eastern Front retained a degree of mobility, as German and Austrian troops steadily pushed the Russians back toward the east. The Eastern Front remained the one theater of war from which the German commanders routinely reported good news, but the vast scale of that region and its primitive communication network meant that even great success could not bring quick victory.

Germany's allies were generally hobbled in some way, industrially or technologically, and required German assistance. German troops thus ended up fighting alongside Austrians, Bulgarians, and Ottomans on the many smaller fronts, from the mountains of the Italian Alps, to the Balkans, to the Middle East, and even in African colonies. At sea the British navy, with its superior numbers and advantageous geographic position, was able to blockade the German coast. Germany may have been an industrial giant, but that power had been financed primarily by exports, and by mid-1915 most overseas commerce had ceased. Thus surrounded, cut off from most world trade, and outnumbered, how did Germany fight on for so long, and often with such success?

All nations changed their economies to a war footing, but few did so as thoroughly as Germany. Initially many bureaus and agencies competed for authority over the hugely important questions of military spending and resources. In 1915 a wealthy industrialist named Walter Rathenau became the director of war production, with a specific portfolio to bring industry into line with the government's military needs. The result was a massive transformation of labor, matériel, transportation, and finance, to the point that by 1917 more than three-quarters of Germany's gross national product was in some way related to the war. Businessmen naturally complained about this odd new form of centrally planned conservative Socialism, and of course no amount of reorganizing could conceal the fundamental problems of being cut off from overseas investments and trade. Overall German industrial production and wages both declined steadily during the war, even as greater percentages were dedicated to the military effort.

Rathenau himself was not an easy man to like. He was famously high-living, usually seen with expensive suits and fine cigars: a man who enjoyed the best of everything. This did not help his reputation when times were hard. Although he was genuinely patriotic, people accused him of giving the most lucrative contracts to Berlin-based companies (he was from Berlin), or of favoring Jewish banks and businesses (Rathenau was Jewish). Some of the accusations were exaggerated, and indicated a building atmosphere of discontent and anti-Semitism. Even though his office was eventually taken over by the army, Walter Rathenau became a scapegoat for the inevitable shortages and suffering of a population trying to support a world war. His methods, however, probably kept Germany in the war longer than it otherwise could have managed.

Private citizens contributed, too. By the war's end in 1918, nearly 60 percent of the government's war bonds were owned by private citizens (compared with only 12 percent in Britain).[5] Germans put up with the rationing and growing shortages and kept buying bonds until the very last months of the war. Whether this was due to natural patriotism, or whether the heavily censored news with its misleadingly optimistic reports of victories kept people uninformed, is not clear. After all, if people had believed that Germany was losing, their patriotism might have resulted in even greater contributions.

The most obvious level of public commitment was found in the willingness of the German public to mobilize men for the front. Only Russia put more men in uniform than did Germany in the period 1914–1918. Germany was relatively late to allow women to work in the war industries, a fact that has been explained variously as social conservatism or the power (and anxieties) of labor unions. Whatever the reason, by the end of war women were indeed working in industry, and by some estimates were nearly one-third of the industrial workforce.

As the war dragged on, it was financed by borrowing, as it was in most countries. By 1917, the German government was running a deficit close to 100 percent of revenues. The huge government contracts awarded to industries for producing war materials, and the high interest rates charged by lenders to a government running deep in debt inevitably resulted in a few people at the top becoming extremely rich. People in several countries began to grumble about "war profiteers." In Germany, the figure of Walter Rathenau became a particularly despised symbol for many groups, who also spread rumors that Jewish investors (like some of Rathenau's colleagues) were deliberately prolonging the war and German suffering in order to get even richer. We cannot say how widely the conspiracy stories spread, but surely they resonated with Corporal Adolf Hitler and many of his comrades at the front.

The government's financial woes did not impress many lower-class citizens. Factory workers saw their hours increase and their wages drop, while the prices of basic goods began to rise. A loaf of bread—the basic staple of the German diet—was three times as expensive in 1918 as it had been at the war's start in 1914, prompting protests in several cities, including a large women's demonstration in Berlin. Germany's huge chemical industry was so completely reoriented to war production that basic lubricants and fertilizers became scarce, reducing farm production. By 1917, hunger became common in a country that had once had plenty of food. During the miserable "turnip winter" of 1916–1917 over half a million people died. That same winter there was a coal shortage, causing much of the national railway system to shut down and causing many cities to cut electricity after certain hours of the night.

Nonetheless, by 1917 it was clear that Russia was collapsing, and that the Germans could plausibly end the war with a greatly expanded empire in the east. The success on the Eastern Front led many Germans to irrationally predict a victorious end to the war, despite all the signs of trouble. Even after the United States entered the conflict in April 1917, German leaders concerned themselves with visions of huge annexations of territory, colonies, and Slavic puppet states. A new right-wing party formed in the Reichstag, the German Fatherland Party (DVP), which supported the government's takeover of industry and the concept of postwar annexations and colonization. Many historians have seen the DVP as a forerunner of the Nazi party, with its right-wing "socialism," hyperpatriotism, militarism, anti-Semitic paranoia, and belief in expansionist war. In fact, one of the DVP's founders, Anton Drexler, was later a founder of the Nazis.

By this point the emperor had virtually withdrawn from the public and from politics, leaving the country in the hands of his two most prominent generals, Paul von Hindenburg and Erich Ludendorff, whom people usually mentioned in one breath as simply "H-L." The line between government, military, and economy had become very blurry by 1917. The German empire was essentially a military dictatorship with H-L at the top, supported by military commanders, bankers, and industrialists. The suffering of common people, and the seemingly endless nature of the conflict itself, finally broke down the "Civil Peace" (Burgfrieden). The Socialists began to agitate against the war in 1917, although at first timidly, given the strong censorship laws and arbitrary powers of arrest the government now had. German workers, who had been much more orderly and obedient than in many other countries, began to go on strike regularly in 1917. Their grievances were not simply about hard times, but also had to do with the ugly realization that not all sectors of society were being forced to sacrifice equally, an unfairness dramatically illustrated by the growing black market. Middle-class people were also no longer willing to accept the lack of democracy or participatory government, particularly when the war was being financed primarily from their savings accounts in the form of war bonds. In the summer of 1917, when the Center Party and the SPD debated a "peace resolution" calling for no annexations, and began to demand changes in the government, it was clear that the German middle and working classes were shifting away from the consensus of the Burgfrieden.

The H-L quasi-dictatorship lasted a little more than one year. In the end, it could not hang on to power when the military situation was collapsing. Germany's allies began deserting early in the autumn of 1918. Germany's own last major offensive on the Western Front that spring had already run out of steam, and the arrival of new American troops finally provided the Allies with the numbers and supplies they needed to break the stalemate. Exhausted German armies began to retreat slowly, back toward the Rhine. Desertion, which had never been a serious problem in the German military, now became an epidemic. Large numbers of German soldiers began to surrender to the Allies.

On October 3, 1918, the emperor asked Prince Max of Baden to serve as chancellor, and to explore the possibility of a cease-fire and negotiated peace. Prince Max was supposed to be a conciliatory figure; he was from an old and important aristocratic family, but had also been known as a liberal before the war. The chaotic situation was ripe for radical change, but Max was probably not the man for the job, and clearly was less than enthusiastic about taking it. Nonetheless his brief term in office set the stage for the collapse of the empire, the end of the war, and the establishment of a republic—all in one month.

Prince Max's new government included, for the first time, the Social Democrats. The SPD felt energized by the rapidly changing situation and pushed for changes in the law that would have been unthinkable a few years earlier, such as the abolition of class privileges, the parliament's right to appoint government officials, and civilian control of the military. That last point inspired Ludendorff to consider a military coup to establish H-L as a true dictatorship. But he never had the time to carry it out. When the admirals of the navy decided to take their ships out on one last suicidal mission and go down fighting, rather than surrender, their furious sailors mutinied, refusing to be sacrificed in that way. The naval mutiny began on October 29 at the bases in Kiel and Wilhelmshaven and quickly transformed into a Socialist revolution spreading across the country, calling for an overthrow of the monarchy, peace, and a new republic modeled upon workers' councils like the Soviets.

In Prince Max's government, a trio of parties—the SPD, the Center, and the Left-Liberals—commanded a majority of votes. The SPD had emerged as the most assertive of the three, and the only party that seemed to have any chance of controlling the left-wing movements that were erupting across the Reich. SPD leader Friedrich Ebert was clearly pushing the pace of change toward a republic. General Ludendorff and many of the other far-right leaders seemed almost spitefully relieved that somebody else was willing to take responsibility for the impending catastrophe, and began to blame the peace settlement on a "stab in the back" by Socialists, intellectuals, Jews, and various other groups, even before there *was* a peace settlement. This was a convenient salve for their egos since everybody, Left and Right, knew that Germany was about to lose the war.

On November 6, members of the military high command met secretly with members of the SPD and trade unions. Despite their mutual animosity, everyone was worried that the revolutionary movements, which were now erupting in major cities, might overthrow the entire society and plunge Germany into a civil war or a Communist revolution. Ebert was understandably nervous about a possible military coup d'état, and the officers were nervous about their role in a Socialist future. The exact words they exchanged are speculative, but in substance they agreed that the military would support the new government if the government agreed to suppress radical left-wing revolutionaries. At the meeting, Ebert suggested that the emperor should abdicate, but the military men refused to ask him to do so.[6] Three days later, however, they persuaded the emperor to do exactly that, and on November 9 William II fled to Holland, never to return. Prince Max of Baden resigned the chancellery the same evening. The Austro-Hungarian Empire, which had already surrendered by this point, was similarly at the mercy of the victors and soon to be broken up. The houses of Hohenzollern and Habsburg, which had shaped German history for centuries, were no more.

Weimar

When Prince Max, the last imperial chancellor, resigned on November 9, 1918, he summoned the SPD leader Friedrich Ebert for a short ceremony and handed over all his duties to him. This was a gesture completely outside the constitution, but perhaps emblematic of the chaotic world of 1918. Germany's leaders seemed to have completely abandoned ship. The emperor and the crown prince fled to Holland. General Ludendorff fled to Sweden. Having enthusiastically pursued war, the leaders of the Second Reich now dumped the defeat onto the provisional civilian government struggling to take control.

Friedrich Ebert was a German patriot who had lost his son in the war. Like many Social Democrats who supported the war, he now had difficulty winning back the trust and cooperation of those Socialists who had opposed it. Ebert tried to shore up his support by asking the members of the Independent Socialist Party of Germany (USPD) to join his government. The USPD was the breakaway faction of the SPD that had split because of the SPD's support for the war. It included true Communists, hard-line Socialists, and simply disgruntled Social Democrats. Together, the two parties could not quite command a majority, but they represented Germany's Left. In essence, they walked a fine line between a Bolshevik Revolution and total chaos, just managing to secure enough support from rebelling soldiers and sailors, unions, and striking workers to hold together a new, left-wing government.

Ebert's provisional government had the unenviable task of asking the Allies for an armistice that everyone knew was a pretext for surrender. Two days after they took power, the SPD leaders declared the cease-fire on November 11. They had little choice but to hope that Woodrow Wilson's Fourteen

Points would be the basis of the peace settlement, and that the Allies would not take out their hatred of Germany's old government upon its new one. Of course, as it turned out, not only the victorious and vengeful Allies, but also Germany's own people blamed the new government for the disastrously harsh surrender terms that came out of Versailles the next year. In the end a large segment of the population chose to eulogize the heroic sacrifices of their defeated military, and nostalgize the nationalist leaders that had led them to disaster, and instead blamed the Socialists and democrats who tried, in the last few days, to clean up the mess they had inherited. It was not an auspicious way to begin a new state.

Although a left-wing government was a revolutionary development in German history, Friedrich Ebert was no revolutionary. He was a moderate who knew he had a very limited window of opportunity in which to create a republic, and knew that he faced fundamental opposition from both Left and Right. In retrospect, he probably made a mistake believing that the radical Left was the more dangerous threat, and focusing upon that, but such was the substance of his agreement with the army, and thus the basis of his security. Ebert had to keep his bargain and crush Communist revolutionaries, or the military would turn against him. Germany—even though defeated on the battlefield—still had millions of soldiers, most of whom were now slowly coming home. Thus in the last weeks of 1918 Ebert called for elections to a new National Assembly to create a new constitution and legitimize the government. And he also used the army to crush the Communist uprisings across the country, most famously in Berlin. There, the Spartacist movement, led by the Communists Rosa Luxembourg and Karl Liebknecht, was defeated by the army and right-wing paramilitary groups. This was the final straw for most German Communists. Although most of them had originally been Social Democrats and supported the SPD, the Communists now believed that Ebert had not only sold out to the conservatives of the military old regime, but that he had even sided with them in the killing of fellow left-wing activists. For the rest of the Weimar Republic's history, the Social Democrats and Communists despised each other and refused to cooperate. The disarray of Germany's two major left-wing movements eventually made it much easier for right-wing radicals ultimately to gain power.

In the National Assembly (*Nationalversammlung*) elections in January 1919, the SPD and USPD received nearly 44 percent of the vote; an impressive plurality, but not a clear majority. The assembly's job was to draft a new constitution, but most of Germany's major cities were too politically unstable to host it. Berlin was simmering after the Spartacist revolt; Cologne was in the unstable and demilitarized Rhineland, where German troops couldn't be used to keep order; Hamburg was considered too "red," having had a Soviet-style revolutionary council; and Munich was soon to erupt into violence after the assassination of its Socialist revolutionary leader, Kurt Eisner. The Ebert government chose instead the city that would forever be associated with this brief but crucial period of German history: Weimar.

Weimar is a small city, but it was the home of Goethe and Schiller, and had been a center of learning, culture, and the arts ever since. Ebert hoped that it would symbolize a new beginning, and of course it did, although not in the way that most people expected at the time. The new Nationalversammlung began to arrive in February 1919. They met at the State Theatre, where the delegates divided up the seating by parties, just as they had done in the Reichstag, with sections of the auditorium sliced off for contending groups. For the first time, a German legislative body included women: there were twelve female delegates from this first German election to grant female suffrage. In his opening remarks, Friedrich Ebert specifically welcomed them and the new female constituency to which they were all now answerable. Ebert's speech was reminiscent of Fichte's *Addresses to the German Nation* in 1808. He didn't shy away from the obvious fact that they had lost the war, and he argued that it was now time for Germans to give up dreams of world power and to concentrate instead on spiritual and cultural strength and development, freedom, and individual rights.

Throughout the deliberations, a limited media access nonetheless leaked substantial details to the public, who began referring to "the Weimar constitution." The little Thuringian city became the temporary de facto capital of Germany. It was surrounded by troops. There was an outer perimeter regulating transit to and from the city, and a literal ring of soldiers surrounding the State Theatre to protect the assembly. Photographs show helmeted troops almost elbow-to-elbow beneath the great statues of Goethe and Schiller in the Theatre plaza.

On February 11, 1919, Friedrich Ebert, the son of a tailor from Heidelberg, became the first president of Germany. Exactly six months later the new constitution was approved and the new parliament convened. As their national flag, the founders had chosen the black-red-gold horizontal stripes of Lützow's Jägers from the Napoleonic Wars, also used as the colors of the Frankfurt Parliament in 1848. Except for the interruption of Hitler's Third Reich, it has remained the German flag to this day.

The Weimar Republic is often seen as a radical break with the past, a moment of political and social emancipation, a "modernist crucible," in Rudy Koshar's interesting phrase.[7] Women joined the electorate, class privileges were removed from the law, and sweeping social reforms were enacted to benefit working people. Radical politics were accompanied by radical new ideas in art, music, fashion, and architecture. But many historians have observed that in politics, at least, the founders of the Weimar Republic tried to preserve as much continuity as possible. The country was still called a "reich," even though it was clearly no longer an empire, and the parliamentarians still met in a Reichstag. There was no more emperor, but the constitution provided for a very strong executive, the president, who commanded the armed forces and could appoint his chancellor.

This was in fact one of the crucial flaws in the constitutional design. It was assumed that the president, in order to get anything done, would have to appoint a chancellor who represented the interests of a ruling majority of parties in the Reichstag, and thus the government would be answerable to the will of the voters at two levels: the election of parliamentarians, and the direct popular election of the president himself. But the design assumed a relatively limited number of strong parties, and thus a ruling coalition should be feasible with two or at most three parties in government. The founders did not foresee the continuing fragmentation of German politics, with many small parties drawing off the votes of the larger ones, making it harder for the major parties to form coalitions without including small, often radical or violent groups in government. And they apparently did not foresee the constitutional ramifications of the president's "emergency powers" (Article 48). These were conceived in the chaotic atmosphere of 1919, in which a directly elected president might have to rule without the Reichstag and even suspend civil liberties in order to restore order. But if the Reichstag could not produce a ruling coalition, and if the president thus could not choose a chancellor who represented a majority, Article 48 effectively gave him an opt-out of the entire system of legislative accountability. The constitution gave the Reichstag the power to impeach a president, but only with a two-thirds majority. And if a simple majority could not be found to form an effective government, there was no hope of finding a two-thirds majority for anything. As we shall see, Weimar Germany only had two presidents, but the chancellery was a revolving door of unstable political combinations. President Ebert had nine different chancellors. His successor Paul von Hindenburg had seven: a total of sixteen governments for a republic that lasted only fourteen years. Not surprisingly, both presidents made extensive use of their emergency powers.

We have observed that the new German government inherited an immense catalog of extraordinary problems, nearly all of which flowed from the military defeat in the First World War. These would have been bad enough in themselves, but in addition the government had to fulfill its duty to sign the surrender terms of Versailles, which were finally publicized in the spring and led to outrage. The Reich lost territory to Belgium, France, the newly created states of Poland and Lithuania, and even to neutral Denmark: a total of 13 percent of its territory and 10 percent of its population. All the German overseas colonies were lost. The air force was eliminated completely, the navy almost totally confiscated, and nearly 90 percent of the merchant marine was seized. The army was cut down to a token force of one hundred thousand men. Germany's ally Austria-Hungary was broken into several small states, including a small German-speaking Austria, but Germany was forbidden from unifying with it. Allied countries, particularly France, demanded huge war reparations and reserved the right to intervene militarily if they were not paid. And of course by signing the treaty, the Germans agreed to the infamous "War Guilt" clause, in which Germany accepted the moral responsibility for the entire war.

Ebert's government, and indeed the entire Weimar Republic, never really recovered from this disastrous beginning.

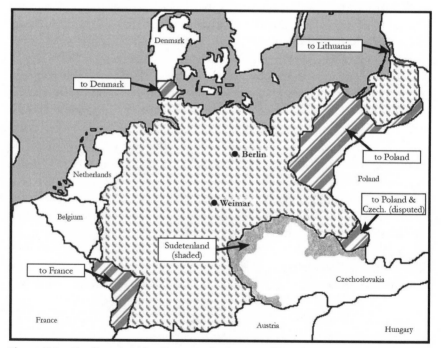

Figure 7.1. Territory Lost by Germany in the Versailles Treaty: Note also the gray/ shaded borderlands of the new Czechoslovakia. This German-speaking region (the Sudetenland) would become a point of dispute.

Survival: 1920–1923

Friedrich Ebert was a short, stout man who did not cut an inspiring figure. Although he was a good public speaker, he lacked the martial swagger of the Hohenzollerns and many right-wing politicians, and he was mercilessly caricatured by the press. Many newspapers and magazines were owned by wealthy conservatives who also funded right-wing parties and political clubs, and the media spread an astonishing assortment of libel and outright lies about Germany's first president. Ebert made matters worse by rising to each challenge with a lawsuit, and then losing in court. After less than a year in power, however, he had still underestimated the extent of the threat to the new republic from the Right.

The first problem had to do with the many paramilitary groups that had formed in the final days of the war, especially in the lawless east, where Germany still ruled over vast stretches of territory in Poland, Lithuania, and elsewhere. Groups of soldiers, anywhere from a few hundred to a few thousand in number, formed "Free Corps" (*Freikorps*) and essentially ruled little fiefdoms like warlords. As these territories had to be surrendered, the Freikorps came home, usually still well armed, with chips on their shoulders, and looking for something to do. They were evolving into little private political armies, and were almost all led by officers with political views on the far right of German society. Many longed for a restoration of the old monarchy, while others wanted some form of military dictatorship, but all shared a hatred of the peace settlement, and the new civilian government that had signed it. In 1919 there were perhaps as many as a quarter million of these men under arms.

According to the Versailles treaty, Germany was supposed to have disarmed these groups, as well as the regular military, but in fact Ebert skirted this issue because he had used these soldiers to put down the far-left movements across the country throughout 1919. Freikorps troops helped crush the Spartacist revolt in Berlin, for example, and took the extra step of executing its leaders. A large number of the future Nazi leaders, including several men prominently involved in the Holocaust, began their political careers in the Freikorps.

In early 1920 the defense minister, Gustav Noske, tried to begin the process of disbanding the Freikorps. The result was a plot to overthrow the government (in German, such a plot is called a *Putsch*). Wilhelm Kapp was an army officer who had been one of the founders of the right-wing Fatherland Party, and Walther von Lüttwitz was an aristocratic general who had enjoyed a successful career in the war. In an ironic twist that demonstrated the

ongoing fragility of the government, Lüttwitz had been one of the commanders who had put down the Spartacists the year before. Kapp and Lüttwitz led
a brigade of troops into Berlin and seized power. Ebert, fleeing the capital and
invoking his constitutional authority as commander in chief, ordered military commanders to put down the putsch, but they refused. In desperation, he
turned instead to the labor unions and called for a nationwide strike. Thus,
the Kapp-Lüttwitz Putsch was ultimately defeated not by the government
and its army, but by workers, unions, and another wave of left-wing revolts.
It was an ominous sign that the civilian government could not depend upon
the military to support democracy.

Three years later the government faced a lesser threat from Adolf Hitler
and his National Socialist Party, who tried to overthrow the government of
Bavaria on November 9, 1923, the fourth anniversary of the kaiser's abdication. The scale of this "Beer Hall Putsch" was much smaller and it lasted only
two days, but it featured prominently among its supporters General Erich Ludendorff, the former commander and de facto military dictator from the First
World War. Ludendorff's return from exile and presence in support of Hitler
gave the Nazis a level of credibility and national attention among right-wing
groups. Hitler's subsequent trial and the media coverage it enjoyed cemented
his reputation as a national political figure to watch. Hitler received a very
light sentence, guaranteeing that he'd be back.

Throughout its often troubled existence, the Weimar Republic was beset
by fiercely patriotic right-wing movements that wanted to bring down not
just the government, but the entire republican system. These groups organized
around veteran associations and Freikorps members, around student fraternities and young men's clubs, and in some cases around churches. The two
major right-wing parties, the German National People's Party (DNVP) and
the German People's Party (DVP—not to be confused with the Fatherland
Party, which split after a poor showing in the 1919 elections) campaigned
in elections and won seats in the Reichstag, yet in their rallies and media
routinely called for the elimination of the republic, which they believed to
be hopelessly corrupted by Socialists, foreigners, Jews, and intellectuals, and
tainted by the shame of defeat and surrender. These groups held marches
and demonstrations, often armed and in military or quasimilitary uniforms,
in which they furiously blamed Germany's defeat and disgrace upon most of
the ills of the modern world as they saw them: modern art, jazz music, homosexuals (although many German conservatives were secretly gay), Socialism,
intellectuals, Jewish bankers, emancipated women, and city folk in general.
Their tone was often so extreme, calling for the "annihilation" of the "trai-
tors" and "criminals" who were supposedly destroying Germany, that their

followers, not surprisingly, often committed violent acts, such as when they assassinated Walter Rathenau in 1923.

Aside from right-wing coups, the Weimar Republic had to deal with a variety of separatist movements and declarations of secession from the moment it began. Regional leaders tried to break away from the central government on various pretexts and often received the help of foreign powers with an interest in keeping Germany weak. The most serious of these was the Rhineland Crisis of 1923–1924. Under the terms of the Versailles peace, several of Germany's border regions, including the whole Rhineland, were demilitarized zones, in which the Germans were forbidden to station troops. In the chaotic postwar world, this obviously made it very difficult for the national government to assert its authority, which—in the case of the Rhineland—is precisely what the French wanted. A local rebellion against the Weimar government, obviously encouraged by French authorities, sparked a counterrebellion. A state of near–civil war ensued, in which the French tried to break the region away from Germany altogether and establish a "Rhenish Republic" as a French puppet state. Ironically, it was French military intervention that actually restored order and a sense of loyalty to the German state. By the time the French troops left in 1924, the worst of the German economic crisis had also passed, and with it the popular anger in the Rhineland.

Weimar Germany might have navigated between secessionists, Communist revolts, and right-wing extremist violence, had it been able to keep the confidence and support of the middle class. But the government injured itself, possibly mortally, when it failed to stabilize German currency in the early 1920s, setting off a period of hyperinflation. The roots of this famous catastrophe lay in the wartime economy of 1914–1918, in which shortages and rationing created a black market and wild price fluctuations. Inflation was already bad when Germany ended the war and had to begin paying reparations to the Allies. The government was desperate for cash and resorted to a combination of risky measures: depreciating the currency (in the hope of making German goods more attractive abroad and thus restarting the export trade), printing more money, and trying to manipulate the financial markets. As prices rose, workers demanded wage increases. For a left-wing government that depended upon keeping the working class happy, this was a demand they had to meet.

In the summer of 1922 the inflation began to accelerate out of control as the Reichsbank, fearing that a currency shortage would cripple businesses and cause mass unemployment, dramatically increased the money supply. By the autumn of 1922, one dollar equaled well over three thousand German marks. When the government informed the Allies that it couldn't make its reparation payments, Allied troops occupied the Rhineland and the Ruhr. The government asked workers to engage in passive resistance against the occupiers, resulting in a near-total shutdown of that entire industrial area, and of course massive new welfare payments for the striking workers. The final component of the disaster was the speculation by investors who tried to get rich quickly by riding the wave of currency inflation.

The German hyperinflation remains one of the greatest economic collapses in world history. Many middle-class people lost both their jobs and their savings. People's faith in government was shattered as they raced from their jobs to spend their pay (now paid every day, or even twice a day, in cash) at stores before the prices changed again. The government's printing presses rolled out ever more absurd banknotes: million-mark notes, billion-mark notes, and finally in November 1923, a 100-trillion-mark note (equal at that time to about twenty-three dollars).[8]

The hyperinflation of 1922–1923 did not destroy the German middle class. But it did destroy any hopes for broad middle-class–based moderate political parties holding a majority in Weimar politics. The wild swings of fortune and despair hardened people's attitudes and made them more willing to look for new and radical political solutions. The three parties of the Weimar Coalition increasingly found themselves besieged by smaller, more radical groups. The hyperinflation also dramatically increased crime and disrespect for private property. Since money was worthless, people wanted *things*

Figure 7.2. A Fifty-Million-Mark Bill: Hastily printed on cheap paper during the hyperinflation. Less than a week after this bill appeared, it would not have been sufficient to buy a loaf of bread.

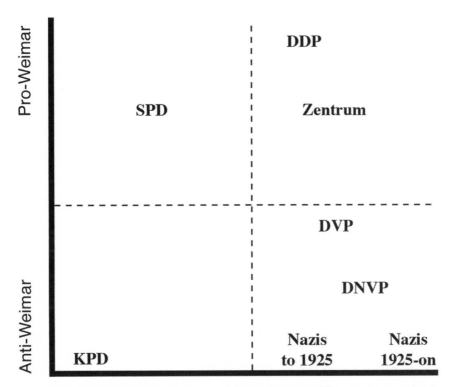

Figure 7.3. The Major Political Parties of the Weimar Republic: One cannot simply place them along a graph from left to right, because an important feature of their ideology was also their level of support for, and willingness to work within, the parliamentary system of Weimar. That, in fact, proved a much wider gulf separating parties than traditional measures of Left/Right ideology; it prevented, for example, a Communist–Social Democratic coalition on the Left.

This graph shows only the handful of larger parties. Weimar Germany proliferated several more, as well as regional parties and innumerable political clubs and associations. The terms are often confusing. For example, the "Center" (Zentrum) Party was actually a fairly conservative party organized by—and mostly for—German Catholics, and thus it was regionally strong in Catholic areas, but not elsewhere. Words like *Liberal* or *Socialist* can be deceptive. For example, Weimar Germany had two Liberal parties, the Left-Liberals (German Democratic Party, or DDP), which were definitely not "left" in the sense of Socialism, and the National Liberals, who evolved into the German People's Party (DVP), a right-wing anti-Weimar party. There were obviously two large "Socialist" parties, too, neither of which would have pleased Karl Marx. The Social Democrats (SPD) were the mainstream left-wing party, supported by trade unions and workers, while the National Socialists (Nazis) were of course a far-right movement supported by nationalists, but also by working people who were anti-Communist for other reasons. The only true far-Left party was the Communists (KPD).

instead. Burglary and especially shop looting became almost commonplace and took on political meaning, and of course became things that the Nazis would later use as social weapons.

Revival: 1924–1929

The economic and political stabilization of Germany in the mid-1920s was due to a combination of sound fiscal and foreign policy decisions by a new government led by Gustav Stresemann. Although he was chancellor for only three months, Stresemann remained in the cabinet (serving as foreign minister) until his death in 1929, and was arguably the Weimar Republic's most successful politician.

Stresemann was a conservative from an improbable background: working-class Berlin. He worked his way through a variety of retail and distribution businesses before entering politics as a National Liberal, and he remained a staunch conservative during the war. By the time of the hyperinflation, he had been in and out of three right-wing parties, and had emerged as a much more moderate and pragmatic figure than many of his compatriots on the Right. He had, for example, reluctantly come to accept the Versailles settlement and the need for Germany to be restored within the normal European diplomatic circles.

The Stresemann government introduced a new replacement currency as a first step toward stabilizing the mark, called off the passive resistance campaigns in the west, and opened meaningful negotiations with the Allies for a restructuring of Germany's reparation debts. Stresemann was particularly interested in establishing a strong new German-American relationship, as a way around Germany's diplomatic isolation in Europe. The Allied troops withdrew, the reparations were set on a schedule and funded by specific taxes, and the government agreed to allow foreign regulators to participate in the restructuring of the Reichsbank. By the middle of 1924, Germany's economy had stabilized, and a degree of normalcy returned to its social and political life that hadn't been seen in a decade.

But what was "normal" in Weimar Germany? The historian Peter Gay famously suggested that the Weimar Republic never really created anything new; it simply liberated many social, cultural, and political impulses that had been suppressed for decades. If that is true, then the liberation that characterized Germany's new cultural life was most brilliantly on display in the major cities. Many historians have drawn a distinction between that handful of big cities (especially Berlin and Hamburg), and the rest of the country.[9]

In this formulation, Weimar Germany was two distinct worlds, each in utter contempt of the other.

In the cities many shocking things happened. Perhaps the most dramatic changes involved the new roles and images of women. First, obviously, the Weimar Republic gave women the vote, and Germany's first handful of female politicians won seats in the Reichstag. Women's fashions became very daring, with short skirts, high heels, and low necklines. Women began to go out at night together, or even alone, and—to the amazement and horror of the older generations—were seen with short hair and smoking cigarettes. A number of new magazines and newspapers and even publishing houses appeared, written and edited by female authors for a mainly female readership. In Germany, as in much of the Western world in the 1920s, the New Woman was a high-profile figure of independence.

Homosexuals took a first few tentative steps out of the closet, as gay nightclubs opened in cities like Berlin and Hamburg. Movie houses began to appear, with films depicting overtly sexual themes, such as Marlene Dietrich's famous *Blue Angel*, the story of a once-respectable middle-class man who becomes infatuated with a cabaret dancer. Jazz music, imported from America, began to appear in German cities, often performed by African Americans or other foreigners whom Germans had never seen before. Plays with controversial topics, such as crime, violence, sex, and corruption, including the works of the Socialist writer Bertolt Brecht, were attended by larger audiences than the traditional theater pieces in the major halls. Buildings and public spaces were transformed by radical new architectural styles that altered the physical environment.

And yet one could travel less than an hour into the countryside and find villages without a single automobile, where farmers pushed plows behind horses and their wives bottled milk fresh from the cow, or churned their own butter. Here the women braided their long hair the same way their ancestors had done for centuries, and certainly didn't shave their legs to wear a skirt and high heels. These hard-working, churchgoing folk had been the backbone of the German empire, and what little time and money they had for entertainment was not spent on a coffee during the lunch hour in some street café, nor on the latest nightclub cocktail. They often looked at the New Woman as a perverse figure, and noted with concern that Germany's birthrate, especially in the urban areas, was in sharp decline, as women were no longer encouraged and supported in their traditional roles as mothers and wives.

The distinction between city life, with its trendy fashions and lively entertainment, and small-town life, with its quiet stability and conservatism, was hardly a new phenomenon and certainly not unique to Weimar Germany. People at the time would have considered it a normal state of affairs. Moreover, the distinction may not have been as sharp as commonly believed. The supposedly left-wing big cities nonetheless had plenty of angry conservatives (many of the leading Nazis, for example, lived in Munich). And the supposedly conservative provincial life of smaller cities and towns nonetheless felt the changes of Weimar's new culture. Movie houses sprang up across the country, bringing a touch of the avant-garde and exotic even to the smallest cities. Between 1924 and 1931, Germans saw an average of 450 new film releases each year, roughly half of which were made in Germany.[10]

Of course, different kinds of movies appealed to different audiences. Not every small-town farmer would have traveled to the city to see Marlene Dietrich stroking her shockingly exposed legs in *Blue Angel*. The big-budget films with the largest national audiences were usually historical epics, often set during the Napoleonic era or the time of Frederick the Great, offering stories of past generations of Germans who rose up against foreign conquerors (usually the French) and redeemed the defeated Fatherland. Cinema may have been a new medium and considered avant-garde by many people, but German audiences still loved traditional heroic and patriotic tales. This was not lost upon the early leaders of the Nazi Party, particularly Josef Goebbels, who grasped the power of film and made extremely effective use of it for political purposes.

The city of Weimar itself provides a fascinating example of the clash between these two Germanies. By the mid-1920s the urban population was about 46,000, making Weimar a small to midsized city. Weimar had always been a cultural outlier, a college town full of artists and writers in the midst of a much more conservative farming community. During the 1920s it became famous simply because the constitution had been written there, but also because of the *Bauhaus*, the radical avant-garde architectural school founded by Walter Gropius.

Gropius had combined two existing art schools into a new university that challenged not only the old neoclassical styles, but also the whole atmosphere and purpose of a university. The students were rowdy and considered disrespectful by everyone except their equally unruly professors. Their style embraced a radical new aesthetic of simple, clean lines; undecorated walls; and buildings that seemed shockingly out of place, as if they had traveled back from the future to land in the stodgy, classical cityscapes of imperial Germany. This style, of course, is still with us, and is arguably now the dominant architectural and interior-design style of the Western world. But many conservatives at the time hated it and associated it, and all the Bauhaus teachers and students, with anarchism and Communism.

The Bauhaus moved to Dessau in 1924, where Gropius designed the famous building that stands as a symbol for the whole movement and era. It was probably inevitable, given Hitler's personal interest in art and especially architecture, that the Nazis would focus early upon rallying German conservatives against the Bauhaus. In Weimar, the local Nazi party chief, Fritz Sauckel, regarded the Bauhaus as an infection that had to be eradicated, and even though the school was no longer in Weimar, he pursued them until their final exile in America.

Fritz Sauckel: A Nazi Cultural Warrior

Fritz Sauckel became the Nazi party chief for Thuringia in 1927, setting up his office in Weimar. One of the loudest anti-Semites in a party that prided itself on anti-Semitism, Sauckel was equally relentless in his attacks against intellectuals, "cultural Bolsheviks," and "degenerate art."

In the confusing redundancy of overlapping portfolios typical of the Nazi regime, Sauckel had his hands in a number of projects during the Third Reich. One of them, the use of slave labor in concentration camps, earned him the death sentence at the Nürnberg Trials in 1946. He went unrepentant to his execution, still praising Hitler as "the most brilliant light in German history."

It is easy for us today to look at the Bauhaus style and shrug. It looks no different from thousands of buildings or interiors in any number of cities in the Western world. That, however, is precisely the point. The things that we now take for granted in our urban landscape—from the streamlined blocks of office buildings to the functional simplicity of a doorknob—were overwhelmingly influenced by these new thinkers and designers from Weimar.

Collapse: 1929–1933

Although Gustav Stresemann's government usually receives the credit for the stabilizing measures that pulled Germany back from the brink in 1923–1924, many of the government's solutions would not have been possible without President Friedrich Ebert invoking his emergency powers under

Article 48. In fact, even Hitler's Beer Hall Putsch had been put down by the president giving the army emergency powers in Bavaria. Observant Germans realized that whether or not the society had muddled through the worst of the crisis, the normal political structure had proved itself unable to cope. The Weimar Republic was a democracy only until its next crisis, at which time it reverted to a constitutional dictatorship. We shouldn't blame many Germans for concluding that the extremist parties like the Nazis or the Communists were right in calling for a revolution and the destruction of the existing system. Regardless of what one thought of parliamentary democracy, it had become obvious that the existing system didn't work.

The constitution established a presidential term of seven years. It is likely that Ebert was not planning to run again, as his health was obviously failing. It was nonetheless unexpected, however, when he died in office on February 28, 1925, from appendicitis, aged only fifty-four. The special election called for his replacement produced, after a second-round runoff, a winning candidate perhaps as unlike Ebert as could be imagined. At the age of seventy-seven, Paul von Hindenburg, one of wartime Germany's military heroes and later a de facto military dictator, had come out of retirement.

Hindenburg, a Prussian aristocrat, was conservative to his core, and had been an unabashed monarchist for most of his years in retirement. Like many military officers, he appeared to be biding his time, waiting for the republic to collapse and be replaced with something more to their liking (a future, ironically, that he would not live to see, but would do much to make happen). Why, exactly, he wanted to be president is unclear. During his retirement he had chaired veterans' organizations that had heaped praise upon him and urged him to enter politics. In a sense, he was "drafted" by the Right. Sworn into office in full military uniform, complete with medals and sword, Hindenburg was a comforting figure to many conservatives. He brought the far-right DNVP into government for the first time; a paradoxical situation in which the republic's fate was now at least partially in the hands of a president and a party that had very little faith in any of its alleged democratic values.

The unease that many people felt with these developments, however, was dwarfed by the relief felt by the recovery of the German economy and the apparent return of law and order. The major diplomatic accomplishments of Gustav Stresemann's tenure as foreign minister did much to return Germany to the community of nations, which in turn improved trade and international finance. As export activity resumed, industrial production accelerated and unemployment decreased. The return of employment and a stable currency encouraged the growth of the retail sector, as German cities again became places to go shopping. By the beginning of 1929 it looked as though the Weimar Republic, as flawed as its politics might have been, was finally past its long, ugly postwar depression and entering a period of prosperity.

On October 3, 1929, Gustav Stresemann, the chief architect of German recovery, died from a stroke. Three weeks later, the share prices of the New York Stock Exchange began to fluctuate wildly and soon took staggering losses. With German banks and businesses so dependent upon the export trade to prosperous nations like America, the crash was felt immediately. In fact, by mid-1929 German exporters had begun laying off workers as the worldwide overproduction gradually became apparent.

The political history of the last few years of the Weimar Republic is an often bewildering tale of government coalitions forming, collapsing, reconfiguring, and collapsing again, over issues that in retrospect seem minor: disagreement over signing a treaty, disagreement over an unemployment benefits bill, and so on. There was rarely a chancellor from the largest party in the Reichstag; more often Hindenburg appointed men who hoped to form grand coalitions or minority governments. All of this played out against the backdrop of the disastrously worsening economic situation, as average Germans lost whatever remaining faith they may have had in the government's ability to address the crisis.

***

The Depression-Era Chancellors

Hermann Müller (SPD) 1928–1930
Heinrich Brüning (Center) 1930–1932
Franz von Papen (Center) 1932–1933
Kurt von Schleicher (independent) 1933
Adolf Hitler (NSDAP) 1933–1945

***

Into this vacuum of leadership stepped Adolf Hitler. Although he is one of history's most infamous individuals, there is surprisingly vast ignorance about his biography and career. This is not the place for long detail, but a brief outline is important. Hitler was born in the small Austrian city of Braunau, just across the Inn River from Bavaria. His father was a minor civil servant; the family was typically middle-class provincial. Hitler's father died relatively young, leaving the family in some financial straits. Hitler left for Vienna when he was only sixteen, with impractical dreams of becoming an artist or architect in the big city, despite his mediocre education and lack of money or connections. The years of his youth were difficult. He worked odd jobs, sold paintings and postcards on the street, and was occasionally a resident in men's (homeless) shelters. His personal habits were somewhat unusual, uninterested as he was in the typical pursuits of young men who spent their pay on dance halls, beer, or prostitutes. Hitler was a nonsmoking, nondrinking, and apparently asexual man who saved his money for the opera and the museums.

Hitler had never respected the multiethnic Austro-Hungarian monarchy, and in 1913 finally found the means to leave and move to Munich, where he could be among Germans. Like many people in the late nineteenth and early twentieth centuries, Hitler saw the world as divided between races that were locked in a brutal struggle for survival, and thought that racial mixing threatened to pollute the pure blood of superior races. He was hardly unique in these views; much of his thinking on race would have been within the norms of most Christian countries at that time. Hitler specifically considered Jews to be a parasitical race that was sapping the strength of the Germanic ("Aryan") peoples. Thus Jews were fundamentally criminal, and a direct threat to Germans, not so much because of what any individual Jew might do or have done, but simply because of who they were. The fact that Hitler was politically conservative and that Jews were often prominent in left-wing fields and politics (as intellectuals, politicians, Socialists, and entertainers) only reinforced the notion that they posed a fundamental threat to all that was good and pure in German civilization.

The German word *Volk* means literally "people," but also implies a racial and cultural bond: nationality, ethnicity, language, shared history, and even values. A Volk is a community of people who share a common culture and ancestry. To be *Völkisch* was to believe that people of the same Volk should share the same pure, "good old-fashioned" values and lifestyle, uncorrupted by the multicultural big cities and their mixed races and religions. It also meant that one believed that one's Volk had to be protected from infection by others.

Nineteenth-century Europeans frequently used words like *race* or *people* to mean nationality, as in "the Irish race" or "the French race." The advent of Socialism challenged this concept by arguing that all working people are basically the same, and that nationality was a learned and artificial concept. But for many conservatives, one's race literally ran in one's blood. There was a biological attachment to the Volk that was as fundamental as a law of nature, and thus patriotism was not just about politics, it was about the survival of your race. Adolf Hitler was one of many people who came of age in the late nineteenth century believing firmly that the German Volk, to which he belonged, was a single biological organism that had to be defended the way one's body fights off disease, or the way an animal fights for survival.

German Völkisch attitudes had not had any particular connection to anti-Semitism in the nineteenth century, notwithstanding certain prominent anti-Semites like the composer Richard Wagner. The historian George Mosse famously observed that at the turn of the twentieth century France, not Germany, seemed to have most of the ingredients for an anti-Semitic, national-socialist movement.[11] But German anti-Semitism spiked during the First World War, along with rumor-mongering and the search for scapegoats on whom to blame the economic woes and the impending defeat. Adolf Hitler's generation, in other words, came of age at the dawn of modern German anti-Semitism, and attached it to the concept of *Völkisch* nationalism.

Hitler initially tried to avoid military service, but once World War One began, he volunteered eagerly. He served all four years on the Western Front and was apparently a very good soldier: brave, motivated, loyal, frequently volunteering for the most dangerous jobs. He was promoted, decorated twice for bravery, and wounded twice in action. His excellent service record is one reason he was able to remain in the vastly shrunken Weimar army after 1918, and trusted with the job of investigating potentially dangerous political movements, even though he was not yet a German citizen. When he investigated one of these groups, the German Workers' Party, he instead found them to be kindred spirits, and soon joined. He discovered that he had a gift for the rowdy, theatrical street speeches that would attract men like himself to the movement. Through his recruiting skills and his bullying, Hitler soon became the party's leader, and changed its name to the National Socialist German Workers' Party (NSDAP.) He left the army and became a full-time politician.

Where Does the Word *Nazi* Come From?

Germans have a habit of abbreviating and nicknaming political parties, so the Communists were usually just the "Kommis" and the Socialists were the "Sozis." The National Socialists' nickname wasn't a perfect spelling of the first two syllables of their title, but it was a phonetic rendering: the "Nazis" (from National).

German parties also are generally very consistent in their use of symbols and colors. People who want to express their support for the Socialists, for instance, would wear red. The Nazi color was brown, and used in a more disciplined style as a full uniform by the party's most loyal volunteers.

In the early days of the Nazi party Hitler's rhetoric was a mixture of populism from both Left and Right. He ranted against Big Business, bankers, and anybody who hurt the Little Man. Very much like a Socialist, he demanded national institutions that would take better care of workers and wounded veterans. On the other hand, he was extremely conservative on questions of patriotism, immigration and race, and militarism, and he loathed much of the modern world of Weimar culture, wanting to return Germany to its folk roots. His low-brow oratory, occasional grammatical mistakes, heavy southern accent, and obvious lack of higher education all endeared him to people much like himself: veterans and working men who had fallen on hard times. Unlike most politicians, Hitler seemed absolutely sincere when he spoke of things like poverty and patriotism, and he clearly spoke from experience.

Hitler's appeal was primarily local, in Bavaria, although the Nazi party did have branches elsewhere. In 1922 Mussolini's Fascist party came to power in Italy, in part due to a dramatic "March on Rome" which saw the Fascists, although small in number, bluffing the police, government, and military with their audacity. Impressed, Hitler attempted the same thing by taking control of Bavaria in a *putsch*, and then planning a march to Berlin. But his "Beer Hall Putsch" was easily defeated and Hitler was arrested. The media coverage of his trial, at which he ranted for days, gave him national attention and sympathy. During his brief and lenient prison term, Hitler and his aide Rudolf Hess composed his book *Mein Kampf* ("My Struggle"), which was part memoir and part manifesto.

When Hitler emerged from prison the hyperinflation was over, and a mainstream right-wing government was in power in Berlin. Support for angry extremists waned. Over the next few years Hitler devoted his considerable energies to building up the party as a legitimate political organization across the country, with a particular focus on trying to recruit new members from other, similar groups. Weimar Germany had a plethora of right-wing clubs and associations, many of which had philosophies similar to the Nazis. In the struggle to win over these people, the Nazis gradually came out on top due to superior grassroots organizing.

The party had a paramilitary organization, the Sturmabteilung (SA), known by their uniform as "brownshirts." This was a sort of Nazi army whose purpose was to turn out en masse for rallies and events, schedule parades and marches, disrupt the meetings and rallies of other parties, and generally wreck havoc upon the opposition. They tended to attract unemployed men, often veterans, and Hitler occasionally had difficulty keeping them under control, although he was normally content to let them run amok, causing street battles with Communists, beating up Jews and homosexuals, and vandalizing the homes and offices of opponents. The SA was theoretically organized top-down from the national level, but in practice tended to operate according to the leadership of each regional or local party boss, a harbinger of the way that the Nazis would rule Germany.

The Nazi Party's growth was limited by its image as a violent fringe group of ignorant extremists. After 1925 Hitler perceived that he needed to modulate his message in order to win over more mainstream conservative voters. The party dropped much of its anti-business rhetoric, for example, replacing it with specifically anti–Jewish-business rhetoric. Hitler stopped speaking of the state as a means to assist the common working man, and instead focused on the need to assist one's own race and people, the "national community." The Nazis consciously moved to the right, and it was clear that of the two dissonant concepts in the party's name, the national was now far more important than the socialist. Nonetheless, the Nazis had very strained relations with the most important conservative institution in Germany: the army. Traditional, often aristocratic officers were very uneasy with the loud Austrian corporal and his brown-shirted thugs marching through the street pretending to be an army.

Historians have studied the demographics of Nazi supporters and attempted to track the electoral success of the party.[12] On one hand, there is not much success to track, since the party's electoral results were meager until 1930, when they suddenly achieved over 18 percent and became the second-strongest group in the Reichstag, behind the SPD. On the other hand, support for the Nazis was spread broadly across the different regions of the country, across different classes and economic levels, across different educational levels, among both Catholics and Protestants, among all age groups, and among both men and women.[13] There was no typical Nazi voter. Instead, what appears to have happened is that the Great Depression created new opportunities for radical extremist parties, and the Nazis had laid the groundwork better than others to take advantage of those opportunities. They thus broadly increased their support among the many kinds of people who had lost hope in the system, particularly in the middle class, or those who had an axe to grind against certain groups, or those who were desperate for a new path and felt reassured by the tone of extreme confidence and certainty exuded by Hitler and the Nazi leaders. If we can conclude anything from the Nazis' stunning emergence as a political force in the 1930 elections, it is that the majority of their new voters appear to have come from the other conservative parties, as the DVP and DNVP both declined.

There is a widely held misconception that Hitler was elected. In fact, the Nazis never received more than 32 percent of the vote prior to Hitler's appointment as chancellor, and their share slipped a bit in the last free election, November 1932, as they dropped below 27 percent of the vote. When Hitler also ran for president in 1932 he received nearly 37 percent of the vote, but Germans gave a clear majority to Hindenburg, thus preferring to reelect an eighty-five-year-old man who was clearly struggling with senility to another seven-year term.

The Nazis were a powerful presence in the Reichstag, distinctively intimidating in their brown uniforms. But they appeared to have reached their peak as a national political force. This helps to explain why other parties were willing to consider forming coalitions with them. Obviously, nobody in 1932 had our hindsight on dictatorship, oppression, war, and genocide. The Nazis themselves had no clear vision of the future, much less a disastrous future. Instead, they were an unpleasant right-wing party that was now large enough that it had to be included in government in some way, and perhaps could be tamed once it had to settle into the difficult and unglamorous business of really running a state.

The Weimar political system had essentially collapsed by 1932. The last three free elections were all called early because of government crises, with two in that year alone. It had become impossible to form a governing coalition, and President Hindenburg essentially ruled by emergency powers and decree. Hitler placed a number of demands upon the composition of a cabinet that resulted in his being passed over for chancellor earlier, but in late January 1933 Hindenburg finally asked him to form a government.

Adolf Hitler was sworn into office on January 30 as chancellor of the German Reich, a title he retained for the remainder of his life.

Suggested Reading

Berghahn, Volker. *Modern Germany: Society, Economy, and Politics in the Twentieth Century.* Cambridge: Cambridge University Press, 1987.

Broszat, Martin. *Hitler and the Collapse of Weimar Germany.* Leamington Spa, UK: Berg, 1987.

Evans, Richard. *The Coming of the Third Reich.* New York: Penguin, 2003.

Feldman, Gerald. *The Great Disorder: Politics, Economics, and Society in the German Inflation 1914–1924.* Athens: Ohio University Press, 1997.

Fischer, Fritz. *Germany's Aims in the First World War.* New York: W. W. Norton, 1967.

Gay, Peter. *Weimar Culture: The Outsider as Insider.* New York: W. W. Norton, 2001.

Weitz, Eric. *Weimar Germany: Promise and Tragedy.* Princeton, NJ: Princeton University Press, 2007.

CHAPTER EIGHT

∼

Downfall

In the spring of 1932 the city of Weimar prepared to celebrate the one-hundredth anniversary of the death of its most famous resident, Johann Wolfgang von Goethe. It was not lost on observers that German democracy also seemed to be dying. The magazine *Simplicissimus* printed a cover featuring a ghostly Goethe closing his eyes in tired resignation as mobs of radicals raged past beneath him, banners flying against a quote from *Faust*.

When Fritz Sauckel, the regional Nazi party chief, learned of the city's program for the event, he sent a memo urging all Nazis to converge on Weimar in response to the "scandal" and "shame" that "a great German cultural hero" was being besmirched by guests of honor like "Thomas Mann and other pacifists . . . a Jew from Paris . . . a Czech" and so on. Sauckel's counterdemonstration involved Nazis parading through the city in tight ranks, holding hands and shouting slogans.[1]

By the time of Goethe's birthday in 1935, with the Nazis now in power in Germany, Sauckel was able to organize precisely the event he'd wanted three years earlier. Despite the Nazis running every aspect of the city and its historical events, they maintained the tone and form of a protest rally, not much different from what they had done under the Weimar Republic. They marched in columns under swastika banners, chanting angry slogans against the enemies of German culture.

A decade later, on April 10, 1945, one of the very last acts of Weimar's Nazi administration was to remove the coffins of Goethe and Schiller to a "safe" bunker under a mountain near Jena, about fifteen miles away. This was accomplished only two days before American troops entered Weimar. These men from the Sixth Armored Division might have arrived earlier, but had been delayed the previous day by their discovery of the immense concentration camp nearby at Buchenwald, where about forty thousand emaciated prisoners still survived; roughly one-fifth the number that had been there a few weeks earlier.

The Trajectory of the Third Reich

The Nazi regime is probably the most written about government in human history, both by serious historians and by enthusiastic amateurs. A brief chapter like this can never do justice to the immensity and complexity of its story and subsequent historiography. Instead we will quickly outline the twelve-year course of the regime and its major acts, and then address certain topics in more depth.

The name Third Reich appeared almost as soon as the Second Reich collapsed, as disgruntled conservatives and monarchists proposed doing away with the Weimar Republic and creating a new entity. We have seen that Germans continued to use the word Reich even during the republic, so it did not require much of an imaginative leap for the Nazis to conjure a new Reich as both a goal and a symbol of German restoration. The Nazis' flag, for example, may have looked very different, with its odd swastika in the middle, but it consciously reverted to the old imperial colors of white, red, and black, thus jettisoning the hated Weimar flag, which to their minds symbolized weak-kneed liberalism.

Where Does the Swastika Come From?

Germans rarely used the word "swastika." It is instead known as the *Hakenkreuz* (sickle cross). The symbol dates to ancient India and was apparently used as a lucky charm as early as four thousand years ago. In the Nazi revision of world history, the ancient "Aryan" peoples began in central Europe (i.e., Germany) and then spread throughout several regions of the earth, thus creating various "white" racial groups. In late nineteenth-century Germany a number of conservative groups began using the swastika as a symbol for the ancient Germanic peoples. It was in this sense that the Nazis appropriated the symbol and Hitler used it for a Nazi party flag and emblem.

When Adolf Hitler became chancellor on January 3, 1933, he was still theoretically bound by the Weimar constitution, still only one of three Nazis in a cabinet that was dominated by other conservatives. His path to dictatorship was a combination of deliberately planned escalations and astute opportunism. Shortly after taking office, Hitler succeeded in placing his friend and loyal deputy Hermann Goering at the head of the Interior Ministry of Prussia. Goering thus controlled the state police and security forces of by far the largest state within the Reich, and he immediately began a rampage against the Communists and Social Democrats. He was assisted by a remarkable stroke of luck: a fire started under mysterious circumstances gutted the Reichstag building. Hitler persuaded Hindenburg to approve a nationwide crackdown against Communists, whom he blamed for the fire, and to use the emergency powers to suspend civil liberties. The ensuing dragnet naturally scooped up more than just Communists, as Goering arrested over one hundred thousand people, mostly left-wing opponents of the Nazis. Hitler depended upon his gifted propagandist Josef Goebbels to persuade Germans that these measures were necessary, and that a state of emergency really did exist.

Thus the parliamentary elections in March 1933 took place in an atmosphere of repression and propaganda, in which many Communists and Social Democrats had been arrested. Even under these conditions, the Nazis still could not get more than 44 percent of the vote. Together with other conservative parties, however, they now commanded a majority coalition. On March 23 the Reichstag (now meeting in an opera house) passed the Enabling Act, which at least theoretically set no limits upon the use of what had been "emergency" powers. From that point, as the Nazis began to outlaw the left-wing parties and bully and coerce the other right-wing parties, Hitler's dictatorship began to take shape.

The Nazi seizure of power played out over the course of several months in 1933 as the party purged local and state governments and civil service positions and replaced them with loyalists. Trade unions were shut down. Hundreds of newspapers were closed and the rest of the media rapidly came into line, expelling Jewish and/or left-wing writers and producers and replacing them with people willing to cooperate with the regime's new storyline.

Throughout this period, Hitler retained his title of Reichs Chancellor, although his own followers had always called him simply *der Führer* (the leader). His power was still not absolute. Old President von Hindenburg may have been broadly sympathetic with many of Hitler's goals, and his failing health meant that he did not interfere too vigorously, but as long as he remained alive, the constitution still reserved true executive powers for his office. And there was one institution that the Nazis could not purge or intimidate: the army. Weimar Germany's small army was an exclusive professional force that had their doubts about Hitler, although they were often broadly in agreement with his larger goals of rearmament and his general tone of patriotism. Nonetheless, as long as the Nazi Party maintained its own private army of brown-shirted SA "storm troopers," the professional army would keep its distance.

Hitler had his own concerns about the SA. By this point it numbered over 3 million men and had become an army unto itself. Its leader, Ernst Röhm, was an old Freikorps veteran whose respect for Hitler had slowly ebbed as his own power had grown. Disquieting rumors reached Hitler that Röhm might have been planning a coup. Hitler had at his disposal another, smaller paramilitary organization, the *Schutzstaffel* ("protection squad"), abbreviated SS, whose task was to escort the führer. The leader of the SS, Heinrich Himmler, was not only totally loyal, but was also extremely ambitious and eager to feed Hitler's suspicions of Röhm and the SA. Himmler had already persuaded Hitler to give him control of the Prussian state police when Goering was promoted to minister-president of Prussia, and by 1934 his SS had over fifty thousand members. But the most important factor was probably that Hitler knew he could not secure the loyalty of the German military unless he did something about the SA. When Ernst Röhm began making declarations about the role and privileges of the SA without consulting Hitler, the führer decided to act against him. On June 30, 1934, in the so-called Night of the Long Knives, Hitler ordered the SS to purge the leadership of the SA through a combination of executions and imprisonment. Röhm and others were shot on the spot. Three days of murders followed, in which the army leadership looked the other way, and President Hindenburg declared the purge to be legal. The SA was defanged, eventually becoming just a social organization. Himmler and his SS began to grow immediately in power and prestige.

On August 2, 1934, Paul von Hindenburg finally died. The Weimar constitution reserved the position of commander in chief for the president, which meant that a vacancy in the post raised questions about the ultimate role of the military. Only two weeks after the old president's death, Hitler pushed two new laws through the cabinet. The first established his new title as "Leader and Reichs Chancellor." The second, which had been some months in preparation and negotiated with key leaders, was the new military oath by which the army swore *unconditional* allegiance personally to Adolf Hitler, not to a constitution, laws, or the nation.

The beginning of the Nazi dictatorship is therefore best dated from the summer of 1934, by which point the party controlled all aspects of the national government, state and local governments, police and security forces, the media, and the military. This chapter will examine several questions about the relationship of the regime to the German people. But first we will conclude a brief outline of the course of the Third Reich.

When Hitler became chancellor, the unemployment rate in Germany stood at nearly 35 percent.[2] The early efforts of the regime were, not surprisingly, focused upon the economic crisis. The Nazis' racial beliefs appealed to a population that needed jobs, since it was always useful to rant against foreigners and immigrants taking opportunities away from native Germans, whether there was any truth to the claim or not. In certain sectors of the economy, Jewish-owned businesses were shut down, or Jewish colleagues were fired from civil service or educational positions, thus creating openings for others. But in general the Nazis offered xenophobia and racism as a useful distraction from the more immediate domestic woes of the Depression. Keeping people busy in large-scale government-funded work projects and redirecting their frustration against aliens was a logical strategy for a regime that had always had trouble with the unionized and left-wing working class.

There were a number of high-profile public works projects, with workers organized in paramilitary fashion by the Reich Labor Service. Many of the Nazi projects were overly ambitious top-down initiatives, such as the building of a network of new superhighways (the Autobahn). They were popular, created jobs, and looked good on newsreels, but Germany had at the time only a fraction of the automobiles that a country like the United States or Britain possessed. Hitler dreamed of creating a "people's vehicle" (*Volkswagen*) to compete against the mass-produced Fords that had captured the world's imagination and money, but the government could not force people to need or purchase automobiles in the midst of a depression. The new highway system remained useful primarily for the military.

German rearmament began to pick up dramatically in 1935. By 1937 the Third Reich was spending twenty times more on its military than the Weimar Republic had spent in 1930.[3] The military expansion also shifted unemployed men from the job market to the government payroll, and naturally meant huge new contracts for industry. The German army remained much smaller than that of any of its potential rivals, but it did not escape notice that Hitler had simply discarded the limitations of the Versailles treaty with apparently no consequences. The German military had the advantage of starting many things from scratch, rebuilding with new weapon systems and developing entirely new tactics for their use. German generals focused upon a new doctrine of mobility (*Blitzkrieg*) in which motorized units would cooperate closely with the air force (*Luftwaffe*), thus avoiding the slow movements that had resulted in the trenches of the First World War. The Germans tested and refined many of their concepts in the late 1930s when they intervened in the Spanish Civil War on the side of Franco's Fascists. By the end of the decade German forces were still relatively small, but they had developed innovative new tactics, were in most cases well equipped with modern weapons, and had a superb system of planning and communication.

In retrospect it is easy to criticize the Allies for their unwillingness to confront Nazi Germany as Hitler increasingly flaunted the restrictions of the old peace settlement. If, for example, the French had invaded in 1936 when Hitler ordered German troops back into the Rhineland, they surely would have overwhelmed the small German forces and dealt Hitler a humiliating blow. Equally, had the Allies been willing to go to war in 1938 when the regime staged a coup in Austria to bring the Nazis to power and thus unify the two states, then Germany would have been unready and probably blockaded and starved out, much as it had been in 1914–1918. But the people and leaders of Britain and France loathed the idea of another war against Germany. Their military preparations had been almost totally defensive in nature, and no politician in either London or Paris wanted to risk his career on trying to persuade the people to support another years-long world war over an esoteric question such as whether or not Germany and Austria should unify. The Allies remained passive primarily because they were democracies, and a clear majority of their people had no desire for war.

The Czechoslovak Crisis was more serious because it involved the fate of a nation with whom the Allies had a military alliance. Czechoslovakia had been created by the Allies from lands in the former Austro-Hungarian empire. The Czech heartland of Bohemia was also home to 3 million ethnic Germans, mostly in the Sudeten region on the border, who were now under Czech rule. Bohemia had been part of the Holy Roman Empire and was considered by most Germans to be a German land in which a Czech population also existed, rather than vice versa. Thus Hitler was expressing another of Germany's longstanding grievances about the Versailles settlement when he demanded that the Sudeten region become independent and have the right to join the Third Reich. His tone grew increasingly hysterical as he claimed that Czechs were actually carrying out genocide against Sudeten Germans. The Czech government predictably refused his demands. Czechoslovakia was a small state but had a modern army and was willing to fight because they believed that their British and French allies would back them up. However, the Allies ultimately pressured the Czech leadership to accept the Munich Agreement, in which the Sudetenland was ceded to Germany. Hitler assured the Allies that he had no further territorial demands.

Czechoslovakia began to collapse. Poland and Hungary demanded and got portions of Slovakia, and the Slovaks finally declared their independence. In the midst of the chaos, German troops invaded the remainder of Bohemia in March 1939, allegedly to restore order, but of course to annex the entire region to the Third Reich. Finally realizing that Hitler could not be appeased, the Allies reluctantly began to prepare for war.

The Second World War began over another crisis that was created by Hitler but which had its roots in the Versailles settlement. In 1919 the Allies created Poland by taking territory from Germany, Austria-Hungary, and pre-war Russia. In order to give the new Polish state access to the sea, they cut a corridor of land through old West Prussia (which, admittedly, had once been Polish in the days before Frederick the Great), thus cutting East Prussia off from the rest of the Reich. When Hitler demanded another territorial settlement to redress this historical grievance, the Poles, and this time the British and French, gave every indication that they were prepared to fight. The war began on September 1, 1939, as German troops invaded Poland. Three days later, the British and French declared war on Germany.

Much of the world was astonished at the speed of the German advance. Within three weeks German forces overran western Poland and completely defeated the Polish military. The Allies received another shock when Soviet troops invaded Poland from the east, revealing the existence of a secret Nazi-Soviet pact. Although they were not allies, the Soviets and Germans agreed on a division of Eastern Europe, and Soviet dictator Josef Stalin agreed to supply Germany with important raw materials in return for technology.

The war was quiet throughout the autumn and winter of 1939–1940. Then in the spring of 1940 the Germans struck suddenly in the north, overrunning Denmark and Norway, thus establishing important new air and naval bases on the North Sea. In May 1940 German forces overran Holland and Belgium. As British and French forces entered Belgium to confront them, the Germans cut behind them, trapping them against the coast of the English Channel. The British made a narrow escape, but lost tens of thousands of men and nearly all their equipment. France lasted only another month, and was totally defeated by the end of June. At that point Italian dictator Benito Mussolini entered the war on Hitler's side, thus bringing the conflict to the Mediterranean and North Africa.

Germany's great victories convinced Hitler of his personal military genius, although in fact his interference had probably cost the German generals their chance to annihilate the British army in 1940. Nonetheless, his popularity was astronomical in the summer of 1940, and most Germans assumed the war would soon be over. Hitler ordered a demobilization of much of the army.

With Germany's tiny navy, there was no way to invade Britain, so Hitler contented himself with bombing British cities and letting German U-Boats (submarines) sink British merchant ships until his enemy finally came to terms. Unfortunately for his plans, Hitler's Italian allies proved themselves repeatedly incompetent, thus drawing German forces into the Mediterranean and Balkans to clean up Italian disasters, and the British appeared in no way ready to surrender.

Believing he had neutralized the British, by the autumn of 1940 Hitler had become obsessed with the Soviet Union. The Nazi-Soviet pact had been a marriage of convenience for two partners who in fact despised and mistrusted each other. Stalin was shocked by the speed with which the Germans had defeated the western Allies, and he wanted to maintain the pact for as long as possible. Hitler, conversely, sensed an opportunity to settle matters in the east on a grand, historical scale. His "strategy" was in fact based more upon his ethnic and racial ideas of history than upon any military logic. Hitler envisioned an immense ethnic cleansing of the east, pushing away or eliminating Jews, Gypsies, and other "parasites"; enslaving the Slavs; and settling the region with German colonists; all while achieving the ideological goal of eliminating Communism. Typically, he asked his generals to draw up military plans and then interfered with them in dramatic and unpredictable ways. The result was a wildly optimistic schedule of operations in which the German forces would supposedly overrun all of western Russia in the summer of 1941 and wrap up the campaign by autumn.

The initial invasion in late June 1941 (Operation Barbarossa) enjoyed overwhelming success, driving hundreds of miles into the Soviet Union, cutting off and capturing millions of Soviet soldiers. But operations in this far-flung region with a primitive road network were very different than what German commanders had experienced in the west, and the supply chain soon broke down. The German offensive was slowed, then halted, more by its own logistical realities than by Soviet resistance. The offensive resumed in early winter, but by then the Soviets had brought up reinforcements and the weather had turned very cold. In the blizzard conditions of the first week of December, large-scale Soviet counterattacks threw back the Germans over one hundred miles and inflicted over a hundred thousand casualties. A few days after this new phase of the struggle began, Japan attacked the United States, and Hitler declared war on America on December 11.

The Germans were now locked in a massive conflict on the Eastern Front, with the British still unconquered in their rear, supported by the Americans. In 1942 the government finally began to mobilize for a total war effort. The Nazis, most of whom had vivid memories of the First World War, had always been reluctant to impose the kinds of sacrifices on the civilian population that had caused such unrest and ultimately the fall of the government in 1917–1918. But in 1942 they began mass conscription, finally began a limited effort to encourage women to work outside the home, imposed strict rationing, and tried to exercise tighter control over factories and war production.

The immense areas of conquered territory and millions of prisoners also afforded the Nazis the opportunity to use slave labor. The regime and the entire German economy became increasingly dependent upon this system, which fell under the aegis of Himmler's SS. By this point the SS had become a huge organization, with control over security, prison camps, the extermination programs, and even its own economy of SS-run factories and enterprises. The SS had created its own military forces, the Waffen-SS, alongside the regular German military, and they enjoyed a prestige and priority with the regime, often being given the pick of the replacements and equipment. The war helped the careers of some Nazi leaders, while frustrating others. Hitler's secretary Rudolf Hess found himself increasingly sidelined and went so far as to escape to Britain in 1941. Hermann Goering, despite his impressive portfolio of jobs, lost Hitler's favor because the *Luftwaffe*, which Goering commanded, was unable to protect German cities from the ever-increasing fleets of British and American bombers. Himmler became steadily more powerful, as the SS swallowed up other bureaucracies and assumed their duties. Josef Goebbels remained indispensable in his job as minister for propaganda, particularly as the war turned against Germany and the regime became worried about managing dissent. And the architect Albert Speer, who initially ascended due to his personal friendship with Hitler, acquired various new jobs until he was minister for war production, which placed him in direct conflict with Himmler over control of the slave-labor economy.

German forces suffered severe defeats in the east and in North Africa at the end of 1942, and the remainder of the war was essentially a long, grudging retreat as the Third Reich was hammered by Allied bombers and pushed from three sides by Allied armies. Hitler no longer allowed his commanders any initiative. He attempted to direct all war operations personally, spending hours hunched over maps with a magnifying glass and sending out increasingly unrealistic and draconian commands to hold every inch of ground to the last man, or to counterattack against hopeless odds. After he survived an assassination attempt by several army commanders in July 1944, his paranoia reached levels that one must equate with insanity.

By early 1945 Germany was a wasteland of bombed cities and wrecked infrastructure. The final Allied offensives across the Rhine began in March;

the final Soviet push against Berlin began in April. In his command bunker under the ruined capital, Hitler finally killed himself on April 30. The Third Reich survived him by ten days, its surrender marking the end of the Second World War in Europe.

Image vs. Reality

The Nazis always depicted Hitler as a firm and decisive figure, driven by an irresistible will and clear sense of direction. They believed that their dictatorial system was superior to the incompetent and corrupt bourgeois democracy that it had replaced, because unlike a democracy, with its petty squabbles and bureaucratic turf wars, a dictatorship could get things done. The term for this—*Führerprinzip* (leader-principle)—expressed the reality that Hitler could inject his will into the system at any point or in any way he desired, by issuing a Führer Directive that could address literally any topic, and which carried the force of law. Indeed, when Hitler's instructions contradicted the existing law, judges and legislators were forced to play catch-up, altering the law retroactively to make whatever Hitler had done legal.

In reality, however, the Nazi system encouraged an extraordinary level of confusion, redundancy, bureaucratic waste, and inefficiency. It was anything but the clearly ordered, smoothly running, top-down machine of its propaganda. The problems were probably inevitable, given the relatively low level of administrative and political experience of many of the leading Nazis, coupled with their ambitious, paranoid, and aggressive behavior. The Third Reich was a government of personalities, not laws.[4]

The Enabling Act of 1933, which gave Hitler his first dictatorial powers, set the tone for what was to come. Its opening sentence reads: "In addition to the methods designated by the Constitution, national laws may be enacted by the government."

We see here that the constitution is not necessarily eliminated, replaced, or invalidated, but rather that a new structure is being built on top of the old one. The Nazis referred to their seizure of power as the National Socialist Revolution, but in fact it was not a revolution, at least not in the radical style of the Soviets, but instead an ad hoc creation of new institutions. The Nazis channeled the existing extremist and right-wing sentiments within the society and created a new layer of administration that reflected that ideology. But it was very irregularly applied and never a complete or even smooth transformation. Nazi Germany still had a capitalist economy, for instance, but it was now allegedly managed in consultation with various new government planning offices. It still had the forms and structures of diplomacy and statecraft, but the dictator could and did cut through them at his discretion.

It still had an army, navy, and air force, but also created a new Nazi military growing alongside them.

Fundamentally, the Nazis never resolved the question of who ran the country: the party, or the state? From the outset, Hitler had two official job titles: Führer and Reich Chancellor. He was simultaneously head of the party and of the state. And in fact the only true synthesis of the two occurred in his person. In almost every other way, the institutions of the state—the civil service, the police, the utilities, the school systems, and so on—remained in place, and eventually were mostly staffed by Nazis. But alongside and on top of them the Nazi Party created its own institutions with essentially the same purposes. In some cases, the Nazis seemed uncertain that they could completely Nazify the old institutions, at least not in one generation, so they created their own ideologically loyal institutions that might one day replace them.

For example, the public school systems did not complete the transition to a Nazi curriculum until 1937—an oddly long wait for a regime that paid such close attention to children and youth training. Yet from the moment they took power, the SS created special private schools nicknamed *Napolas*, whose purpose was to pick and train the most promising boys in a completely ideological environment, with a heavy emphasis upon total loyalty, paramilitary exercise, and frequent brutality.

This duplication and redundancy was felt even at the highest levels. As chancellor, Hitler was directly served by Hans Lammers, his "Chief of the Reich Chancellery." But as führer, he was served by Rudolf Hess, his most immediate deputy within the party, replaced by Martin Bormann after Hess's treason in 1941. (Bormann, in fact, got his new job in the classically Nazi way, by inventing it and then convincing Hitler it was important, through his access to the führer at his vacation home in the Alps, where Bormann was the manager.) So if Hitler issued a command, or wanted a briefing on something, or needed to meet with people . . . who arranged it? Through whom did the paperwork and communication flow? The answer, as with so many things in the Nazi dictatorship, was usually whomever was present at the moment.

At the national ministerial level, it was often impossible to determine who had authority in fundamentally important fields. Consider, for instance, the management of industrial policy. There was a minister of economics, Hjalmar Schacht. Then there was Hermann Goering, who—in addition to his many other jobs—was given authority to implement the Four Year Plan, the supposed direction of economic policy. In 1938 Fritz Todt set up his Organization Todt, which coordinated industry with government and military policy, and when the war began, he became minister for armaments and munitions. Himmler's SS soon controlled not only its own factories, but also most of the slave labor supply. Josef Goebbels, the Propaganda Minister, also became "Minister Plenipotentiary for Total War on the Home Front," which gave him authority to mobilize workers for war-related projects. Local administrators all had their pet industrial projects, often run on their own initiatives. And on it went. Consequently, Nazi administration often became a competition for the attention of Hitler himself, because only the führer could issue a directive that could cut through the chatter and backstabbing. But even Hitler had his frustrations with the limits of the system. In 1941, for instance, he issued a Führer Directive to the Daimler-Benz company to change the armament on one of Germany's main battle tanks. The company ignored him because the change would have been expensive and difficult. Their refusal went unnoticed for months, until an exasperated Hitler had to threaten and rant to get his way.

These problems were not restricted to the highest circles around Hitler. Nazi Germany retained much of the old Weimar-era state administrative boundaries and services. A governor was still a governor, and a mayor still a mayor, for example, even though there were no free elections. On top of this, however, the Nazi Party layered its own subdivisions of *Gaus* (regions) managed by *Gauleiters* (party chiefs in large regions), who answered directly to Hitler. Local administration was also overseen by *Kreisleiters*, who supervised their districts within each gau. The borders of a gau often didn't match the old state borders. Needless to say, the old state administrative offices continued to function, yet now had to do so in a constant rivalry with the party administrators over who actually had the authority to do what.

Not only was there frequent conflict between state and party, but there was often no logic or system in the creation of the party institutions themselves. Virtually any prominent Nazi could take the initiative, perhaps getting Hitler's ear and approval for some new project, and then creating an administrative structure for it, even if some other prominent Nazi had already done so. This was, in fact, the most common way that rivals within the party tried to maneuver each other out of power and influence, by starting bureaucratic wars with one another.

For example, in the early days of the regime Heinrich Himmler wanted to create a national police force from within his SS organization. He persuaded Hitler that the presence of so many internal enemies (Communists, Socialists, and foreign spies) necessitated a security apparatus outside the normal police and courts. Thus he created the SD (security service), which soon had tens of thousands of employees, its own directorate, and eventually its own prisons, motor pool, recruiting, training, supply services, and so on. However, Hermann Goering, as minister-president of Prussia, the largest state in the

Reich, had also decided to create more or less the same kind of national police force by recruiting from his Prussian interior ministry forces. He also received Hitler's approval. Thus he created the Gestapo (an abbreviation for "secret state police"). The two large institutions had a rivalry for a few years until Himmler finally got control of the Gestapo as well, and yet he simply allowed both to continue in existence. The results would be comical if they didn't ruin so many innocent lives; it was not uncommon for a suspect to be arrested, imprisoned, and tortured by the SD in one of their prisons, then released and picked up the same day by the Gestapo, and sent to one of their prisons for the exact same treatment.[5]

Figure 8.1. Hermann Goering. Photograph courtesy of the United States Holocaust Memorial Museum. Used with permission.

Hermann Goering: A Nazi Ministerial Portfolio

Behind his back Germans called him *Der Dicke* ("the Fatty"). Goering's administrative responsibilities are a case study in the illogic of Nazi officialdom. He was president of the Reichstag, minister-president of Prussia, head of the Luftwaffe (air force), Reichs protector of forests and wildlife, head of the Four Year Plan, chief of the state police of Prussia, and founder of the Gestapo.

A notoriously lazy and self-indulgent man, Goering rarely worked more than a few hours a day, or more than a few days a week.

It remains anybody's guess how long the Nazi regime would have lasted, had it not started the Second World War. One could argue, of course, that a vengeful war of conquest was such a fundamental desire within Nazi ideology, and that the regime's rhetoric and worldview was so militarized and so obsessed with contests of strength, that a European war was inevitable. But at least until the war began to turn against Germany in 1942, the Nazi governing model, despite all its waste, confusion, and internal conflict, sufficed to keep many people happy, and most people at least content. Some historians, in fact, argue that a substantial majority of Germans felt that their lives had been improved by the Third Reich, at least until the hardships of the Second World War.[6]

Who Supported the Regime?

After the Second World War, Allied occupation authorities were often disgusted and angry to find that Germans virtually never admitted to having supported the Nazis, much less to having been members of the Nazi Party. For years the party had displayed propaganda films of thousands of cheering Germans waving flags and shouting "Heil Hitler," but as soon as the government was no more, miraculously few actual Nazis could be found. This is due to two proximate causes. First, obviously, is the fear of Allied retribution. Secondly, most of those big Nazi rallies were in fact carefully staged and scripted, and filmed to look bigger and more impressive than they were. Josef Goebbels, the minister for propaganda, loved wide-angle crowd scenes, particularly with throngs of people in motion, as if the entire nation was joyfully and spontaneously marching behind their führer. It is an important question, however, particularly in light of the horrible crimes perpetrated by the Third Reich, to ask who actively supported the regime, and to what extent.

The Nazis obviously did not do public opinion polling or measure approval ratings, but Hitler and Goebbels were often surprisingly sensitive to questions of popularity. Hitler frequently made policy decisions out of a concern for his public image, and Goebbels's diary is full of fretting over what the public will think of this or that initiative if it is not properly sold to them. It is not as simple as saying that the more structured and hierarchical the organization, the more often one could find loyalty to the regime. In the army by 1941, the average nineteen-year-old soldier would have been twelve years old when Hitler came to power, and his entire coming-of-age experience would have involved a Nazified school environment, probable membership in the Hitler Youth, and a fair amount of formal and informal indoctrination in his military training. The average soldier was not a Nazi—not a member of the party, nor particularly driven toward the party's goals—but he was basically loyal and often enthusiastically confident in Hitler's leadership.[7]

On the other hand the churches, despite their traditions of hierarchy and service, remained skeptical of the regime, and their loyalties were not solid or monolithic. Several of the early inmates in the first concentration camps, alongside the Communists and Socialists, were Catholic priests and Lutheran ministers. The church leadership might have embraced Nazism, but that embrace did not always encompass the churches' employees. The naive courage of the Scholl siblings (Hans and Sophie), who resisted the regime and were executed in 1943, stemmed largely from their religious convictions. And of course some of the more famous individual resisters included pastors like Martin Niemöller and Dietrich Bonhöffer.

German civilians often grumbled about the increasingly obvious incompetence of the government. While Hitler as an individual remained popular, people often expressed their dismay about the behavior of other Nazi leaders. After bombs began to fall on German cities, for instance, Hermann Goering stopped making unscripted public appearances, having experienced some uncomfortable moments with angry crowds. His rival Goebbels commented upon this with spiteful pleasure, although Goebbels himself was one of the leaders whom people increasingly referred to as *Bonzen* (privileged fat cats).

The Nazi regime seemed content, even happy, to expel or persecute members of various elites who disapproved of them, such as media entrepreneurs, scientists, professors and other intellectuals, and of course politicians. But they were much more careful with elites in the two areas they felt they could not afford to alienate: business/industrial leaders and the military high command.

Some prominent business and industrial leaders were in fact convinced Nazis. Others were probably more cynically motivated. Of course many things the Nazis did proved a boon for big companies. There were huge new contracts for civil and military projects, often awarded through personal connections to a Nazi official or through bending Hitler's ear. Labor was cheap for much of the Nazi period because of the high unemployment rates in the 1930s and the fact that the regime had crushed labor unions. When manpower became scarce during the war due to the mass mobilizations for the front, the regime compensated by offering companies the use of prisoners and then slave labor. In some regions, by 1944, tens of thousands of prisoners and forced workers, housed in camps or even on the factory grounds, kept German industry moving.

Businessmen generally dislike government regulation and "interference," so they were often unhappy at the Nazis' various attempts to structure and manage production. Fortunately for them, the bureaucratic jumble of Nazi administration often left loopholes open for business leaders to do as they pleased, particularly if they could bet wisely on which Nazi officials might come out on top in the administrative conflicts. The ever-astute Himmler sensed the money that could be made in this way, and established a "Friends of the Reichsführer-SS" association, which business leaders could join by making financial contributions to the SS. Many who joined undoubtedly did so out of a desire to get a share of the government's large contracts and many perks, and also to avoid any trouble with the SS. Since the SS was also the nation's largest supplier of slave labor, being friends with Himmler, or at least bribing him, was good for one's payroll.

The Nazi government was likely to interfere in industry not through regulation, but often through simple theft. Nazi officials had a tendency to take over private enterprises to add to their personal empires. Historians disagree on the degree to which the Nazi regime respected private property and contracts, but most agree that Goering and Himmler were profligate confiscators, and not simply of Jewish-owned businesses (which after 1935 were perfectly legal to steal).[8] On the other hand, business leaders were often pleased with the opportunities afforded by the regime's casual relationship to the law, workers' rights, and private property, particularly when Jewish competitors were run out of business or plundered, and their assets taken at bargain rates.

Figure 8.2.   Heinrich Himmler with His Daughter, Gudrun. Photograph courtesy of the United States Holocaust Memorial Museum. Used with permission.

The Nazi Party's relationship with the military high command was as complex and conflicted as its relationship with churches and business leaders. The generals of the Weimar Republic had comprised a very small, cliquish, aristocratic circle who were broadly conservative, but who generally turned up their noses equally at ranting right-wing populists and Socialists. The Nazis promised an expansion of the military, however, which was at least appealing enough for the generals to consider making deals with Hitler. Of course the massive expansion of the military democratized the institution, in the sense that it brought in men from all social strata, and thus many of the aristocrats had to share generals' rank with men whose surnames did not have the preposition "von."

Among the aristocratic commanders there were some enthusiastic Nazis, or certainly happy fellow travelers. Walter von Reichenau, who commanded German forces in the Polish, French, and Russian campaigns, was one of Hitler's favorite "political generals." He ordered soldiers on the Eastern Front not to consider the Soviets as "fighters under the rules of war," but rather as "bestial . . . sub-humans." Other generals never got over the odor of Nazism, but nonetheless served because they were patriots. Erwin von Witzleben, for example, whose family had produced generals since before Frederick the Great, objected to the Nazis' abolition of the rule of law, and plotted against Hitler on several occasions, finally paying with his life in 1944.

Interestingly, being a Nazi did not appear to increase one's chances for promotion, except, obviously, in the Waffen-SS, where ideology and party loyalty were a sine qua non. The regime rarely exerted any pressure on military leaders to toe the party line. Even though he disliked aristocrats, Hitler was usually willing to tolerate a non-Nazi general, if that general achieved results that made Hitler's own leadership look good. Thus he indulged the cantankerous Erich von Manstein, who brought him such success in France and Russia, and even dismissed the evidence that Manstein had enough Jewish ancestry to qualify him as Jewish under the race laws.

There were three serious crises between the Nazis and the military high command, and Hitler won in all three cases. In 1938 he approved the purge of the two highest-ranking generals in the army, based largely on false or exaggerated moral "crimes." In the shake-up that ensued, Hitler restructured the high command more directly under his authority and replaced the leadership with men whom he knew to be loyal. The second crisis occurred in the winter of 1941–1942, when the German offensive in the Soviet Union ground to a halt and then was thrown back by Soviet counterattacks. Hitler sacked a number of his highest-ranking commanders and took personal command of the Eastern Front himself. From that point on, his role as führer was increasingly circumscribed by military affairs, and very few commanders dared to make major movements without his approval. And in July 1944 a group led by a number of high-ranking officers came very close to assassinating Hitler with a bomb. The explosion left Hitler with light injuries, but a lasting paranoia about the officers of the regular army. For the remainder of the war he preferred only those commanders of whose political loyalties he could be sure. A number of high-ranking commanders were executed, and others were forced into retirement. In the end, military operations became the sole prerogative of the führer. Yet despite all of the abuse he heaped upon his generals, the large majority remained loyal to him.

Strength through Joy

The process by which German civil and social institutions were absorbed and integrated by the Nazis is known as the *Gleichschaltung*, which loosely translates as "synchronization." The Nazi regime was constantly pulling in multiple directions, but it was broadly consistent in certain obvious ways. All media, for instance, had to reflect the party's ideology. All social organizations that were allowed to continue eventually had to demonstrate that they supported the regime's goals and worldview. And of course the Nazis created their own organizations to channel existing social activities in politically acceptable ways.

The Nazi regime was a very activist government when it came to the lives of everyday people. The Third Reich was the first government in Europe, for example, to launch public health campaigns to persuade people to stop smoking and to dissuade children from starting. They had a more difficult time persuading people to abstain from alcohol, given the importance of Germany's beer industry, but they did indeed try. And they incessantly encouraged people to get more physical exercise. This all fell under the rubric of the national program "Strength through Joy" (abbreviated in German as KdF), the administrative structure established to structure leisure time, culture, health, fitness, and sports. The KdF sponsored activities that ran the gamut from Baltic cruises to skiing in the Alps. It also encompassed sedentary recreation such as concerts and theater, although in those cases it often competed against Josef Goebbels's Ministry for Propaganda and Enlightenment, which asserted its control over nearly all entertainment media.

It is of course ironic that a regime like the Nazis could be so casually brutal with the lives of its people, and yet simultaneously so concerned with their physical health and spiritual wholesomeness. The KdF is an example of the totalitarian impulse to control all aspects of civic life. The Nazis succeeded on many levels, although they knew that adults had habits and lifestyles that neither oppression nor enticement could change. Not surprisingly, then, the regime focused more intensely on the social and civic lives of children.

The Nazis were not the first political party to create a youth auxiliary or to focus on politicizing youth movements. Communists and Social Democrats had extensive youth organizations, and of course the concept dated back even before the Prussian use of student/militant groups in the Napoleonic Wars. As they had done in Prussia after the Napoleonic defeat, youth groups proliferated again following the First World War. Many of them were patriotic, often with religious affiliations, and they were usually on the Right of the German political spectrum.

The early Nazi youth groups thus had to compete in a fairly crowded field. There were dozens of similar groups, not affiliated with the party, with comparable goals and agendas. The Nazis themselves, with their typical confusing redundancy, even created multiple and overlapping groups. But by 1930, the large majority of these groups had been absorbed into and reorganized under the umbrella of the *Hitlerjugend* (Hitler Youth, usually abbreviated HJ). As soon as the Nazis secured power, all other rival youth organizations were banned.

By 1936, membership in some HJ-affiliated group became theoretically compulsory, although in many cases children's names were simply inscribed by their schools. It is not clear what percentage of German children routinely took part in HJ-related activities, but their general level of exposure to them was undoubtedly high. As with other social activities during the Nazi *Gleichschaltung*, a combination of attractive opportunities and peer pressure probably sufficed to involve most people in one way or another. A young person might find a place to play tennis with a friend, but to play on a team, or to use many courts, or to become competitive in the sport, meant having a proper coach and joining an organization. One might enjoy swimming in a local lake, but to join the swim team meant adhering to the HJ. In short: it was possible to live a normal childhood without participating in any Nazi organizations. But it was increasingly difficult to take any active role in society without being in some way affiliated.

The Nazis created a parallel female organization, the *Bund deutscher Mädel* (League of German Girls, abbreviated BDM). In many ways this was a revolutionary concept: encouraging physical fitness and exercise for girls, developing female sporting leagues, and even training young women in pre-professional and business skills. Nazi Germany was undeniably a patriarchal institution, emphasizing women's most important contributions in the traditional roles of motherhood and family. Nonetheless, in their desire to create new, superior Aryan wives and mothers, the Nazis achieved a level of social activity and engagement for young women that most democracies didn't reach until decades later.

Nor did the Nazis neglect the intellectual development of youth. The party's official press in Munich devoted an imprint specifically to books for children and young adults. With time these publications became quite elaborate and ubiquitous, reaching down even to kindergartners, who had coloring books featuring the great heroes of German history. Although they were slow to produce school textbooks, the party's affiliated presses were very productive with other publications for children and youth.

By and large, these were high-quality productions. Magazines and journals were often targeted at specific age groups of boys and girls, well written, lavishly illustrated, and filled with youth-oriented content: sports, adventure tales, puzzles, and often simplified and highly politicized historical excerpts to teach young people patriotic stories about the heroic Germans of the past. (Girls read about the noble Queen Louise of Prussia, while boys read about the valiant fighter pilots over the trenches of the Great War, and so on.) These publications were full of "message" as well as content: get outside and exercise, serve your country, don't drink or smoke, watch out for Jews and foreigners.

Despite the popular imagery of them at the time and thereafter, Nazi youth were not simply brainwashed automatons, marching in formation and shouting "Heil" at Hitler's public events. Many became involved because the organizations provided them with a rich social experience, and often, with *fun*. It was fun to go hiking in the mountains, camp out, and sing folk songs into the night. It was fun to join the track team and travel to cities they'd never seen before, to compete in athletic events. Given the choices for distraction and entertainment in Weimar Germany, we must also imagine that many parents were probably relieved to know that their children were engaging in these more wholesome, old-fashioned pursuits.

As the war progressed and turned against Germany, the theme of sacrificing for one's country gradually came to dominate youth instruction. School textbooks by 1944 offered examples of heroic young Germans who had given their lives for the Fatherland. Girls of the BDM were trained to operate antiaircraft guns. And the boys of the Hitler Youth increasingly found themselves on the front lines at ever younger ages. The last known film footage of Adolf Hitler is a broadcast of him congratulating a group of adolescent HJ boys who have knocked out Soviet tanks during the desperate fighting near Berlin in the spring of 1945.

Oppression and Murder

The twentieth century was crowded with oppressive dictatorships. In retrospect, the Nazis were not remarkable or unusual in the way they treated their political opponents or people whom they suspected of disloyalty or nonconformity. What makes the regime stand out is the way that their race-based ideology was enacted as a state policy of genocide. The process was fitful, and one could argue that it was not really a true nationwide policy until 1941, being until then a series of pogroms, often inspired by some event or at the whim of a Nazi leader, and sometimes linked to the persecution of other groups. Indeed, the Nazis originally did not intend an entirely separate program for the extermination of Jews, considering them simply one of several undesirable groups they wanted to remove from Germany. By 1942, however, a full-scale nationwide program was underway to commit genocide. Because this topic has received so much attention in popular media, often with confusing or inaccurate depictions, it is important to define some of the key terms and concepts.

The Nazi state practiced incarceration without legal due process from the moment it began to take power. It became a massive industry unto itself. Over the years the regime proliferated nearly twenty thousand "camps" with different purposes. The term concentration camp is therefore a broad term that can mean several things. For purposes of clarity we should distinguish between six distinct kinds of institutions:

Special prisons or detention centers were set up by the SS, the SD, the Gestapo, and in some occupied regions by the local Nazi authorities. Their purpose was generally torture and interrogation, not prolonged incarceration, although some people did indeed spend long periods there. (The Communist leader Ernst Thälmann, for example, spent eleven years in three such prisons before being transferred to Buchenwald, where he was killed.) There were hundreds of special prisons across Germany, from early in the regime.

Concentration camp could refer to any number of institutions where people were imprisoned as punishment, often for political crimes, but in some cases simply for being "undesirable." Many dissident churchmen, for example, were sent to Dachau, the first big camp, built near Munich in 1933. Homosexuals, Jehovah's Witnesses, Jews, Socialists and Communists, all could be found in these camps, where their punishment was—in addition to the extremely harsh treatment—usually some form of manual labor. Although their official purpose was not to kill their inmates, the terrible conditions and constant violence meant that inmates routinely died in large numbers. Some concentration camps became huge. At one point Buchenwald held over two hundred thousand inmates, several times more than the population of the nearby city of Weimar.

The word **stalag** was an abbreviation for the German word meaning "base camp" or "holding camp." These prisons were run by different branches of the German military and used for Allied prisoners of war. However, the treatment of prisoners varied widely, and the SS-run camps in the east were essentially concentration and slave-labor camps where hundreds of thousands, mostly Soviet prisoners, perished.

Labor camps were built all over Germany in various sizes. In some cases, particularly in regions with a lot of industry, there might be a central camp and then several "satellite camps" (*Aussenlager*) holding only a few hundred inmates who were being used to work in a single nearby business or factory. Some of these smaller camps were very obvious and in the midst of urban areas. In Braunschweig, for example, nine regional satellite camps routinely received prisoners from Auschwitz, Neuengamme, and other larger camps, to work in over fifty local businesses, with one of the satellite camps being practically in the midst of downtown, only four blocks from the main city government buildings. By 1943 labor camps had become the most numerous type of Nazi prisons.

Transit camps were established across occupied Europe, where people were held for varying lengths of time prior to being sent on to some other fate. (Many people who would otherwise have been killed managed to survive because they were rerouted for slave labor.)

Death camps (the Germans later named them "Annihilation Camps") were the largest and least numerous of the institutions. A half dozen were established by the SS beginning in early 1942, and located outside the borders of Germany, in the occupied eastern territories formerly in Poland. Their purpose was entirely genocidal, for "Jews and other enemy races," although some political and other types of prisoners did end up there. Although there were only six such camps, they accounted for the majority of people murdered during the Holocaust. Auschwitz-Birkenau alone killed over a million people. Transport to a death camp usually resulted in execution by poison gas within forty-eight hours.

The typically ad hoc nature of the Nazi system does not make these classifications easy or simple, since many camps existed that performed multiple functions, or changed over time. The reason there were proportionately more survivors from Auschwitz than from the other death camps, for example, was that it was simultaneously a labor camp, a concentration camp, and a death camp, with three large institutions operating side by side. Nor is it easy to find a single responsible party for the imprisonment and death of people. The Nazi regime had no shortage of organs of oppression, and prisoners could end up in a camp for any number of reasons. By 1942, however, the SS had become the principle actor in the running of death camps and the transferring of millions of their victims.

Even before they came to power, Hitler and other prominent Nazis spoke in melodramatic, draconian terms about how Jewish power over Germans would be "destroyed" or how the Jews would be "obliterated." But it is unclear whether they literally had any intention of mass murder. Their initial goal, to make Germany *Judenrein* (free of Jews) could just as easily have been accomplished by forced expulsion. Germany had only a very small Jewish population (less than one percent), and many Nazis were satisfied with turning up the pressure on them by boycotting Jewish businesses, regulating them out of existence, and/or creating regulations barring Jews from various sectors of the economy, civil service, or public life. These measures were both an argument for Jews to leave (without, of course, their money or possessions) and simply a way of focusing anger and resentment upon an "alien" minority during the hard times of the Depression. Anti-Semitic sentiments were found in many democracies during the 1920s and 1930s, including very prominently in the United States, where Henry Ford occasionally spoke of Jews in terms similar to those used by Hitler. Even if anti-Semitism had not been a factor, however, the high unemployment during the Depression meant that it was unlikely that any nation would have been willing to take in a refugee population, and thus an exodus was never truly feasible.

By 1935 several Nazi leaders had become worried that disorganized and arbitrary abuses and discriminations were hurting German economic recovery, and also encouraged general lawlessness. Thus many of the practices that the regime had already begun were codified as the Nürnberg Laws (also known as the Race Laws). This was a far-reaching set of rules that had implications beyond simply the Nazi obsession with Jews. The laws regulated marriage and sex, travel and passports, employment, and issues of citizenship and public life. Definitions of races were established, setting a legal precedent for future persecution, but also again trying to encourage Jews to leave (their passports did not permit them to reenter Germany if they left).

In November 1938 a young Jew assassinated a German diplomat in Paris. Hitler and Goebbels discussed possible reactions and decided to incite pogroms across Germany that began on the night of November 9—that crowded date in German history that included the anniversary of Emperor William II's abdication and the Beer Hall Putsch. Many SS and SA men had already been drinking and celebrating the latter anniversary when Goebbels sent out the call for a "spontaneous" demonstration of rage against Jews. The result was a series of rampages across the country as Jewish businesses were damaged or destroyed, synagogues were burned, Jews were beaten and arrested, and nearly a hundred people were killed. The night acquired the nickname *Kristallnacht* ("night of the [broken] glass"), and is regarded by many historians as a turning point for Jews in Nazi Germany. As a result of Kristallnacht, for the first time large numbers of Jews—approximately thirty thousand—were taken to concentration camps. The pogrom did have one effect desired by the Nazis; over one hundred thousand Jews fled Germany in the following months, reducing the overall Jewish population by about one-fifth.[9] By the end of 1938 Himmler was apparently optimistic that the "Jewish Problem" would soon be solved, and he asked the SS to begin planning for the expulsion of Germany's small but persecuted community of "Gypsies" (Sinti, Roma, and Lavelli).

When the Second World War began, borders closed, sea and air travel became almost impossible, and it was clearly no longer feasible to expel unwanted minorities. Moreover, the sudden German conquest of Poland meant that the Third Reich now controlled regions populated by nearly 3 million Jews, many times greater than the number in Germany before the war. The initial attempt to create a massive Jewish ghetto in Warsaw (whose population was already one-third Jewish) proved untenable. The ghetto became a vast, chaotic island of misery, poverty, and disease that German occupation authorities did not want to deal with. The invasion of the Soviet Union in June 1941 greatly exacerbated the Nazis' problems, as they conquered several million more Jews across a huge area, and Germany's Balkan allies contained at least 2 million more, plus another 2 million Gypsies.

Because there was never any single order for the Holocaust, no one set of instructions or policy from Hitler or anybody else in high command, historians have long debated when the decision was made—or even whether just one decision was made—to begin in earnest with a policy of mass killing. In early 1941, during the planning for the invasion of the Soviet Union, some Nazi officials were already planning large-scale killings of both Jews and Communists in their anticipated newly occupied lands in the East. As the invasion opened in the summer of 1941, the SS and SD experimented with mobile death squads called *Einsatzgruppen*, which cooperated with local pro-Nazi militias in Poland and the former Soviet territories to locate rural Jewish communities and massacre them. In many cases, the Poles, Lithuanians, or Russians assisted in these killings. Not satisfied with the slow and inefficient methods of the Einsatzgruppen, and still worried about the Polish ghetto, the SS General Reinhard Heydrich called a meeting of mid-level Nazi administrators and some occupation authorities at a villa in the Berlin suburb of Wannsee in December 1941.

Heydrich was one of Himmler's most important deputies in the SS, the leader of its Security Service (SD), whose job was to control internal dissent. Since Germany had begun expanding, Heydrich had been building his own bureaucratic empire in the occupied territories, in classic Nazi style. It is not clear on whose authority he called the meeting. Speculation has ranged from Goering to Himmler to—less likely—Hitler himself, or Heydrich may have simply acted on his own initiative. Although Heydrich indicated Goering's approval, Heydrich did not take orders from Goering. The question is significant because the result of this Wannsee Conference is the clearest evidence we have of a decision to enact a "Final Solution to the Jewish Problem"—in other words, to enact the Holocaust as it is now generally understood.

During 1942 most of the death camps were established and began killing by means of Zyklon-B poison gas, delivered to groups of victims in gas chambers. Bodies were then cremated. By 1943 when the transportation networks for the camps were fully established, the entire procedure was similar to mass production in a factory. Precise numbers will never be known, but historians can make educated guesses based upon the Nazis' own records and testimony. Altogether the different kinds of camps resulted in the death of at least 12 million human beings: 6 million Jews, 3.5 million Soviet prisoners, perhaps a million Gypsies (mostly Romani), and at least 1.5 million others, including homosexuals, Communists, Jehovah's Witnesses, people with disabilities, and political prisoners.

The Ethical Basis for Genocide

The disorganized structure of the Nazi regime makes it impossible to point a finger at one individual or decision and to say exactly when, where, and why the state began a policy of genocide. Mass killing occurred in a variety of places, under a variety of authorities, for a variety of reasons, and evolved over time.

It is significant, however, that the regime had already taken some ideological steps in that direction long before the systematic mass killings of the Holocaust. As early as 1934 the regime practiced forced sterilization of mentally and physically handicapped people. Although shocking today, similar laws existed at the time in the United States and other countries. The Nazis, however, expanded this practice to forced abortions and euthanasia on a large scale, ultimately killing at least two hundred thousand Germans.

The regime's propaganda openly advocated this practice on the basis of sound racial policy as well as saving the taxpayers' money. Unlike the Holocaust itself, a document survives in Hitler's own handwriting authorizing these procedures, which he referred to as "mercy killings."

Figure 8.3. The Case against the Disabled: An advertisement from the Racial-Political Bureau of the Nazi Party and its magazine *Neues Volk* (New People), endorsing euthanasia on the basis that it saves taxpayers' money. The headline reads: "This genetically diseased person will cost society 60,000 Marks over the course of his life. Fellow Citizen: that's your money, too." Original in the German Historical Museum, Berlin. Digital copy in public domain.

Historians have been fascinated by the question of what the perpetrators of the Holocaust thought of their own actions, and whether their families, friends, and communities approved of it. In other words: what did "ordinary" Germans think about this activity that in retrospect appears to be the most extraordinary and important legacy of the entire era? It is significant that very few men were conscripted by the SS until late in the war; the rest were volunteers. Even so, we cannot simply assume, as some historians have done, that volunteerism for an organization like the SS was the same thing as an active desire to commit murder.[10] Both men and women (about 11 percent of camp employees were female) had a variety of reasons for their service in Holocaust-related activities. In many cases the simple promise of a well-paying job could have been sufficiently attractive, especially for a man who might otherwise have been drafted and sent to the Russian front.

Given the wanton cruelty of many perpetrators, there can be no question that the regime endorsed and encouraged racial violence and thus attracted amoral people or those whose natural prejudices inclined them toward persecuting others. On the other hand, complicity in the Holocaust is an extremely complex issue because so many people were peripherally involved. Was a train conductor, for example, guilty of crimes against humanity if his job was to transport Jews and Gypsies to death camps? Was an industrial manager guilty if he filled a government contract for cement to build crematoria? How directly involved in killing must a person be to be "guilty"? It is probably fair to say that several thousand people were directly involved in the Holocaust, actively and even enthusiastically killing. And many hundreds of thousands were enablers of some sort, perhaps in a minor way, but associated enough for their consciences to smart and for their natural human reaction to be to stubbornly deny their guilt or even their knowledge.

Even at the very top it is evident that the Nazis had some troubled consciences. Leaders of the regime frequently commented that their actions would be judged correct by future generations or vindicated by history, an implicit admission that *present* generations did not approve. The persecution of Jews and other groups was carefully suspended during the 1936 Olympics, when the world's media was turned on Germany and Berlin in particular, which clearly indicates that the Nazis recognized that civilized nations would regard their behavior as bad. Even while conservative Germans frequently wrote to friends and relatives about their pride in Germany's returning strength, they nonetheless asserted passionately that the stories about Germany circulating in the foreign media were complete fabrications; the lies of Jews and Socialists and other enemies of the Volk, and that Germans would never commit such atrocities. That indicates, obviously, that they believed that such atrocities were wrong in the first place. Even Heinrich Himmler, arguably one of the most amoral people to hold power in the twentieth century, addressed SS officers in Poland in 1943 with the tone of "it's a dirty job but someone's got to do it":

I also want to refer here very frankly to a very difficult matter. We can now very openly talk about this among ourselves, and yet we will never discuss this publicly. . . .

I am now referring to the evacuation of the Jews, to the extermination of the Jewish people. This is something that is easily said: "The Jewish people will be exterminated," says every Party member, "this is very obvious, it is in our program—elimination of the Jews, extermination, will do." But then they turn up, the brave 80 million Germans, and each one has his decent Jew. It is of course obvious that the others are pigs, but this particular one is a splendid Jew.

But of all those who talked this way, none had observed it, none had endured it. Most of you here know what it means when 100 corpses lie next to each other, when 500 lie there or when 1,000 are lined up. To have endured this and at the same time to have remained a decent person, has made us tough. This is an honor roll in our history which has never been and never will be put in writing.

When the end came in 1945, the revelations about the camps were staggering even to people who had just fought the most destructive war in human history. Most of the top-ranking Nazis were dead. Hitler, Goebbels, and Himmler had killed themselves; Bormann died in Berlin; Heydrich had been assassinated in 1942; and Goering would kill himself in his prison cell in Nürnberg. Lacking any leading Nazis who would speak for themselves (except Albert Speer, who skillfully dissembled during his trial), the Allies demanded answers from the German people.

Suggested Reading

Bartov, Omer. *Hitler's Army: Soldiers, Nazis, and War in the Third Reich*. Oxford: Oxford University Press, 1991.

Broszat, Martin. *The Hitler's State: The Foundation and Development of the Internal Structure of the Third Reich*. New York: Longman, 1981.

Browning, Christopher. *Ordinary Men: Reserve Police Battalion 101 and the Final Solution in Poland*. New York: HarperCollins, 1992.

———. *The Path to Genocide: Essays on Launching the Final Solution*. Cambridge: Cambridge University Press, 1992.

Burleigh, Michael. *The Third Reich: A New History*. New York: Macmillan, 2000.

Burleigh, Michael, and Wolfgang Wippermann. *The Racial State: Germany 1933–1945*. Cambridge: Cambridge University Press, 1993.

Evans, Richard. *The Third Reich in Power*. New York: Penguin, 2005.

———. *The Third Reich at War*. New York: Penguin, 2009.

Kershaw, Ian. *The Nazi Dictatorship: Problems and Perspectives of Interpretation*. London: Arnold, 1985.

Longerich, Peter. *Holocaust: The Nazi Persecution and Murder of the Jews*. Oxford: Oxford University Press, 2010.

Mason, Tim. *Social Policy in the Third Reich*. Providence, RI: Berg, 1993.

Mommsen, Hans. *From Weimar to Auschwitz*. Cambridge: Polity, 1991.

Overy, Richard. *War and Economy in the Third Reich*. Oxford: Clarendon Press, 1994.

Tooze, Adam. *Wages of Destruction: The Making and Breaking of the Nazi Economy*. New York: Viking Press, 2007.

Weinberg, Gerhard. *Germany, Hitler, and World War II*. Cambridge: Cambridge University Press, 1995.

CHAPTER NINE

◦

Zero Hour

In Wolfgang Borchert's haunting, semiautobiographical short story *Along the Long, Long Street*, a young veteran walks through the rubbled wasteland of a German city in the days after the war, trying to find a yellow streetcar that he remembers from his childhood. His mind is jagged from hunger and profound exhaustion, and he can't seem to stay in the present. One moment he is on the ruined street, the next he is marching through Russia, or returning to the visions that he can't drive from his head: a little girl begging for bread, the burial of half his company in a mass grave after a Soviet artillery bombardment. The reader begins to realize that the young man is so profoundly lost, in both time and space, that he will in fact never get where he is going. Does the yellow streetcar even exist? Is he in fact really going anywhere at all? Or is he perhaps already dead, having, like the city itself, passed from the world of the living into something else?

Wolfgang Borchert was one of the lucky German soldiers who made it home relatively quickly at war's end. His psychological wounds were the inspiration for his brief but brilliant career as one of postwar Germany's first great authors of poetry, plays, and short stories. But his physical wounds caught up with him, particularly the wartime injury to his liver that finally killed him in the autumn of 1947. He was twenty-six years old.

The stories of Wolfgang Borchert remain as examples of what the Germans call "Rubble Literature" (*Trümmerliteratur*). In the wake of the defeat and occupation, Germany was a vast sea of desperate people, millions of

whom were in flight, wounded, and/or starving, moving between ruined cities in search of shelter and food, or fleeing the vengeance of the victorious
enemy. It was an historical moment of unprecedented upheaval and destruction, in which Germany as it had been known virtually ceased to exist. To
this day, Germans call it *Stunde Null*: "zero hour"—the time when history
itself was reset to the beginning.

The Rubble Women

In the old Hanseatic port of Bremen, where the medieval canal around the
city center had been transformed to a wooded park, the trees were so completely incinerated that they looked like stacks of grey cigarette ash, and
people could push them over with their hands. In the lower-Rhine industrial
city of Wesel, 97 percent of the buildings had been destroyed and fewer than
two thousand people remained alive in the city limits: about 7 percent of
the prewar population. In East Prussia's old royal city of Königsberg, home
to the great Enlightenment philosopher Immanuel Kant, 80 percent of the
urban center was in ruins, and those residents who had not been killed in the
fighting or starved to death, or escaped, were tormented by their conquerors
and then expelled. In Mainz not one building in the city center still had a
roof. In Berlin desperate people carved up the corpses of horses that had been
killed in the fighting, or went to the city zoo and killed the few remaining
animals for food. Disease, starvation, and child mortality reached levels not
seen since the seventeenth century. The average woman in Berlin was raped
twice a week by the Soviet occupation soldiers, for more than two months.

This was Germany in the spring and summer of 1945. And yet people
survived. There is no "greatest generation" for German twentieth-century
history, since the generation of the Second World War will forever be associated with Nazism and the Holocaust. But there is a certain mythic lore
about these years of terrible poverty and suffering, when tens of thousands
of "rubble women" cleared the ruined streets with their bare hands, brick by
brick. With 4 million men dead or missing in the war, another 3 million in
Allied captivity, and over 1.5 million men permanently disabled, Germany
was a predominantly female society in 1945, and women had to take on
roles and responsibilities that they had never expected. With virtually no
legitimate formal economy, people resorted to black market trade and barter
to survive: alcohol, cigarettes, and sex were traded for food, clothing, and
medicine.

After an initial period of severe abuse and violence against the civilians, Soviet occupation forces settled into a reasonably reliable system that

managed to keep people alive at subsistence levels. Nonetheless the Soviets continued to dismantle much of the remaining industrial plants and machinery to take back to Russia as reparations for the astronomical damage the Germans did during *their* occupation in 1941–1944. People in the west did somewhat better under American, French, or British occupation. Violence against civilians was nowhere near as widespread or vicious as it was under Soviet occupation, but it did happen. The French occupation forces were often vengeful, and many American soldiers proved to be creative smugglers and black-marketers who took advantage of desperate people.

In 1945 Germany was fundamentally at the mercy of a few powerful personalities who had decided its fate and future borders in midwar, at a pair of high-level conferences at Teheran and Yalta. At those meetings Winston Churchill, Franklin Roosevelt, and Josef Stalin had made a number of agreements about the future borders of Europe and the postwar situation in an occupied Germany, but much was left unsettled. By the summer of 1945 Roosevelt was dead and Churchill out of power, leaving Stalin as the indisputable political survivor. The Soviet dictator also had the plain advantage of millions of soldiers occupying Eastern Europe, in the zones that he wanted to alter.

Stalin met with the new U.S. president Harry Truman and with Churchill and the incoming British prime minister Clement Atlee in July 1945, at Potsdam, that former residence town of the Hohenzollerns, surrounded by ruined palaces and Frederick the Great's home at San Souci a half-hour's stroll away. Here they settled many of the outstanding issues, as well as resettled many things that the Americans and British thought had already been agreed upon, in almost every case to Stalin's advantage. The Soviet war reparations, which were already underway by force, were legitimized. Many of the wartime ideas of the Allied leaders were applied, at least in theory: that the future Germany should be a completely demilitarized zone, subservient to Allied control.

The most dramatic agreements concerned borders. A new Poland was finally created after years of midwar haggling. Stalin annexed more than a third of pre-war Poland to the Soviet Union, and compensated the Poles by giving them German territory: Prussia, Pomerania, and Silesia.

Thus ended five centuries of Prussian history and the inheritance of the Hohenzollerns. The names of the places were changed and many cities and towns vanished altogether in the destruction and forced re-settlement as Germans were expelled and replaced by Poles. Prussia was officially eliminated in 1947. At a stroke, eastern Germany (Silesia, Prussia, Pomerania) ceased to exist, and the old center (Saxony, Brandenburg, Mecklenburg) became the new "East." The Oder and Neisse rivers became the new border.

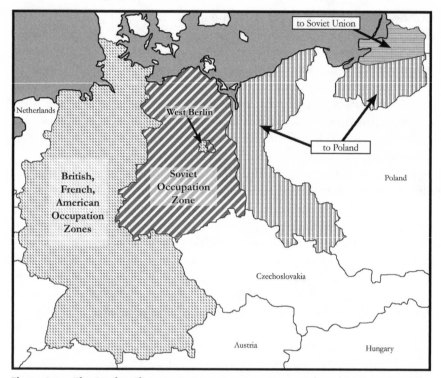

Figure 9.1. The Border Changes: Eastern Germany was transferred to Poland and the Soviet Union, while western and central Germany were occupied by the victorious Allies. West Berlin was an island of Western occupation in the Soviet zone.

Unlike the end of the First World War, when people could argue that the surrender was unfair because Germany hadn't really been defeated, this time nobody could possibly argue that Germany had been "stabbed in the back," or that it hadn't really lost the war. Not only were Germans in no position to deny their defeat, but the shame and guilt of Nazi atrocities was so massive that it cancelled any right for Germans to plead their own grievances. This was especially true for the millions of refugees from the eastern lands of the Reich, who suffered terribly from the Soviet vengeance and then the expulsion to the West. Many of these people faced the retribution of the Poles, who of course had every reason to feel hatred against Germans for what the Third Reich had done to their country.

"Ethnic Germans" (*Volksdeutsche*) living elsewhere in Europe were forcibly expelled, or fled for their lives. Many of these people had lived in these regions for two or three centuries, but their presence was now associated with the hated Nazi occupation. They fled from Romania, Hungary, Yugoslavia,

Czechoslovakia, and elsewhere, often terribly abused, having been robbed of all their property and possessions. In the ruins of Germany, where people were already desperate for food and shelter, nobody was glad to see more refugees, much less to assist them.

In all, nearly 12 million refugees fled to the western regions of Germany. Historians estimate that about one-fifth of the population of the future West Germany had fled from elsewhere. In a cruel twist of historical irony, many were housed for years in concentration camps originally built by the Nazis. Those who did not flee were often forcibly expelled by their conquerors, with orphan children given to Polish, Lithuanian, or Russian parents, given new names, and forbidden to speak German. Called "Wolf Children" or "Little Hitlers," many youngsters actually wandered for more than two years, abused, occasionally used for hard labor, and then ejected and forced to move on. Marianne Beutler, a teenaged girl from Königsberg, concluded that Germany had ceased to exist, and that she and her brother were all that remained of the German people. Adolescent Heidi Hermann survived gang rape and beatings, and witnessed men crucifying a German woman to a wagon for fun, before she and her battered mother escaped Pomerania and settled in the west. Anna Paapke lost every male relative in her extended family in East Prussia, including her fiancé, who never returned from a Soviet prisoner camp, before she escaped and settled in Braunschweig.[1]

In the immediate aftermath of the war, Germany was occupied by the Allied military forces and under martial law. The occupiers monitored virtually everything, although Germans did create new institutions for themselves. As early as the summer of 1945 a new free press began to emerge in the west, although American authorities reserved the right to inspect and possibly censor it. New political parties began to coalesce in the winter of 1945–1946. Some of these, like the Communists and the Social Democrats, were restorations of old parties. Others, like the Free Democrats and the Christian Democrats, were new creations. The latter example, the Christian Democratic Union (CDU), represented an attempt to unify mainstream conservatives of both Catholic and Protestant denominations. It was founded in 1946 by Konrad Adenauer, a former Catholic Center Party leader and mayor of Cologne who had been imprisoned during the Nazi years.

Adenauer was aware, as were all the emerging political figures in occupied Germany, that his range of action was severely limited by the occupation powers. The first and most obvious limitation was the incipient Cold War division between the Communist east and the capitalist west that ran through the middle of Germany. The Soviet zone was complicated still further by the presence of Berlin under "four-power" administration, and thus West Berlin was a little island of the capitalist world in the midst of the Communist world. In the early months after the war these divisions remained vague and ideology was less important than survival. (Neither capitalism nor Communism existed in a world without goods or legitimate markets.) But as time went on, it became clear that the Western occupying powers were deeply suspicious of left-wing politics, and that the Soviets were deeply suspicious of everyone except their own approved German Communists.

In theory, at least, the Allied powers could agree upon the elimination of the vestiges of the Third Reich. "Denazification" was an explicit goal agreed upon at the Potsdam Conference, but its implementation proved tortuous. It was relatively easy to arrest a small number of leading Nazi officials and military commanders. It was a much more complicated thing to determine the degree of nazification of lower-level civil servants or citizens. Because so many everyday activities in Nazi Germany had required some kind of party affiliation, most citizens were connected to the regime in some way or another. Was a small-town mayor, for instance, culpable for the regime's crimes? A postal official? A bureaucrat for the national railway?

There was no way to punish or even account for all the people who had been involved with the Nazis in small ways. Although a number of panels and some trials were established, inevitably a great many people who had been active Nazis and even low-level party officials went on to live influential and productive lives. The same was true in cultural life; professors at universities who had expelled their Jewish colleagues stayed on in the faculties, actors and directors who had made anti-Semitic and propaganda movies for Josef Goebbels remained active after the war. (One film director, Veit Harlan, stood trial for crimes against humanity, for his role in creating intensely anti-Semitic films like the infamous *Jud Süss*. He was acquitted and returned to work for another decade.) Many people simply kept quiet, or dared not raise their voices against others, for fear of their own complicity becoming an issue.

It is even more difficult to determine whether common people were nazified and then denazified after 1945. The regime had always enjoyed the support of a significant minority who shared its views, and it then spent twelve years indoctrinating a generation of young people. Gerhard Hennes joined the German army in 1939 as a patriotic teenager. Although he was never a member of the Nazi Party, he admired Hitler and believed in the war effort. Captured by Free French forces in Tunisia in 1943, he spent three years in a prisoner of war camp in the United States, and gradually concluded that everything he had learned had been a terrible mistake. When he returned to Germany in 1946 he was a changed man, comprehensively ashamed and disgusted by the Nazis, but when he encountered other veterans and German civilians, he realized that a wide variety of views existed, and not everyone had been as thoroughly denazified as him.[2]

On both sides of the Cold War line exceptions were made for "useful" people, regardless of their political pasts. Nazi Germany's leading physicists and experts on rocketry and synthetic fuels, for example, were eagerly sought by both the Soviets and Americans. The U.S. Army employed over 2,500 former German officers, mostly for studying Soviet military capabilities. Hitler's former chief of the general staff, Franz Halder, was even decorated for "meritorious service" to the United States. Reinhard Gehlen, head of Hitler's military intelligence, was taken along with his whole staff—SS members and all—into the service of the American Office of Strategic Services (OSS), the precursor to the CIA. The Soviets preserved a large number of Nazi officials, who switched rather effortlessly from Nazi dictatorship to Communist dictatorship. This galled many German Communists who had suffered under the Nazis and watched their friends perish, but there was little they could do. As Germany began electing new local/regional governments under Allied supervision in 1946, people under both Western and Soviet occupation took office, despite having been members of the Nazi party.

The showpiece of Allied denazification efforts was the long process known as the Nürnberg Trials. Deliberately held in the city associated with huge Nazi rallies, the trials represented the efforts of the victorious Allied nations to cooperate in the investigation, exposure, and conviction of Nazi leaders for "crimes against humanity." This was a relatively recent concept in international law, dating back only to the First World War. The court, comprising judges from the four occupying powers, indicted two dozen men for crimes committed by the regime during the war. This covered both civilian and military affairs, although the most obvious goals of the trials were to assign responsibility for things like the use of slave labor, genocide, and the killing of civilians. The presence of the Soviets on the court was unavoidable, and they obviously had the greatest grievances against Nazi Germany, which had devastated their country. But equally obviously the Stalin regime was in no moral position to judge others for the very same crimes it had committed, and continued to commit, in many cases on an even greater scale.

The accused at Nürnberg represented a cross-section of upper-level management from the Third Reich. The star defendant was Hermann Goering, who probably was never in any doubt about his fate. He managed to smuggle cyanide into his cell with which to kill himself shortly before his execution. Some of the guilty sentences were obviously chosen for their symbolic value. Joachim von Ribbentrop, Hitler's foreign minister, was a boorish anti-Semite who frequently expressed ugly opinions on the regime's behalf, but executing such a relatively powerless sycophant for crimes against humanity and for complicity in starting the war stretches the imagination. Had he not been so haughty and unrepentant, he might have ended like Albert Speer. That man, who as minister for war production had the deaths of hundreds of thousands of slave laborers on his hands, performed such a skillful combination of humble apologia and cover-ups that he managed to secure only a twenty-year prison sentence and eventually died in freedom in 1981.

Creating the Federal Republic

In 1947 the occupying powers shifted from their earlier views about stripping Germany down to a demilitarized, deindustrialized farming land and began instead to accelerate activities that seemed destined to create two separate German states. The Soviets created an administration to develop the basis for a Communist economic system in the east. In the west, the British and American zones merged, and American reconstruction money began flowing into western Germany under the Marshall Plan. This provided desperately needed funding for infrastructural repairs such as roads, bridges, railways, electricity, water, and sewage. The American government's goals were political: to make sure that capitalism could recover and that Communism would not become attractive to Germans. If judged by these criteria, the Marshall Plan must be considered a tremendous success. American funding for infrastructure gave the western zones the ability to re-create the conditions for new businesses and residential construction. Within a year the French agreed to merge most of their administrative supervision with the Americans and British, and thus the outline of what was to become West Germany had taken shape.

Berlin remained a key sticking point. As the Soviets began to realize that the much larger, more populous, and more productive western regions would not be assisting their eastern zone, Stalin grew impatient over the four-power occupation of Berlin. The former capital city lay deep inside the Soviet zone, and was more than just an irritant. It was a haven for western spies and smugglers, as well as an escape route for people fleeing from Soviet rule. In June 1948, when western Germany introduced its new deutsche mark currency, the Soviets refused to accept it and created their own alternative. Stalin raised the stakes by announcing a blockade of West Berlin; access over land was completely shut down.

Stalin assumed that more than a million West Berliners and the handful of western military forces would back down and not start a war, nor allow the civilians to starve. The Truman administration's response, which was in fact first suggested by the British, has become known as the Berlin Airlift. In an extraordinary feat of endurance and logistics, the U.S. Air Force, assisted by the British, Australians, and even former German air force personnel, flew cargo planes into the besieged city for eleven months, even through the worsening weather of autumn and winter. The flights provided basic food, clothes, medicine, and heating fuel for more than half of one of Europe's great cities, entirely by air. Seventy pilots were killed in crashes. In May 1949 the Soviets finally gave up on the blockade and allowed land transportation again, along three regulated rail and road lines from the west. For the citizens of West Berlin the Americans in particular were heroes, and an entire generation of West Berliners fondly remembers the "raisin bombers," "Uncle Chocolate," and other nicknames for the pilots who often threw sweets out of their low-flying aircraft to crowds of hungry children gathered near the airfields.

Often seen as the first skirmish of the Cold War, the Berlin Blockade and Airlift are remembered in German history as the last crisis before the founding of the two German states in the east and west. In May 1949, as the crisis abated, the Federal Republic of Germany (*Bundesrepublik Deutschland*) came into being (sometimes abbreviated FRG in English, or using the German letters, BRD). Its creation was the result of more than two years of preparation.

In 1947 most of the old German state boundaries had been abandoned or reconfigured and new *Länder* were created. A *Land* was a state, although some were very old and traditional (such as Bavaria), while others were entirely new creations (North Rhine-Westphalia). Their size varied tremendously, from the little city-state of Bremen to the sprawling Lower Saxony. The capital, Berlin, also became a Land, although it was effectively divided into East and West. In 1948 the western Länder sent delegates to a constitutional convention, with the approval of the Allies, to create a new West German state.

The late 1940s were a time of near-constant challenges for the United States in foreign policy: fearing the spread of Communism, the revolution in China, the incipient conflicts between Greece and Turkey, the Arab-Israeli conflict, and the realization that Soviet spies had obtained nuclear secrets and thus Stalin would soon have an atomic bomb. The Truman administration concluded that it could not possibly afford the cost of occupation and maintaining a huge army in western Germany without assistance, yet their British and French allies were overstretched by conflicts in their African and Asian empires. Thus the Americans concluded that not only should a West German state be created, it should be armed and locked into alliance with the United States and other democratic nations.

Persuading Europeans to accept Germans with guns, however, only a few years after Hitler, was a tall order. The Allies held several conferences in 1946–1947 and, pushed by the Americans, approved the process by which the Germans began to draft the "Basic Law" (*Grundgesetz*). This document became, and remains, the constitution of modern Germany.

The framers of the Basic Law were motivated by a number of factors, but above all were haunted by the failure of the Weimar Republic. Many of these men had in fact been statesmen or politicians during Weimar, and had seen that republic collapse in the face of extremism. Thus they wanted to create a new system that would safeguard the large, mainstream parties and make party politics "normal," hopefully shutting out small extremist groups and preventing them from gaining a national stage. This resulted in some rules that remain controversial to this day, such as the "5-percent hurdle." A German political party must receive at least 5 percent of the popular vote, or it gets no seats at all in the legislature. Moreover, if it doesn't get 5 percent, then whatever votes it did receive are divided and given to the parties who *did* clear the 5-percent hurdle. This law has prevented occasional small fringe parties from gaining power in Germany, but it is obviously in some ways undemocratic. In the early days of the Federal Republic, the law persuaded many right-wing groups with grievances who had formed small parties (a party for expellees' rights, a party for families of MIAs and POWs, etc.) to give up on their minor parties and join a mainstream conservative party.

The Federal Republic has a weak president, whose job is mainly a supervisor of the system, rather than an active participant in it (although his/her ruling can be invoked to settle certain constitutional disputes). The federal president is not directly elected by the people, but rather by a Federal Assembly appointed by the Bundestag and the state legislatures in each Land. There is an independent Constitutional Court, similar to the U.S. Supreme Court, to hear cases that have direct bearing upon the Basic Law. Unlike its American counterpart, however, the German high court has the ability to review any law or case it wishes, without having to wait for that law or case to reach it by appeal. The German framers, wary of the breakdown of justice under Weimar, wanted to ensure that a strong, activist high court would keep an eye on the other branches of government.

The upper house of the legislature, the *Bundesrat*, is chosen by the Länder, and is thus supposed to represent the interests of the states. The heart of the federal system is the lower house of the legislature, the *Bundestag*. Roughly one-half of its members directly represent a voting district, in the same way as the members of the U.S. House of Representatives do. The other half are "party list" candidates. German voters get two votes: one for a direct representative, and the other for a political party. The parties get party list members based on that second vote. Thus although the system is designed to shackle tiny extremist parties, it can also reward small parties because they might pick up a number of "second votes."

The majority party in the Bundestag may choose the federal chancellor, which is the closest thing Germany has to a chief executive. The chancellor is head of the government (similar to a prime minister in many democracies). Although the office lacks many of the powers of an American president (the chancellor is not commander in chief of the armed forces, for instance, and does not have his or her own executive branch or budget), on the other hand a German chancellor has the power to choose his or her own cabinet without any confirmation votes or hearings.

The Basic Law thus created a strong and well-balanced democratic structure that represented both the states (*Länder*) and the nation as a whole, and allowed for both direct democratic representation and enshrining stable large political parties. In May 1949, only two weeks after the end of the Berlin Airlift, the Basic Law came into effect and the Federal Republic of Germany, soon known throughout the world as West Germany, became an independent state.

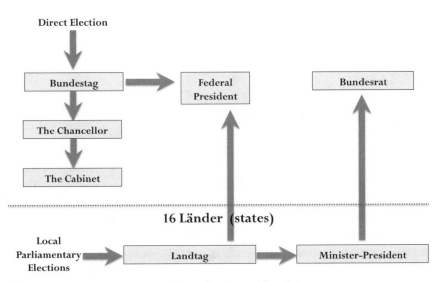

Figure 9.2. Political Structure of the Federal Republic of Germany

The Old Man

On the final page of the Basic Law, the first and largest signature is that of the president of the convention, Konrad Adenauer. Already seventy-three years old, the former mayor of Cologne was a Catholic conservative who had been imprisoned twice by the Nazis. The party he founded, the Christian Democratic Union (CDU), was the first mainstream conservative party to unite German Catholics and Protestants, although he had to negotiate a special agreement with the Bavarians, who insisted upon retaining their own semi-independent version of the party called the Christian Social Union (CSU). Together, the two parties effectively function as a single parliamentary faction that Germans usually call "the Union." In the 1949 elections the Union won a plurality, but not a majority, and formed a coalition government with the Free Democrats (FDP). They chose Adenauer as the first federal chancellor. Since then it has been normal for German elections not to result in a clear majority for any one party, and with only a few exceptions, governments have been chosen by multiparty coalitions.

Liberals in the European Sense

The FDP is also known as the Liberals, in the European sense of that word, meaning something more like "libertarian" in American parlance. They support free-market capitalism and smaller government (which would be on the "right" in U.S. politics) but also free choice on many social issues, such as privacy rights, abortion, and gay marriage, and other things that would be "left" in U.S. politics.

Many people assumed that because of his age, Adenauer would serve only a few years as a caretaker, until the Federal Republic got on its feet. No one expected the extraordinarily long career that ensued, and he did not leave office until 1963, when he was eighty-seven years old. If modern Germany has a founding father, it is surely Konrad Adenauer. *Der Alte* (the old man), as he was called both by supporters and opponents, often ran the administration from his house in the little riverside town of Bad Honnef, a few miles upstream on the Rhine from Bonn, the small city that had been chosen as the new capital. Indeed, some people grumbled, semi-seriously, that Bonn— whose only claim to fame had been as the birthplace of Beethoven—had been chosen as the new capital primarily because it was an easy morning commute for the Old Man.

The early West German government existed under close supervision of the Allied powers. Even though Adenauer did not have to answer to German voters in his ministerial choices, he nonetheless had to have them vetted by the Western Allies. From the outset, Adenauer recognized and embraced these constraints. In his view, the only hope West Germany had to rebuild as a normalized democratic society was in unison with existing Western democracies. He was thus a strong advocate of permanent alliances with the United States and with France. The American relationship meant that West Germany would commit to building a military and placing it under the command of the new North Atlantic Treaty Organization (NATO) alliance, as well as committing West Germany to anti-Communist activity in general.

It is hard to exaggerate the importance of the German-French rapprochement. Since the time of Napoleon, these two nationalities had defined themselves as existential enemies, and had fought three major wars in living memory. Much of the credit for the alliance is due to the French foreign minister, Robert Schumann, whose own lifetime and career was complex and entangled in both countries, and who was determined to end the ancient rivalry between the Germans and French. Other French and German statesmen laid the groundwork, but Adenauer must also receive credit for embracing and pushing the concept of a new alliance based upon shared economic and social goals, rather than plans for war. Starting with treaties on coal, steel, and energy production, the alliance steadily strengthened, embraced other nations, and grew into the European Community, which eventually grew and evolved by the end of the century into the European Union.

Adenauer's government walked a fine line between the French alliance and the American alliance, particularly as Washington and Paris increasingly fell out of step with each other on military policy. Throughout the 1950s the new West German military, the *Bundeswehr*, slowly took shape under close American supervision. Germans themselves had mixed emotions about having a military at all. Federal President Theodor Heuss was famously opposed, and often said so in public. Some of this opposition to rearmament was the fault of the Western Allies, who had insisted upon overseeing the reconstruction of German youth groups and schools to demilitarize the society and deromanticize war and military service. The result was an inconvenient new pacifist movement that lobbied the government to end conscription and allow for conscientious objector status. Bundeswehr officers went through a rudimentary form of political reeducation, and men of colonel's rank or higher were investigated for possible complicity in Nazi-era crimes, but one of the new army's founding fathers subsequently found himself convicted. Ironically, it was Heuss who pardoned him.

West Germany's population represented about three-quarters of the total German population, and in the eyes of most of the world, it was "Germany." Consequently, it faced questions about the degree to which the new republic was responsible for the Nazi past. Obviously, none of the West German leaders had been Nazi officials. But equally obviously, some kind of ongoing atonement was necessary to reassure the world that Germans had turned a new page. The most sensitive questions dealt with Germany's relationship to Israel. In 1951 Chancellor Adenauer declared that West Germany had special obligations to the Jewish state, and would begin to pay reparations. This touched off a furious debate in Israel over both the amount of reparations and the method of payment. Menachim Begin, a former terrorist who became the leader of Israel's Likud Party and later Israel's prime minister, demanded that Germany compensate individual victims and families, rather than paying lump sums to the Israeli government. In 1952 Begin sponsored an assassination attempt on Adenauer, in which a bomb package was mailed to the German chancellor. It exploded in a post office instead, killing a policeman.[3] Thanks to help from French intelligence, Adenauer's government knew the identities of the would-be assassins, but did their best to "bury" the

Figure 9.3. Konrad Adenauer (seated left) Signs the Reparation Treaty with Israel. Photograph courtesy of the United States Holocaust Memorial Museum. Used with permission.

story, out of fear that it would reignite anti-Semitic feelings in Germany. Over the next fourteen years billions of deutsche mark were paid to Israel, constituting a large portion of their national income. Germany began a program of other compensations that have remained in place to this day. Israeli goods, for example, are sold in Germany with "most favored nation" status that not even the products of the American allies are granted. Germany has built a number of weapon systems for the Israeli military at no cost to Israel, including large items like submarines for the Israeli navy.

All questions of statesmanship and politics aside, the most important consideration for Germans during the 1950s was the pace of reconstruction and economic recovery. By any measure it was astonishing. Much of the credit here is usually given to Adenauer's minister of economics, the Bavarian Ludwig Erhard, a cigar-smoking former salesman and marketing expert who provided a remarkably steady hand and sound policies for recovery. Erhard was well aware that the failure of Germany's last democracy, the Weimar Republic, was largely due to the government's incompetence at managing the economy and providing a stable currency. He proved very adroit at dealing with foreign bankers and the Allied occupation authorities to set up the new West German financial system, currency, and stock exchange on a solid footing, fully integrated within the Western capitalist system. At the same time, Erhard was committed to what he called a "Social Market Economy," which promised to gradually increase social services and safeguards as conditions improved, so that—again unlike Weimar—nobody would be left behind. Thus by 1957 the West German government established a generous retirement plan, and over the next decade added socialized medicine, publicly funded higher education, public assistance for families with dependent children, and paid vacations. Government, business, and labor unions developed a system of negotiated settlements that kept workers on the job, at good wages, and reestablished many German industries as export leaders.

The restoration of the West German society is known as the *Wirtschaftswunder* (the economic miracle). Growth accelerated at a dramatic, almost shocking rate, yet without inflationary spirals or speculative bubbles. The rates of growth in the 1950s in particular were astonishing, over 10 percent per year in some cases. Capital investment increased more than 100 percent in a single decade. By the early 1970s, West Germany had repaid all of the Marshall Plan aid, in the form of war reparations. During the 1960s unemployment was near zero, and Germany became an attractive destination for immigrant laborers, mostly from Turkey, who acquired the name "Guest Workers" (*Gastarbeiter*). Although some of these workers were migratory and returned to Turkey for part of the year, most remained and raised families. By the end of the 1980s they represented nearly 10 percent of the West German population.

Happiness with economic recovery persuaded Germans to return the CDU/CSU "Union" government to power in several elections, and helps explain "the Old Man" Adenauer's impressive political longevity. He finally stepped down in 1963, was replaced by Erhard until 1966, and then a "grand coalition" of Union and SPD under Kurt Kiesinger ruled until 1969. In all, the Union, usually in coalition with the FDP, led West Germany for twenty years, at the end of which the western state had one of the most powerful economies in the world, certainly the largest in Europe.

Historians have debated whether the "new" Germany was really new. Some have pointed out that most of its founders came of age in the Weimar Republic and used that as their model.[4] Others have argued that West Germany may have been a democracy, but the Old Man himself ran the government in a semidictatorial way, or at least as an oligarch, thus showing that West German democracy was only skin-deep.

Historians also disagree, often sharply, about the nature of West German society in the 1950s. Some see it as a fundamentally conservative time, in which most people who had Nazi guilt on their hands walked away from it and resumed their lives, and the Americans encouraged this because they wanted to establish a conservative military ally that would reliably help hold back Communism. The society was fundamentally conservative in ways that transcended politics. Citizenship laws remained based upon ancestry and ethnicity until the end of the century. Women in the 1950s had to have permission from their husbands to hold a job outside the home, and didn't receive the right to keep their maiden names in marriage until the 1990s. Shopping and business hours remained tightly restricted for years after much of the capitalist world began moving toward a more flexible retail economy.

On the other hand, West Germany was indeed a new republic, committed in word and deed to the rejection of the nationalist, militarist past. The Federal Republic of Germany celebrated pacifists or the anti-Hitler conspirators of 1944. By 1954, the tenth anniversary of the failed plot to assassinate Hitler, Chancellor Adenauer described the resisters in a radio address as "victims . . . worthy of everyone's esteem and reverence."[5] The symbols and gestures of Nazism became illegal (in one famous case, a bookstore owner went to prison for selling copies of Hitler's *Mein Kampf*). Poets and composers appeared on the national currency and postage, replacing men in military uniforms. Past victories went unmarked, streets and plazas were renamed, and schoolbooks were rewritten under the supervision of a new United Nations commission on the dangers of nationalism in school instruction.

Perhaps the most important consideration is simply that West Germany was a democracy. It exhibited all of the conflicting impulses and varieties of opinion that one can expect in a democratic society, and it provided for freedom of expression while simultaneously keeping a watchful eye on the possibility for extremism. This is understandable given the failure of Germany's last attempt at democracy during the Weimar Republic. It is also notable given what was happening on the other side of the Iron Curtain.

The Creation of the German Democratic Republic (DDR)

Five months after the founding of the Federal Republic in the west, German Communist leaders under the supervision of the Soviet occupation authorities created an East German state: the German Democratic Republic (DDR—sometimes abbreviated in English as GDR). Unlike in the west, where the Americans had committed to a sovereign state, Stalin seems to have been hedging his bets. It is not clear how seriously he took the long-term future of the DDR, or if he considered it simply a stopgap measure of some sort. The Soviets remained in control of many aspects of the DDR's daily life, from state security to grade-school administration, until 1955, and even after the granting of "sovereignty" it was clear that the DDR leadership was far more beholden to Moscow than Adenauer was to Washington. It is tempting, therefore, to see the DDR as simply a Soviet puppet state, occupied by nearly half a million Soviet soldiers. But East Germany did develop its own unique character and style, as well as a considerable amount of sovereignty within the Soviet bloc.

Communists had been the first victims of the Nazis, and in Germany and other occupied wartime countries, Communists had been the most resolute resisters. A great many had paid with their lives. They thus had a certain moral credibility in the post-Nazi era, and could claim that their hands were unstained by Fascist crimes. Of course, most of the German Communists who founded the DDR were hand-picked by Stalin after long periods living in exile in the Soviet Union, and thus they were subservient to a system that was in many ways just as bad as the Nazis. Nonetheless, German Communists, returning from their exile after the Second World War, made a strong case that only they could truly create a new "anti-Fascist" Germany.

In all of the regions of Eastern and Central Europe that the Soviet army occupied, Stalin took steps to eliminate anti-Communist forces and movements, and even those Socialist/Communist movements that were not directly loyal to him. Germany, of course, already had long traditions of Socialist and Communist parties, and Stalin was quick to bring them into line with his goals. By 1946 the left-wing parties in the Soviet zone of occupation had been unified as a new Socialist Unity Party (SED), which was effectively a way of expressing that Soviet-approved German Communists were the only acceptable leaders. Throughout the existence of the DDR, voters' ballots included a variety of parties, some of which were "shadows" of western parties (there was an eastern CDU, for example), but the SED was unequivocally in charge of the state, and tightly regulated the other parties to ensure they remained tiny minorities with no power. (In the 1950 elections, for example, the SED received over 99 percent of the votes for the *Volkskammer*, the national legislature.) Describing his goals for the SED's structure, the future leader Walter Ulbricht wrote, "It must look democratic, but the power must remain in our hands."[6]

East Germany comprised only five Länder plus East Berlin (compared with eleven Länder in the west). It had less than one-third the population of the west, and few natural resources except farmland and lignite coal. Most significantly, it had no Marshall Plan; the Soviets instead extracted wealth from these regions as war reparations. From the outset, then, creating a viable state was a challenge. East Germany also suffered from a disastrous population drain, as skilled workers and professionals fled to the west in search of opportunity and a higher standard of living, not to mention political freedom. More than 2 million easterners left before the Wall was finally constructed to stop them.

Communist rule in eastern Germany achieved a level of centralized planning and organization that the Nazis had never attained. The government of the DDR was based on the Soviet model, with an executive committee (Politburo) whose decisions were then acted upon by the Central Committee of the SED, which also had some limited power to debate and even criticize, although the pressure of consensus and fear of losing one's position (or worse) usually limited such dissent. The First Secretary of the latter was usually also head of the former, and thus the effective leader of the state. East Germany had an elected legislature, the People's Chamber (*Volkskammer*), whose initial purpose was to elect a "president" of the DDR, although a constitutional change eventually eliminated that position and the Volkskammer became a largely ceremonial body. In essence, the DDR was a "dictatorship by committee," and virtually no power was left to regional authorities, certainly not to popular elections. The Politburo and top-ranking Central Committee members answered to the First Secretary. They all answered to Moscow, although—with one exception—the Soviets interfered less in East Germany than they did in many of their other satellite states.

That exception came relatively early. As in the west, the pressing issue for the new administration was economic recovery. In East Germany, with fewer people, fewer resources, and certainly less money, the reconstruction programs were far more difficult. The centrally planned economy was a zero-sum proposition; every worker directed to build a new bridge was a worker who could not be directed to build refrigerators or radios or bicycles. East German workers were organized into "brigades" and given particular assignments and quotas, but the state was often unable to provide them with the equipment and resources they needed to complete their tasks. People often wasted valuable time unable to work, simply because the ramshackle transportation network was unable to supply them with materials on schedule, or even because the electrical grid had to be shut down, unable to power the factories. The regime focused so heavily on large-scale infrastructural and industrial projects that there was virtually no consumer-goods sector worth mentioning, and many people continued to live at subsistence levels. They grew increasingly angry and dissatisfied with their low pay, the inability to use their pay to purchase much of anything, and the slow pace of reconstruction. A joke that haunted East Germany throughout its existence reflects this conundrum of workers sitting idle on a stalled assembly line: "We pretend to work, and they pretend to pay us." In the spring of 1953, a few months after Stalin's death, the state announced that working hours would be increased. The result was a strike by workers in East Berlin that rapidly became a large-scale uprising. More than twenty thousand Soviet troops were used to crush the demonstrations, with thousands of striking workers arrested and over four hundred killed. It was the last serious challenge to the Communist leadership in the DDR until the fall of the Wall in 1989.

The Socialist writer Bertolt Brecht, who had returned to Germany after the war and moved to East Berlin full of hope for a new beginning, expressed the anger and disappointment that many left-wing intellectuals felt at the realization of what the Socialist German state had become. In his poem *"Die Lösung"* ("The Solution"), Brecht's bitter satire was on full display:

> After the June 17 uprising
> The Secretary of the Writers Union
> Distributed leaflets along Stalin Boulevard
> Stating that the people
> had lost the confidence of the government
> And could only win it back
> by redoubled efforts.
> Wouldn't it just be simpler

> for the government to dissolve the People
> and elect a new one?

The Communist authorities were not blind to the implications of the June 1953 uprising, but their range of action was limited. Even though Stalin was dead, the Soviet policy toward the DDR remained essentially unchanged: East Germany had to develop large-scale Soviet-style heavy industry and create a powerful military, while also paying reparations for the war. This all but doomed any chances for developing a consumer economy or meaningfully improving the standard of living, but few of the DDR's leaders were inclined to do so in any event.

By 1953 the man who had emerged as the true leader of the regime was not the president, Wilhelm Pieck, but rather the First Secretary of the Central Committee, Walter Ulbricht. (In fact, the position of the president was eventually abolished, and the first secretary became leader on paper, as well as in fact.) Ulbricht had been a loyal Stalinist and showed no inclination to change his views now that his master was gone. Although he did make serious efforts to develop public housing, the majority of his economic program was a top-down industrial plan, divorced from the realities of the day-to-day needs of his people. East Germany became a maker of reasonably good industrial equipment that was useful to other Communist states, but in return had to import basic items like fuel, medicine, clothing, and even food.

Ulbricht was a cold political operator who had proven himself adroit in the Stalinist system, denouncing enemies and destroying the careers of rivals. It is not surprising, therefore, that his response to the 1953 unrest was to strengthen the state's grip on the lives of its people. Within two weeks of the departure of the Soviet troops, the DDR gathered the intelligence and police services from several bureaus into a new Ministry for State Security that would forever after be known by its German abbreviation, "Stasi."

The Stasi became one of the world's most elaborate and thoroughgoing instruments of social and political repression. With a quarter-million employees and at least 2 million "unofficial collaborators" (informants), the Stasi monitored a population that was never greater than 19 million people. The agents were literally everywhere. A typical university classroom had at least one student informer somewhere in the room (and the professor himself or herself might have been an informant). Most work brigades had at least one informant. Agents bugged apartments, monitored the daily activities of people to the most minute details, even gently questioned small children in day care about the conversations and activities of their parents. Wives spied on husbands, brothers upon sisters, friends upon friends. Many public places had cameras hidden in streetlights and even garbage cans, monitoring people on streets and sidewalks.

East Germans could be arrested and taken for questioning for a variety of reasons and often held indefinitely. Typically, people were suspected of criticizing the SED or the state, or of some kind of treasonous activity such as circulating Western media, trying to leave the country, or most ironically for an allegedly Socialist state, for trying to organize labor unions. Although the Stasi was not an instrument of mass murder, it did kill several hundred people. More often it simply ruined lives by ejecting people from employment, terminating their educations, or incarcerating them for long periods under duress.

The Stasi also had an elaborate foreign operation, spying in the capitalist states and particularly in West Germany, where its agents infiltrated major media companies, corporations, labor unions, universities, and especially political offices. In one infamous example in the 1960s, a radical left-wing student activist in West Germany was shot dead by a German policeman, causing widespread violence and rioting in the west. Only in recent years has it been revealed that the policeman was in fact a Stasi agent, who may have been on a mission to foment left-wing unrest in the west. In another high-profile example from the 1970s, the Stasi recruited one of Chancellor Willy Brandt's personal advisors as a spy, and thus had an informant at the very top of the West German government.

The DDR tried to create an East German national identity, with mixed results. Children were politicized to an even greater degree than in the Third Reich. All schooling and recreational activities were regulated by the state, and the Communist youth organizations structured free time with an ideological bent. East Germans were told that theirs was the true anti-Fascist state, that nearly all the Nazis had come from the west, and that the west was harboring Fascism still, in the service of American imperialism. But although this propaganda was relentless and although most people didn't dare to contradict it, nonetheless East Germans could hear West German radio, could often watch West German television (with the volume turned *very* low!), and could even find people to smuggle West German magazines and newspapers. It was clear that the westerners enjoyed a higher standard of living and wider variety of products—although as later events would show, easterners were astonished and furious when they finally discovered just how dramatically better life in the west really was.

On the evening of August 12–13, 1961, West Berliners realized that the eastern authorities were constructing a wall along the line that divided the city in half. Up to that point, border controls had been rudimentary; usually some sort of simple barrier, no more sophisticated than a tollbooth. Since the western edges of the city stretched for twenty-six miles, it was physically impossible to secure every block, and people could easily pass between buildings, especially at night. The Berlin Wall was a comprehensive program, ultimately involving over fifty thousand workers, to tear down buildings, block streets, close subway tunnels, block canals, and finally to construct a brick wall around all of West Berlin to tightly restrict access to and from the East. The wall, officially designated the "Anti-Fascist Protective Barrier," evolved over years to become one of the most heavily guarded zones on earth, with minefields, barbed wire, watchtowers with machine-gun emplacements, electronic surveillance, and of course troops with dogs and armored vehicles on constant patrol.

As a propaganda asset, the West German government couldn't have asked for a better symbol. When the American president John F. Kennedy came to West Berlin in 1963, he purposely staged his speech with the Wall as a backdrop, to contrast the difference between the Communist and "free" worlds. But as a practical matter, the Wall immensely complicated German-German relations. Families were divided and travel became virtually impossible. And of course each escape attempt now became a dramatic international incident. Perhaps most simply, the Wall was an immense and ugly slash running through and around one of the largest cities in Europe, slicing streets and blocks abruptly and focusing attention upon the few remaining checkpoints where NATO and East German or Soviet troops met in a dramatic, heavily armed standoff.

"Ish bin ein Bee-linnah"

Kennedy's famous speech at the Berlin Wall in 1963 was a brief but moving address on the subject of hope and freedom. He wanted to conclude with a phrase in German, but of course Kennedy spoke no German, so he asked his speechwriters to spell the words out for him phonetically. With his strong Boston accent, Kennedy mangled most of the German, but everybody knew what he meant when he said, "I am a Berliner!"

In most of Germany the word *Berliner* means a sweet puff pastry or a man from Berlin; just as a "Hamburger" can be a man from Hamburg or an American sandwich. Thus the legend grew that Kennedy accidentally told the world, "I am a sticky bun!" In Berlin, however, the pastry is not called a *Berliner*, but rather just one of the many kinds of *Pfannkuchen*, so JFK's Berlin audience was never confused.

Technically, the Wall sealed West Berlin off from the rest of East Germany, and was simply part of the equally fortified German-German border. In reality, of course, the DDR had walled in its own citizens, primarily to prevent them from escaping at the rate of more than fifteen thousand per month, which had been going on for over a decade. Behind the wall, the SED regime got on with "building Socialism." By the end of the 1960s it had driven nearly all small and/or privately owned businesses, farms, and stores out of existence. In 1971 Walter Ulbricht was forced to step down, allegedly because of age and ill health, but in reality because he had fallen out of favor with the Soviets. He was replaced by Erich Honecker, but by this point the regime was essentially a self-sustaining bureaucracy, and the individual personality at the top was not particularly important.

Two Germanies

Historians disagree over the normalcy of the division of the two Germanies during the Cold War. Some have suggested that since so much of German history is the story of multiple states and fragmented politics, the division between east and west was not a particularly abnormal situation. Certainly for people who grew up during the Cold War (like this author) the concept of East and West Germany seemed normal simply because it was part of the larger division of Europe. We became accustomed to two Germanies on the map, two Olympic teams, and two regimes with two militaries and two currencies as part of two great Cold War alliances. Having a German-German border was normal only in the sense that people had grown accustomed to the rituals associated with it. Most television news stations in West Germany, for instance, offered tomorrow's weather forecast only for the west, sometimes also for Berlin, but usually with the symbols of clouds or sunshine stopping abruptly at the Iron Curtain.

On the other hand, Germans themselves always seemed uncertain about the future of a divided nation. In both the east and west politicians, scholars, journalists, and others spoke of eventual reunification as an historical inevitability, even if they could no longer envision how it might occur in their lifetimes. While the Americans had given up on the idea even before the Berlin Crisis in 1948, Stalin offered as late as 1952 to create a unified Germany if it could be completely neutralized. By then, however, the United States was too heavily invested in West Germany as a key NATO member. After the Wall went up, politicians and intellectuals continued to pay lip service to the concept of German reunification, but most people simply got on with their lives as citizens of one "Germany" or the other.

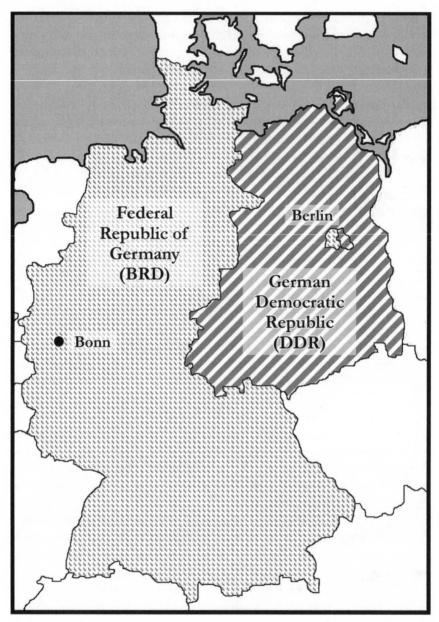

Figure 9.4.   The Two Germanies, 1949–1989

By the 1960s West Germany had performed a remarkable economic recovery and was a valued member of the Western democratic community. It was also showing the same signs of fatigue with conservative government and society that were emerging in France, Britain, and the United States, a generational struggle that finally exploded on college campuses. The proximate cause was the anger over Germany's complicity as an American ally during the Vietnam period, and the presence of thousands of American soldiers on German bases. But students and other young people were also simply tired of the austere conservative government of the CDU/CSU that had run the country for two decades. A German pacifist movement had begun to grow on the political Left, inspired by the ugly scenarios of American and NATO planners that the next war in Europe would be fought primarily in Germany, and probably with nuclear weapons.

The generation of German youth who joined protests and radical groups in this period is known as the "sixty-eighters," named after the violent protests in the spring and summer of that year on college campuses and in public plazas across the Western world. The German sixty-eighters were broadly in sync with the "hippies" and the other left-wing youth movements elsewhere, and shared many of the same desires for a more open and democratic society, women's rights, environmental protection, denuclearization, and an end to the Vietnam War, as well as sharing the same lifestyle and aesthetics: rock and roll, a freer sexuality, recreational drugs, long hair, and so on. In the German case, there was also a specific desire to find some sort of reconciliation with the east. It was in this environment of change that the SPD finally came to power in West Germany, led by Willy Brandt.

The son of a poor, unmarried woman, Brandt had been a young Socialist who resisted the Nazis and had a number of close calls against Fascists in Germany and Norway, and in the Spanish Civil War. The name "Willy Brandt" was in fact only one of his many aliases during those years, but he decided to keep it. He spent most of the war in Sweden, returned after 1945, became active again in Social Democratic politics, and ultimately became the mayor of West Berlin. There he became a local hero for his efforts to improve living conditions, especially for the poor and working class.

In 1961 Willy Brandt was at the top of the SPD's party list and thus effectively their nominee for federal chancellor. For many young Germans he represented a new, hopeful generation. (Brandt was in his forties, while Adenauer was by that point eighty-five years old.) Although the SPD lost the election, Brandt was clearly a rising star. He was part of the "grand coalition" government from 1966 to 1969, and in the very close 1969 elections he negotiated a coalition government with the FDP. Thus West Germany had its first real change of parties in a democratic transition as the Social Democrats came to power.

Willy Brandt's government is seen as signaling a moment of change in German society and politics, in the way that John F. Kennedy's election did in the United States. Like Kennedy, Brandt was seen as a younger, more attractive, and more energetic leader with new ideas and a new moral compass. Early in his administration, Brandt signaled his desire to travel to the East; not just to East Germany, but to meet other Communist leaders and to establish a new relationship. He coined the word *Ostpolitik* to describe this initiative.

Ostpolitik

This word is untranslatable to English. It literally means "East politics." What Brandt meant was a new look at West Germany's relationship with the Communist world, and especially with East Germany. In Brandt's view, since Germans were split down the middle by the Cold War, they had a unique opportunity and responsibility to try to reduce tensions and bring the two opposing camps into closer cooperation, or at least more friendly dialogue and trade.

On a rainy day in December 1970, Willy Brandt visited Poland, and at the site of the former Warsaw Ghetto he surprised everyone by getting down on his knees to symbolize all of Germany begging forgiveness for the crimes of the Third Reich, particularly the killing of Jews and Poles. "I just had the feeling," he later said, "that standing wouldn't do." Reaction in Germany to this striking gesture was mixed and often hostile, but over time it came to be seen as a remarkable and genuine expression of Germans' desire to accept responsibility for the past. It was one of the reasons that Brandt was later awarded the Nobel Peace Prize. Brandt's visit to East Germany was equally groundbreaking and caused the DDR some embarrassment when enthusiastic crowds greeted the chancellor of the "Fascist" west by chanting, "Wil-ly! Wil-ly!"

For all the high-profile gestures and talk of peace, Ostpolitik changed rather little about the Cold War that wasn't already changing anyway. And even though German conservatives criticized Brandt constantly for his alleged "softness" on Communism and for the various small agreements that mainly benefitted the DDR, in fact, Ostpolitik was not tremendously different from what the conservatives had pursued when they were in power. On

Figure 9.5. Chancellor Willy Brandt on His Knees in Warsaw. Photo by Hans Hub-mann, provided in digital format by German History in Documents and Images, German Historical Institute, Washington, DC (www.germanhistorydocs.ghi-dc.org).

both the Left and Right, the West German leaders remained fixated on two contradictory yet necessary criteria: that Germany must one day be unified, and that the west must not threaten the Communist leadership or provoke disturbances in the DDR that would result in repression and probably violent Soviet intervention à la 1953. Thus West German leaders mollified themselves by believing that these contradictory goals were benign and would one day lead to a "modest humanization" of the DDR.[7]

Willy Brandt stepped down from the chancellery after a scandal involving one of his closest aides spying for the East German Stasi. The SPD/FDP coalition continued in power throughout the 1970s under the leadership of Helmut Schmidt, a less charismatic personality but an effective chancellor. By this point, the "German miracle" looked permanent. West Germany had the third-largest economy in the world, with a generous social system. The late 1960s and early 1970s were a time of social unrest, for many of the same reasons as in other Western nations: struggles over civil and women's rights, the emergence of the environmental movement, and demands for more social mobility and access to higher education. An extremist left-wing terrorist group emerged in the early seventies led by Andreas Baader and Ulrike Meinhof (the famous "Red Army Faction"), and carried out a number of high-profile bombings and assassinations. And the worldwide economic slump following the 1973 Arab oil embargo gave West Germans their first taste of a recession. But any fears that radical groups or economic trouble might bring the system down like Weimar proved unfounded. The Federal Republic was fundamentally stable.

In the early 1980s German left-wing politics began to fragment over the controversy about increased American military presence and the use of nuclear power. A treaty for deploying American medium-range nuclear missiles in West Germany was worked out during the presidency of Jimmy Carter, but finally implemented by Ronald Reagan. The result was a fresh round of demonstrations, many sharply anti-American in tone. A new Green Party emerged on the left, with a pacifist/environmentalist agenda. The Greens represented the generation of the sixty-eighters, who were by this point entering middle age. They were the first major political party in Germany to include women in leadership positions (indeed, one of the party's cofounders, Petra Kelly, had been a prominent pacifist and women's rights activist). They took support from the SPD on the left, but what finally undid Schmidt's government was the defection of his coalition partner, the FDP, in 1982. The conservatives returned to power under the leadership of Helmut Kohl. His power was cemented with a stunning election victory in 1983, and West German politics again pivoted to the Right.

It was the fortune of Helmut Kohl to be chancellor of the Federal Republic of Germany at one of the most important moments of transition in the history of Germany, Europe, and the world.

Suggested Reading

Anonymous. A Woman in Berlin: Eight Weeks in the Conquered City. New York: Picador, 2006.

Ash, Timothy. In Europe's Name: Germany and the Divided Continent. New York: Vintage, 1994.

Berghahn, Volker. Modern Germany: Society, Economy, and Politics in the Twentieth Century. Cambridge: Cambridge University Press, 1987.

Fulbrook, Mary. The People's State: East German Society from Hitler to Honecker. New Haven, CT: Yale University Press, 2008.

Jarausch, Konrad. After Hitler: Recivilizing Germans, 1945–1995. Oxford: Oxford University Press, 2008.

Marshall, Barbara. Willy Brandt: A Political Biography. New York: St. Martin's, 1997.

Parrish, Thomas. *Berlin in the Balance: The Blockade, the Airlift, the First Major Battle of the Cold War*. Cambridge, MA: DeCapo, 1990.

Schwarz, Hans Peter. *Adenauer: From the German Empire to the Federal Republic*. Oxford: Berghahn, 1995.

Steege, Paul. *Black Market, Cold War: Everyday Life in Berlin, 1946–1949*. Cambridge: Cambridge University Press, 2008.

Taylor, Frederick. *The Berlin Wall: A World Divided*. New York: Harper, 2008.

CHAPTER TEN

~

Ode to Joy

About fifteen miles north of the city of Leipzig, there is a lake by the town of Bitterfeld. For decades the local chemical industries used it as an open sewer, dumping byproducts from brown coal processing, as well as the toxins used in the production of photographic chemicals. By the 1980s the lake was a disgusting "cocktail" of shimmering metallic slime that gave off a stench that could be smelled for miles. Less than one hundred yards from the lake, screened by a thin curtain of trees, were the homes and shops of the town. Fifteen thousand people lived within walking distance of what they called "Silver Lake" because of the toxic sheen of its swirling surface.

Today the Silver Lake is once again blue, and is surrounded by a green cordon of new trees and grass. After German reunification the federal government spent millions dredging the lake (the toxic metals had penetrated nearly fifteen meters below the lake's bottom, meaning that they were in all the surrounding groundwaters). The air no longer smells rancid, the homes are no longer stained by pollution, and fish once again swim in the water. Although it has been comprehensively cleaned, the lake remains off-limits for swimming and fishing, probably for decades still to come.

As with so many places in the former East Germany, the Silver Lake is a controversial symbol of the outcome of German reunification. At first glance, it has obviously been dramatically improved, and what was once ugly is now attractive. But the improvements came with a price that others had to pay, which they ultimately resented paying, and when all is said and done, the traces of the past linger deep in the ground and won't be going away any time soon.

Palace of the Republic

During the Honecker years of the 1970s and 1980s, East Germany tried to create a consumer economy. In some ways they succeeded. The chronic housing shortages were finally overcome by building huge new apartment complexes in the cities (and by the fact that the population kept shrinking). The DDR developed a reasonably efficient system for creating apartment buildings in prefabricated sections that were assembled on-site by "work brigades." Although not attractive, these buildings provided some of the best housing that average people could obtain anywhere in the Communist bloc, and they were subsidized at very low rents. This shifted the demographics of the DDR to a nation of tightly packed apartment dwellers in a few large cities.

Getting decent food in the DDR was always a challenge. The produce sections of stores famously stocked "cabbages, potatoes, and cabbages." Restaurants were few and generally awful (although the small Vietnamese immigrant population, despite being frequently mistrusted and discriminated against, provided some spicy alternatives in East Berlin). Fresh fruit was a seasonal rarity, and even bread—that German staple food—was available in limited variety and mediocre quality. Nonetheless, East Germany was again well ahead of the other Communist nations at the time. Romania, for example, still had postwar food rationing in place through the 1970s.

Figure 10.1. Marzahn: A suburb of East Berlin constructed in the 1970s and 1980s, eventually with over 55,000 rental units. It is so big that it has three commuter rail stops and is served by several bus lines. Photo courtesy of the Bundesarchiv and Wikimedia Deutschland. Public domain.

In the Honecker years most East German homes acquired the basic trappings of modern life: a television, a telephone, a record player, electrical kitchen appliances. Even though the regime generally discouraged its citizens from traveling, vacation spots were created in the hilly south or on the Baltic coast. Getting there, of course, was another matter, since relatively few East Germans had cars. The DDR had two major automobile producers, Wartburg and Trabant. The latter, whose cars were nicknamed "Trabis," inadvertently became one of the symbols of East Germany, in the way that the Volkswagen Beetle came to symbolize the west.

The Trabi came in various models, and eventually 3 million were sold in the Communist world and even a few western lands. The Trabant factory in Zwickau was a relatively low-tech affair, with one-tenth the productive capacity of Volkswagen's Beetle assembly lines in the west, and people who had saved up for their Trabis usually waited years. The object of their desire was a little two-cylinder, two-door sedan with flimsy interior panels, a manual transmission, and twenty-six horsepower. Filling the six-gallon gas tank was a complex affair that required adding oil under the hood. With only rudimentary muffling and no catalytic converter, the Trabi had a distinctive sound, and odor.

Figure 10.2.   A Trabi: Preserved by a collector in the West German city of Braunschweig.

The Trabi

A few years after the Wall fell, your author was driving on a small country road with an East German colleague when a little white car passed in the opposite direction.

"Was that a Trabi that just passed us?" I asked.

My friend rolled down his window, stuck his head out, and inhaled deeply.

"Yep," he said.

The Trabi is now a beloved nostalgic souvenir for German collectors, but at the time it was the best available car for most citizens of the DDR. Despite years of concerted effort and a huge investment, the East German state-run economy could not produce material goods in sufficient quantity or quality, nor even guarantee their availability. Anyone who dared to watch western television or read western magazines could not help but be struck by the contrast. The east was relentlessly grey: a land of crumbling small towns and prefabricated apartment slabs in the big cities. And of course complaining about it—or even indicating that you were aware of it—could get you in trouble with the Stasi.

By the early 1980s a few people in the East German leadership had begun to raise some alarms. There were three fundamental problems. First, the emphasis on the quick build-up of heavy industry was turning the East German landscape into a toxic dump. Air pollution was a serious problem in many areas, rivers and lakes were contaminated, and public health was in jeopardy. Second, the advances in new technology in the West, particularly the creation of fiber optics and personal computers, threatened to render all eastern industries obsolete within a few years, meaning it would be impossible to compete for exports. But most importantly, the state was running out of money.

Erich Honecker and other top SED leaders didn't want to hear it. They were warned by several economists and bureaucrats during the 1980s that East Germany had become fatally addicted to foreign capital.[1] A vicious cycle had developed. In order to raise the standard of living for its people, the DDR had to spend money it didn't have. The only way to do this was to borrow from the west. But many of the improvements in the consumer sector were only marginal; better than in Poland or the Soviet Union, perhaps, but certainly not producing any goods that westerners would want to buy even if they could. Thus the regime was purchasing the contentment of its citizens on borrowed western money that it could not possibly pay back.

The SED government was not totally ignorant of the problem. They scrounged western capital any way they could. Limited sections of East Berlin were upgraded as tourist attractions—indeed, they had the best hotels and restaurants anywhere in the DDR—and westerners were required to exchange a minimum of currency that they couldn't get back. The regime actually "sold" people to West Germany. One way of getting rid of eastern dissidents—anybody from a skeptical academic writer to a punk-rock musician—was to extort western relatives or the West German government for a fee to extricate this person from detention or house arrest in the East.

East German attempts to create a new export economy were costly failures. One of the dramatic examples occurred in Dresden, where the government invested massively in an electronics company named Robotron, expanding it to build personal computers. The SED leaders hoped to steer East Germany's economy in a new direction: high-precision machine tools and technology products whose quality was good enough to compete in the West. But the Robotron personal computers were based upon technology copied from South Korean copies of American and Japanese hardware and software, and were thus already obsolete in the fast-changing business of computing. The Robotrons were large and clunky machines with low-resolution monochromatic screens. More to the point: what Westerner would want to buy an East German computer? How would they upgrade the software? How could they get replacement parts for servicing? Robotron had some modest success building printers that were used primarily in other Communist countries, but the venture was an enormous expense that never achieved anything like the results the regime hoped for.

If one structure can symbolize the futility of the DDR's attempt to create the veneer of prosperity, it is surely the Palace of the Republic in central Berlin. After the war, the old Prussian royal palace was relatively intact. Nonetheless, repairs would have been expensive, and the Communists had a general contempt for the aristocratic past, so they demolished the structure in 1950. Much of this prime, central real estate (an entire large city block) became a park, but the SED leadership held out hope for a major new government building on the site. Their original concept was to place all government ministries in a single immense building, but the huge scale of the project ensured delay, and the various ministries of the DDR thus found homes elsewhere around the city. When Erich Honecker came to power in 1971 the great project was still simply a twenty-year-old argument.

The Palace of the Republic was finally completed in 1976: an immense, copper-colored rectangle. It was very much Erich Honecker's baby. It housed his administrative offices, part of the Foreign Ministry, and the Volkskammer, the East German legislature, which met only two or three times per year and thus did not require full-time offices. Most of the palace was intended as a multiuse cultural space and was used for entertainment. It had two dance halls, two concert auditoriums, a swimming pool, a skating rink, and oddly enough, one of the world's first video-game arcades. The fifth floor housed one of the world's first food courts, with fifteen restaurants and cafés that served some of the best food in East Germany, relatively inexpensively. That was because none of it came from East Germany. Since the palace was one of the few places where Western tourists were taken, the regime showed off for them. The coffee was from Cuba, the "German" food was from West Germany, and there were Japanese, Chinese, Indian, and South American restaurants. The average citizen had to wait for hours for a table. Gaining admission to the bowling alley in the basement (one of three bowling alleys in the entire country) could take as long as a year. Western tourists, however, never had to put up with the paperwork and lines because the government desperately wanted their money.

Figure 10.3. The Palace of the Republic in the 1980s. Photo courtesy of the Bundesarchiv and Wikimedia Deutschland. Public domain.

"Erich's Lamp Shop"

Everything about the Palace of the Republic was overdone. The unofficial nickname for the building came from the extraordinary number of lamps in the large rooms. The larger of the two dance halls had ten thousand lamps, with two full-time employees whose only job was changing lightbulbs.

Because the regime wanted the best of everything for the building, virtually every bit of it came from outside the DDR. In this showcase of the Communist state, the ventilation system was from West Germany, all the kitchen and dining equipment was from Sweden, the public-address and audio systems were from the United States, the marble floors were from Italy and Turkey, and even the beams holding up the walls were West German Krupp steel. The pinnacle of architectural and cultural achievement for the German Democratic Republic was a building made possible by Western firms, paid with borrowed Western money, hoping to attract Western tourists.

The Wende

The German word *Wende* means a turning point, a moment when everything seems to reverse or change. For nearly all Germans living today, the expression "the Wende" means the events of 1989–1990 that brought down the Berlin Wall and reunified the country.

Many of the problems in the DDR existed in all of the Communist states, and on a grand scale in the Soviet Union, which was additionally feeling the strain of an ongoing war in Afghanistan. In 1985 a new Soviet leader, Mikhail Gorbachev, came to power promising policies to renew Communism and reinvigorate the Socialist system. The two most important elements of his program were *Perestroika* (restructuring), a new economic program to encourage more individual initiative and higher productivity and to create new democratic government institutions that were not necessarily part of the Communist party, and *Glasnost* (transparency), a liberation of Soviet citizens to allow dissent, criticism, and open discussion of new ideas. Historians have debated the degree to which Gorbachev realized he was unleashing forces that would be impossible to control, or if he really believed that such radical changes could be channeled and ultimately controlled for an orderly transition to a better society.

The SED leadership was very uneasy with perestroika and glasnost. Honecker and other East German leaders assured their Soviet colleagues that there was no need for such sweeping measures in the DDR, as all the necessary reforms had been enacted in the 1970s. When Gorbachev announced in 1988 that the Soviet Union would no longer use military force to intervene against popular unrest in the satellite states of Eastern Europe, democratic movements already underway in Poland and Czechoslovakia became emboldened. Similar movements emerged in the DDR.

There had always been dissidents in East Germany. A handful of writers and academics, often people who had once been devoted Socialists but were now disillusioned with the regime, remained under constant Stasi scrutiny. A few rebellious pop and rock bands made secret recordings and sent them to the West for distribution. A number of Lutheran pastors maintained a quiet dissent for years, knowing that Stasi men were in the congregation every Sunday recording their sermons. Actual protest demonstrations, however, were extremely rare in a state that monitored almost everyone's whereabouts. The first significant demonstrations of the Wende began in the city of Leipzig in the summer of 1989. These were relatively small, involving a few hundred people: "neighbors would call neighbors," as one activist later remembered. Unafraid of the small groups, Stasi agents easily broke them up, in some cases arresting more than a third of the protestors.[2]

What were they protesting? In the early days of the movement, the right to travel freely was of prime concern. In an era when Soviet and some other Eastern European citizens were apparently winning this liberty, East Germans in particular wanted the right to come and go as they pleased, obviously including visiting the west. Many demonstrators also demanded the right to form new political parties, or demanded that the government legalize the New Forum, a group that was already trying to coordinate a peaceful resistance to the regime. It is important to recall that the early protestors in the DDR wanted to reform their society, not eliminate the state or join with the west.

In early October, protesters mobbed the main train station in Dresden, demanding the right to go to Czechoslovakia or Hungary, whose governments were loosening travel restrictions and thus would allow these people to pass into the west. By this point protests in the two big Saxon cities were numbering in the tens of thousands, and the Stasi was no longer attempting to make arrests. Demonstrations had begun elsewhere in the country. On October 6 Mikhail Gorbachev arrived in East Berlin to attend the celebrations for the fortieth anniversary of the founding of the DDR. When he appeared in public with Honecker, the crowd cheered "Gor-bi! Gor-bi!" and "Freedom!" Two days after he left, seventy thousand demonstrators gathered in Leipzig, where church leaders were now helping to coordinate the peaceful demonstrations.

In the town square of Zwickau, an angry crowd forced its way into the city hall and out onto the balcony to interrupt a speech by the local Communist party boss. In Plauen a pair of Stasi agents who were trying to arrest a man fled in terror when an angry mob surrounded their car. In Prenzlau a worker walked up to a panel of seventeen Communist officials who were about to speak, grabbed the microphone, and said, "I would like to have some questions answered!" as the crowd cheered him.

In retrospect the most striking thing about the autumn of 1989 was the seeming paralysis of the East German leadership. Both Honecker and his Stasi chief Erich Mielke seriously considered a brutal crackdown, inspired by the Chinese example of Tiananmen Square that spring. But they were deeply worried about the ramifications; Gorbachev would not help them, and the neighboring Communist governments in Poland and Czechoslovakia were clearly crumbling. If the SED cracked down, it would have to stand alone. Most likely, the leadership was simply stunned by the speed and size of the movement. In a few weeks the demonstrations in Leipzig had grown from a thousand people to half a million. The Western media was now fixed upon the story and increasingly speaking of the possibility of German unification.[3] A violent crackdown would have caused an international crisis.

On October 18, in an unprecedented scene, members of the Politburo rose to speak in condemnation of Erich Honecker and to demand his resignation. He was replaced by a younger man whom he had groomed as a successor: Egon Krenz. Although Krenz had been a hard-liner who had recommended a "Chinese solution" (i.e., crushing the demonstrators), he now presented himself as a conciliatory figure who would try to reach an understanding with the protest movements. The regime's first attempt at conciliation—calling town meetings—had been a disaster, as angry crowds refused to be lectured by party chiefs and instead harangued them. Their second attempt at conciliation was to be their undoing.

The regime began experimenting with changes in the laws for travel and the access to passports and other documents necessary to leave the country. After several confusing and contradictory announcements, crowds began to gather at crossing points on the eastern side of the Berlin Wall, demanding that security troops let them through. At a press conference on the evening of Thursday, November 9, 1989, Politburo spokesman Günther Schabowski tried unsuccessfully to summarize the new travel rules and inadvertently gave the impression that all restrictions were lifted. Asked when the change would go into effect, Schabowski frowned, leafed through some papers, and said, "As far as I know . . . immediately."

The night of November 9 was of course fraught with anniversaries in German history. It was the night the Kaiser abdicated in 1918, bringing down the empire. It was the night of Hitler's Beer Hall Putsch. It was the Kristallnacht, the nationwide pogrom against the Jews in 1938. And it was a moment of supreme tension and uncertainty at the Berlin Wall border checkpoints, as troops were armed, had instructions to shoot to kill if threatened, and could not figure out what their orders were.[4] At 8:30 p.m. the guards at the Waltersdorfer Chaussee checkpoint lifted the barricade, and a mass of excited people surged through, cheered from the western side.

Where did the Wall first "fall"?

For many years people assumed that the first break in the wall came later in the night, on the other side of the city, at the Bornholmer Street checkpoint. Books written as recently as 2009 reproduce this error. However, German researchers interviewing guards and reviewing border police phone calls have learned that the Wall "fell" hours earlier, at the Waltersdorfer Chaussee checkpoint.

Although no one could say exactly what was happening, how, why, or whether it would last, there was a general sense that it was wonderful. West Berliners were already in the streets celebrating, and when the news reached the Bundestag in Bonn, which was meeting in a special late session, the delegates suddenly rose and began singing "Deutschland über Alles." The federal chancellor, Helmut Kohl, was abroad on a state visit to Poland when the news reached him. He refrained from making any substantive statement until he returned the next day, November 10. By that time the world watched astonishing scenes of demoralized DDR border troops standing in a line staring at mobs celebrating on top of the wall. That afternoon an elderly Willy Brandt, who had been mayor of West Berlin in 1963 when Kennedy made his famous speech, gave a passionate address to the huge crowd and vowed, "Berlin will live and the Wall shall fall!"

In October, when the big protests began in the DDR, mobs often chanted or held up signs reading "We are the people!" By November, observers began to notice people chanting, "We are *one* people!" Because the fall of the wall did ultimately result in German reunification, it is hard to remember that nobody at the time was sure that it would be so. Many Europeans were understandably nervous. The prospect of a reunified Germany inevitably brought to mind images of the Second World War, and the reception to the idea was cool in France, Poland, and Czechoslovakia. In Britain, Prime Minister Margaret Thatcher was prominently opposed to German unification, and her government even tried to persuade the Soviets to oppose it, arguing disingenuously that the Americans shared her view.[5]

In fact, however, the Americans were solidly behind the idea. President George H. W. Bush's administration supported Chancellor Kohl's West German government to press for reunification as soon as possible. It was a staggeringly complicated issue. There was still a DDR, and even though its leaders had obviously lost control of the situation they were still potentially dangerous. Nobody was sure whether a majority of East Germans actually wanted to be reunified. For that matter, nobody was sure if a majority of West Germans wanted it, either, but their opinions were not considered as important, a fact that later caused a great deal of resentment when the massive bill came due for the expenses of the reunification. Finally, there were over four hundred thousand Soviet troops still stationed in East Germany. Gorbachev secretly informed the Western leaders that the crumbling Soviet economy simply lacked the resources to relocate these men on new bases in Russia. He managed to extract a substantial sum from Kohl to pay for the departure of the Soviet army.

Helmut Kohl's government spent the winter of 1989–1990 in an extraordinary campaign to persuade other European leaders and media that Germans were no longer a threat, and that a united Germany would be an asset to Europe and to the NATO alliance. But probably the most convincing argument was simply that *something* had to be done because East Germany was obviously collapsing. People became aware that the DDR's leaders had lived comparatively lavish lifestyles at the state's expense. Most damningly, the men who had ordered ordinary citizens arrested and often tortured for contact with the West had filled their homes with expensive Western goods. In the ensuing rage against them, the entire Politburo resigned on December 3. Two weeks later many former members reinvented themselves as the Party of Democratic Socialism (PDS), declaring that they had abandoned "Stalinism" and that they were willing to accept the existence of other parties. Effectively, the East German government had ceased to exist.

Nine million people—more than half the East German population—had crossed into the west in just the first week after the wall was breached, to see the forbidden land for themselves. They came home laden with candy, fruits and vegetables, junk food, music, and sex toys. More than a hundred thousand had decided to stay permanently.[6] The West German government initially favored a "confederation" approach that would gradually bind the two states together, in the meantime allowing easterners to have free elections. But after a visit to the DDR in December, Kohl was deeply impressed by the passion of the crowds and sensed that the moment for reunification was now or never.

On January 16, 1990, angry crowds gathered outside the Stasi headquarters in East Berlin, as the agents inside desperately tried to shred and incinerate millions of documents. The crowd stormed the building and vented years of anger upon it. Amazingly, no Stasi personnel were killed, and the mob began to calm when members of the PDS leadership, the police, and leaders of the new democratic movements all called for order. The taking of the Stasi headquarters is often seen as the final act of the East German Revolution and the humiliation of the regime that had intimidated its people for four decades. The revelations that came from the opening of the Stasi files have haunted Germans to this day. The millions of files revealed the incredible level of surveillance of people's lives, and most importantly, the activity of people as informers and collaborators. Families were shattered at the realization that a spouse had spied on a spouse, or a child on a parent. Careers were ruined as it became clear that a worker had spied on a boss, or a teacher on a student, and so on. The revelation of the Stasi files confirmed in many people's minds their worst fears about the nature of the regime under which they had lived, and did more than anything to discredit the entire idea of an East German nation. From that point, reunification seemed to most people to be the only logical course. West Germany would essentially absorb East Germany, and the DDR would cease to be.

In July 1990 Kohl's government offered East Germans the chance to exchange their now worthless East German marks for West German currency at an artificially inflated rate, to prevent the easterners from becoming instantly impoverished in the new capitalist economy. And in September 1990 the unification treaty was finally approved. On October 3, 1990, Germany was reunified. In the 1990 German elections, politicians therefore campaigned on both sides of the former wall for the first time. The result was a clear victory for Kohl's conservative government, substantially supported by the new eastern voters, and the Union returned to power with the FDP. Helmut Kohl had prevailed in his campaign to unify the two German states and he enjoyed a period of great popularity. He was nicknamed the Unity Chancellor.

The Wende is understood by most Germans as a marvelous episode in their history. Coming at the end of a century filled with war, dictatorship, and suffering, common people in East Germany conducted a peaceful revolution that impressed the world and changed Europe. It was justifiably celebrated at the time. But as with most great celebrations, the morning brings quite a mess to clean up.

The Construction Site

At roughly the same time of the Wende, the nations of the European Community had entered discussions on how to bind themselves closer together and create new institutions, including a single West European currency. By the time they finished their negotiations in 1991 and created the European Union, they were presented with the stunning historical development that "Europe" as they understood it had basically doubled in size over the course

Figure 10.4. A Crane Removes Part of the Berlin Wall: The Brandenburg Gate is in the background. Graffiti on the wall reads: "Sooner or later, everything falls." Public domain.

of a few months, and the former Communist states of the east wanted to join the club that had helped bring such prosperity and stability to the west. The European Union spent much of the 1990s debating how to set up entrance criteria for the eastern nations and how to integrate these much poorer lands, with their young democracies, into the organization. One former Communist state, however, was admitted instantly. East Germans, by virtue of suddenly just being "Germans," were the first of the Eastern Bloc nations in the European Union. Many people therefore looked to Germany to see how the transition would play out. After forty years of Communism and Soviet-style oppression, did these people belong in the West? Could they adjust? Was it simply a matter of giving them hamburgers and nice cars?

Even before the wall came down, Germans had used the nicknames *Wessi* (Westy) and *Ossi* (Easty) to describe each other. There were three times as many Wessis as there were Ossis, and they were many times wealthier, so the new unified society was dramatically lopsided. In the immediate euphoria over unification, especially when the German national soccer team won the World Cup, people's jubilant patriotism and hopes for the future had superseded other concerns. Indeed, the very thought that Germans were allowed to *have* patriotism at all was a source of wonder after four decades of careful antinationalism in both states. Very soon, however, the Wessis began to realize that their taxes were increasing to pay for the staggering cost of reunification. It is impossible to overstate the scale of the task. Almost every mile of eastern roads had to be repaved, expanded, or improved. Millions of miles of electrical and telephone cable had to be laid or brought up to code. Millions of pounds of asbestos had to be removed from thousands of buildings. Public transportation systems had to be completely renovated. The main train station in Dresden, for example, had to be gutted and rebuilt, while still somehow remaining in use for all the commuters in a major city.

In addition to the massive outlay by the state for public works, the state-owned businesses in the east also required complete overhaul by any potential buyer. Nearly all eastern factories were obsolete, or produced goods that could not compete in a western marketplace. Unemployment skyrocketed as workplaces were shut down across the country. The new jobs that were created were usually in the service sector, as western chain stores and restaurants appeared. People who had been highly skilled, often with graduate degrees, suddenly found themselves unemployed, or were humiliated to be selling underwear in a department store or serving fast food while being told they were lucky to have found a job at all. Unemployment in the east averaged 20–25 percent in many cities for years.

West German entrepreneurs came east quickly to buy the cheap real estate and start or expand businesses. The initial results were visually jarring. In the Alexanderplatz in East Berlin—one of the main hubs of shopping and transportation—soon after the fall of the wall, a sparkling TGI Friday's restaurant suddenly appeared in the midst of the gray slab buildings on all sides. Your author was in Potsdam after the reunification and saw one block that had been renovated with trendy boutiques, cafés, and an ice cream shop, while the blocks on both sides still had grey crumbling walls, boarded windows, and huge potholes in the street. For years, East German cities—indeed much of the country—seemed to be a single vast construction site. Berlin in particular, which had the massive task of undoing the wall and reconnecting the severed halves of the huge city, had a skyline dominated by construction cranes and cement silos for more than a decade.

The Ossis inevitably began to resent being handled like poor country cousins who had to be bailed out, reeducated, and told what to do. They had displayed great courage and patience in peacefully bringing down a dictatorship, and now they felt they were being treated with contempt. The Wessis, meanwhile, resented having to pay for the reconstruction of the east, particularly when that often meant that eastern cities got the newest and best of everything. Taxpayers in cities like Bonn, Hamburg, and Braunschweig, for example, were angry to find that their money had created an ultramodern new streetcar system for Dresden, when the streetcars and subways in their own cities obviously needed upgrading, too. Soon West German media, particularly in Bavaria, began to print anecdotes about Wessis wanting to rebuild the wall. These stories were humorous, and obviously not serious, but they stung.

Germans were shocked to find that radical right-wing movements appeared to be taking root in the former East Germany. West Germany had always had a few small far-right parties, none of which ever scored more than a few percentage points in national elections. Some of these groups were connected to the "skinhead" movement, and were closely watched by the authorities, since making use of any Nazi-era symbols is illegal. In retrospect, it should not have been surprising to find some of these groups emerging in the East, where confused, frustrated, and/or unemployed people now had the additional shock of seeing foreign immigrants moving into their neighborhoods.

West Germany already had a large immigrant population, mostly Turkish and Kurdish, of so-called guest workers. By the time of unification, many of these people were second-generation, bilingual, and beginning to integrate into mainstream German life. Most, however, still stood out. They looked different, they spoke with a heavy accent, the women often wore Islamic headscarves, and they tended to cluster in their own neighborhoods, although almost every West German city had Middle Eastern fast food and small shops. The east offered inexpensive opportunities for these people, as well as for refugees from conflicts in Africa and from the war in Yugoslavia.

In September 1991, in the small Saxon city of Hoyerswerda, whose unemployment rate after the Wende shot up to over 40 percent, a large group of skinheads attacked African and Vietnamese immigrants, and firebombed a refugee hostel. Witnesses reported that onlookers cheered the attackers, and police were able to find only two of the perpetrators. In Rostock the next year, a similar firebombing attack occurred, this time bringing on a full-scale battle with police in which hundreds of people were injured. This wave of violence was not limited to the east; skinheads attacked Turkish immigrants in western cities like Mölln and Solingen, and the highest death toll came from an attack in Lübeck. Right-wing extremist groups sensed a moment of political opportunity and felt encouraged by the frustrations of people on both sides of the former Wall.[7] The German media, however, tended to focus upon the attacks in the east. Huge demonstrations against the skinheads, at which German politicians spoke, took place in the context of unification: that is, things that had become a problem since the east joined the west. The media focused upon the existence of a burgeoning radical scene in the former DDR, particularly among young men, symbolized by things like a skinhead punk-rock band in Brandenburg named The Turk-Hunters. Inevitably, people made fearful comparisons to the Weimar Republic.

But the Federal Republic was not Weimar. It was a stable democratic system with a functioning judiciary. In fact, long before the courts had to deal with the perpetrators, the public reaction against the attacks was in many ways a bigger story than the attacks themselves. Hundreds of thousands of demonstrators reaffirmed the respect for human rights and the immigrants certainly did not leave Germany. Very much unlike the Weimar Republic, Germans in the 1990s came out into the streets to demonstrate peacefully against intolerance, bigotry, and violence. A few far-right politicians managed to get elected in local and state government in the east, but in general as the economic situation slowly improved, the social troubles slowly dissipated.

In the spring of 1991 the Bundestag took up the question of whether or not to move to Berlin. In some ways this was a strange debate, because the treaty of unification had already declared Berlin to be the capital. Debating now whether or not to move the government there seemed odd to outside observers. But within the context of German history, the debate was a crucial test of how Germans saw themselves, their government, and their society. Bonn is a quiet little city, an ideal location for the government of West Germany, a state that had always tried to keep a low profile in European and global politics, a state that felt the heavy burdens of a criminal past. Berlin is a great global city, but of course it is also haunted by the ghosts of two world wars, the Nazi oppression, and the Cold War. Moving the government "back" to Berlin would mean once again inhabiting the physical space (and in some cases, the same buildings) of that unhappy past. It would also run the risk of sending the wrong signals to the world. The vote that June was hair-raisingly close. In the end, they chose Berlin, although a handful of offices from some of the smaller ministries remained in Bonn. Over the next several years the government slowly trickled into the old/new capital, as old buildings were restored and new ones constructed. In the kind of tortured political debate that seems strange to anyone outside Germany, politicians and scholars now argued, often fiercely, over whether Germany was a "normal" country.

The move to Berlin naturally raised questions about how the Federal Republic would deal with its twentieth-century past in the public space. Although the reconstruction of the capital was astronomically expensive (the local government of Berlin teetered on the verge of bankruptcy for twenty

Figure 10.5.   The Paul-Löbe-Haus

Figure 10.6.   The Reichstag

For its new buildings the German government wanted to convey openness and transparency. Despite being massive, many of the structures seem fragile or delicate because they use so much glass and natural light. The Paul-Löbe-Haus holds the offices of the parliamentarians and their staffs. The Spree River actually flows through the midst of the structure, symbolizing the unity of east and west. Nearby the old Reichstag building has been restored, and its heavy imperial-era architecture has been crowned by a transparent cupola with hundreds of mirrors that refract sunlight in a blue glow.

years after the Wall came down), in a sense Berlin was also fortunate to have so much empty space to work with. The city is geographically huge but relatively underpopulated (it is the size of New York City, but with only half the population). The destruction of the Wall opened miles of prime central real estate. Some decisions were easier than others. Many of the new government buildings, for example, fit nicely into what had been abandoned freight yards and no-man's-land along the wall. The old Potsdamerplatz—a sort of Times Square before the war—had to be rebuilt from scratch and emerged as a cluster of tourist attractions and office towers. Nearby, the site of a former Gestapo prison was excavated as an open-air museum so that visitors can walk through the interrogation cells while listening to recordings of survivors' testimony and reading informational plaques.

By the 1980s, West Germany had a large number of Holocaust-related memorials and historical markers. Most West German cities had some sort of commemorative public space. After reunification there was broad consensus that the new Berlin needed a national Holocaust monument of some kind, and this discussion vexed the country for years as people argued over the location and style of the structure. It finally took shape in the midst of downtown, and covers an entire city block, a few hundred yards from the Reichstag and the Brandenburg Gate. Half a block away, the site of Hitler's old chancellery and bunker is noted with a simple historical marker. Today people can walk the sidewalks of downtown Berlin and find small brass squares in front of doorsteps, noting that a Jewish family or business owned that building before the war and listing their names and their fates.

As hard as it was to reach agreement on many Nazi-related historical structures, the fight over the legacy of the DDR proved even harder. Unlike the Nazi past, the DDR still had a large number of unapologetic supporters, and a great many people who resented being told that what they had believed their whole lives had been false or worthless. To some disgruntled observers during the Wende, the Ossis had voted "for Coca-Cola and porn."[8] Obviously, some Ossis were smitten with material goods, while others were simply angry at the mismanagement, corruption, and oppression of the Communist regime. Although German reconstruction was remarkably fast by historical standards, for people who were unemployed it seemed slow at the time, and markedly unfair, as some people and some places enjoyed its benefits more than others. Not surprisingly, many Ossis chose to remember the good things about the DDR and to deemphasize or even deny the bad things. This phenomenon acquired a name: *Ostalgie* (a pun combining the word for "east" with the word for "nostalgia"). Soon popular movies and television shows gently poked fun at life in the DDR, and it even became trendy and

Figure 10.7.   The Holocaust Monument, Berlin: Officially known as the Monument to the Murdered Jews of Europe, the Holocaust memorial in central Berlin is a large field of tombstonelike monoliths that gradually undulate, giving one the sense of becoming lost in their shadows as one walks amongst them.

cool to wear the old clothes and listen to the old bands. The Trabi became a prized collector's item, as did Soviet-made wristwatches that never worked very well, but now declare you to be Cool (unless you're just wearing one of the many subsequent imitations, sold on the streets or in shops).

When the SED dismantled itself in 1989, it reemerged as the Party of Democratic Socialism, or PDS, led by a new generation of middle-aged former Communists (although how "former" some of them were, and are, is debatable). The PDS immediately became a major force in East German politics, while it was generally loathed in the west. People who supported the PDS recalled that the old East Germany had been a place with a slower, more communal pace of life, where crime was almost nonexistent, where children had free day care, and where people enjoyed simple pleasures. They contrasted this rosy and selective memory with the fast-paced materialism of the new capitalist Germany. For years the PDS remained a party of dissent, since they weren't arguing for secession, and since they obviously couldn't convert the Wessis to Communism. But they provided a voice for disgruntled Ossis who resented the dismantling of their past.

The flash point of these arguments about the past was that ultimate symbol of the DDR: the Palace of the Republic. The huge building lay empty, with a leaky roof, infested with mold and filled with asbestos, in the midst of

Berlin's museum quarter, where tourists gawked at its great copper-colored hulk. The city decided to tear it down and replace it with a reconstruction of the old Prussian palace that had once stood there, to serve as another museum. The planned demolition rallied the Ossis, and it became a test case of Ostalgie as large crowds, encouraged by PDS politicians, fought to have the building saved and restored as a museum to the DDR, instead. The Ossis won the argument for many years, simply because the cost of sanitizing and demolishing the building was so prohibitively high. (Nicknamed "Erich's Revenge" by many people, the palace got the last laugh by costing the capitalists three times as much to tear down as it had cost the Communists to put up!) For a few years it became a strange display platform for large-scale avant-garde art. The demolition finally got underway in earnest in 2007, nearly twenty years after the fall of the Wall.

The N-Word

In 1998 Helmut Kohl's Union government suffered a heavy election defeat, ending his eighteen-year career as German chancellor, the longest term of any leader since Bismarck. Voters were disgruntled for a variety of reasons: higher taxes, the economic slowdown, high unemployment, and the ongoing difficulties of unification and reconstruction. They also simply wanted a generational change. The SPD leader, Gerhard Schroeder, was a skillful politician and effective campaigner. His new coalition also marked the first time the Green Party was included in the federal government. Schroeder and the Green leader Joschka Fischer represented a transition in German politics: for the first time the country was led by men who had no memory of the Nazis or the Second World War. (Both had been born in the 1940s.) Schroeder and especially Fischer were also symbolic of that sixty-eighter generation that had cut its teeth in politics in the 1970s and 1980s, supporting environmentalism, nuclear disarmament, women's rights, and pacifism.

In addition to the focus on this new generation of postwar German leaders, the "Red-Green" coalition also tiptoed into a minefield of controversy over the "N-word" in German politics: *normal*. Was Germany—two generations after Hitler—finally a "normal" country again?

Politicians and the popular media generally don't take the time to dissect semantics, so the debate had less to do with the whole concept of what a "normal" country is supposed to be in the first place and more to do with whether Germans had somehow compensated for the Nazi past. The argument surfaced in a variety of ways. It had implications for the Jewish community in Germany, the huge majority of whom had immigrated after the war. When the writer Martin Walser accepted an award in 1998, he gave an address in which he complained that much of the world used the Holocaust as "a routine of threat . . . a moral club" to beat Germans with for all eternity. Walser entered a high-profile media war that not only pitted him against German Jewish leaders (one of whom referred to Germany as "the land of the murderers"), but also spilled over into Left-Right controversies on matters such as whether Germany had a special obligation to accept refugees from war and dictatorship, as a way of atoning for its own crimes. For example, when the Green Party proposed new, more liberal laws allowing refugees to seek asylum in Germany, conservatives opposed the measure. In a 2001 interview on the topic, the general secretary of the CDU told a reporter, "Yes, I am proud to be a German." A leading Green politician accused him of having "the mentality of a skinhead."[9]

In most democracies, no one blinks when someone declares that they are "proud" to belong to that nationality. Indeed, in many democracies, particularly in France and the United States, regular declarations of patriotism are requirements for nearly all political figures. In Germany, however, such proclamations were extremely rare and generally considered in bad taste, harkening back to the discredited era of nationalism in the early twentieth century. The late 1990s and early 2000s thus occasioned a fair amount of controversy as Germans began to fly the national flag more. (Bonn had been remarkable in that German flags were actually hard to spot, whereas the new public buildings in Berlin are often bedecked with them.) Chancellor Schroeder used the word *proud* more than any of his predecessors, although in carefully sited contexts. He was "proud" of German scientific accomplishment, for instance, when he spoke at the European Space Agency in 2005. He was "proud" of German democracy and rule of law, and was "proud to be allowed to lead a government" that was concerned with the environment and ecological conservation.[10] There is some irony in the fact that it took a sixty-eighter from a Socialist party to get Germans to begin expressing a bit of national pride without angst. In the autumn of 2002, Schroeder's government actually named its platform "Germany: A Normal Land in Europe," although again hedged its bets by explaining that the integration of all Germans, East and West, into a single society was the test of "normalcy."[11] In 2004 Schroeder became the first German leader invited to the annual D-day commemorative celebrations in France, and he laid a wreath on the tomb of an unknown German soldier.

As the new century unfolded, American leaders grew frustrated with Germany's abnormalities in a way completely unexpected to most Germans. In September 2001 Islamic terrorists belonging to the group al-Qaeda carried out devastating attacks in Washington and New York City. Sympathy for the Americans was widespread throughout Germany. In Berlin, two hundred thousand people gathered by the Brandenburg Gate for a candlelight vigil. It soon became apparent that many of the terrorists had lived for some time in Hamburg, and a few had been observed by German intelligence, which had passed along warnings to their American colleagues. Shortly after the 9/11 attacks, the American president George W. Bush declared a "Global War on Terror" and invoked the NATO alliance to summon assistance for an invasion of Afghanistan, where al-Qaeda had its main bases.

This placed the Germans in a quandary. German law forbade the use of its military outside the national borders. In the 1990s the government had skirted the issue by sending only noncombat units (medical, for example) to assist the other European peacekeepers in the Balkans. In 1998 the Bundestag spent weeks in anguished debate over whether it could send troops to assist the other NATO allies in the Kosovo conflict. Immensely relieved that a cease-fire agreement was reached at the last minute, the German troops arrived as peacekeepers, not combat soldiers. But now the Bush administration was asking Germany and the other NATO allies to participate in a shooting war thousands of miles from Europe. Germany offered to take on additional peacekeeping roles in Europe and Africa, in order to free American troops for operations in Afghanistan. And German intelligence services tried to cooperate with the CIA to find other al-Qaeda cells in Europe. But the Bush administration wanted full involvement.

Although it should not have come as a shock, since all members of the NATO alliance, America included, had dramatically cut back their military spending since the end of the Cold War, nonetheless the Americans were surprised to realize that Germany's defense spending was minuscule for a country of its size and wealth. The Bundeswehr had outdated Cold War–era equipment and lacked the budget for a prolonged overseas operation of any size. Moreover, the Bush administration discovered, somewhat to their disgust, that the Bundeswehr was a parliamentary army; it could do virtually nothing without the approval of the legislature. Since the 1990s Germans had enjoyed a remarkable rarity in their history: for the first time they were allied or on friendly terms with every nation they bordered, indeed with every nation in Europe. Many Germans understandably wondered why they needed a military at all. But in the wake of the 9/11 attacks, a narrow majority prevailed to vote for direct involvement in Afghanistan. Schroeder and Fischer both campaigned for it, to the anger of many in their left-wing parties. Thus German troops went into combat for the first time since 1945.

The Afghanistan War continues at the time of this writing, and indeed has even been expanded. More than four thousand German troops were stationed there as of 2010, the third-largest NATO contingent after the United States and Britain. Polls showed that German voters gradually shifted to disapproving of the ongoing involvement, yet most politicians remained in favor of the mission. They broke company with the United States in a dramatic fashion, however, over the war in Iraq.

In 2002 the Bush administration began preparing for an invasion of Iraq, arguing that the Iraqi dictatorship was a sponsor of terrorism and possessed weapons of mass destruction, including a nuclear program. Few Europeans were impressed with these arguments. Polls in Britain, Spain, Italy, Germany, and France routinely showed 80–90 percent disapproval for a war. The governments of the European Union countries, however, were more divided. Britain, Spain, and Italy joined the United States, while France and Germany did not. Smaller nations were similarly divided. Several East European states were more willing to provide some contribution, in some cases in return for substantial financial incentives from the Bush administration. The American secretary of defense, Donald Rumsfeld, dismissed France and Germany as "Old Europe" (as opposed to the new democracies of the east), and American conservative media produced numerous accusations that Europeans were "appeasing" a dictator in Iraq, just as they had appeased Hitler before the Second World War. All of this made Germans seethe. The German foreign minister, Joschka Fischer, confronted Rumsfeld, even shouting at him in English that he did not believe the American claims of imminent danger from Iraq. The Bush administration declared that future lucrative development contracts in Iraq would not be forthcoming to Germany, France, or others who didn't help in the invasion.

The Iraq War marks the lowest point of German-American relations since 1945. President Bush was despised in Germany, and Gerhard Schroeder squeaked out a narrow election victory in 2002 specifically by campaigning against Bush and the coming war. As the Iraq conflict became a long and difficult occupation, Germans felt vindicated that they had made the right decision, although German troops remained in Afghanistan for much the same purpose as the troops in Iraq.

Ossis, Wessis, and Germans

The great Czech author Milan Kundera wrote that "sooner or later, everyone lets everything be forgotten." Students in German schools and universities today have no memory of the Wende, nor indeed of most of the complex issues of reunification. Researchers at the Free University of Berlin spent two years conducting a survey of German high school students in both east and west, testing their knowledge of recent German history. As with many surveys of students (or adults, for that matter), the results can often be disheartening. More than a quarter thought that Konrad Adenauer and Willy Brandt had been East German leaders. Only 22 percent could correctly identify Erich Honecker. Two-thirds of the Ossi students thought that the east had been the larger economy, and half thought that the Stasi had been a normal police force.[12] In some ways, these are positive developments, since they mean that the things that vexed their parents' generation are for young Germans today no more or less contentious than anything else learned and forgotten in history class.

One could argue that German reunification was a process that took at least sixteen years. It began in the autumn of 1989 and seemed fraught for many years thereafter. West Germans transferred nearly two trillion dollars to the east, and yet the Ossis still suffered from high unemployment and incomes that were on average only three-quarters as high as incomes in the west. The much larger western population dominated the Bundestag and thus national politics. But in 2005 a remarkably close election brought down the Red-Green government of Gerhard Schroeder. The results were so close, with no party able to form a ruling coalition, that finally the SPD and the Union agreed to share power in a "Grand Coalition." As a result, the new CDU leader, Angela Merkel, came to power. She was the first woman ever to govern a unified Germany. That was history-shattering in itself, but perhaps even more important for German political life, she was the first Ossi to become chancellor.

Merkel was actually born in the west, but her father, a Lutheran pastor, moved the family east when she was a child, and she grew up in Brandenburg. With a doctorate in physics and speaking fluent Russian, her career options in the DDR were good, despite her insistence on maintaining the rituals of her religion. Joining the CDU during the Wende, Merkel began her political career representing poor fishing communities and shipyard workers on the Baltic island of Rügen. She rapidly became a protégé of Helmut Kohl, a relationship she soon outgrew, and she became the Union's first female leader.

Angela Merkel is not a charismatic leader or a dramatic campaigner. She speaks without much feeling, and almost never allows her temper to show. This easterner, woman, and Protestant, at the head of a traditionally western, patriarchal, and heavily Catholic party, slowly won over German voters with

Figure 10.8. Chancellor Angela Merkel, 2008. Public domain.

her quiet intelligence, stability, and reputation for honesty and simplicity. The German Everyman, it turned out, was a woman.

The 2005 and 2009 elections confirmed Merkel in power, but also illustrated the shifting political landscape of Germany. The older, mainstream parties have steadily lost membership and voters. The SPD, Germany's oldest party, dropped to a shocking 23 percent of the vote in 2009, and Merkel's Union received only 35 percent. As they have declined, the smaller parties have steadily grown. The Greens can now count upon at least 10 percent in most elections, the FDP anywhere from 5–15 percent. The new force on the scene, however, is the controversial Left Party (*die Linke*). This group was created by joining the PDS (the former Communists) with a far-left breakaway faction from the SPD. Thus, a quasi-Communist party now has a substantial presence in West Germany for the first time since before Hitler, and the Left Party has received between 10 and 15 percent nationwide. Its heartland of support is still the east. Many Wessis sigh and shake their heads to note that places like East Berlin's Lichtenberg district, where the old Stasi headquarters and prison used to operate, have the highest levels of support for the former Communists of any region in the country.

For years after the Wende, a traveler moving between western and eastern Germany noticed the change instantly. Today, with the passing of a generation, it often takes considerable effort to find the former line that once separated them. Even the generations that grew up with the Wall have become used to living in a single nation. Ossis and Wessis watch the same television shows, listen to the same music, read the same magazines and novels, go to the same movies, sprinkle their speech with the same American slang words, and go shopping in the same chain stores. Now that Germany's East European neighbors are also members of the European Union, the sense of belonging to "Europe" is equally strong, whether one crosses the border into France, or into the Czech Republic.

A nation which once aspired to be a leader among the great powers of the world now aspires primarily to be a good neighbor and a conscientious custodian of history and the environment. Europeans who once feared German ambition now sometimes express frustration at the difficulty of coaxing the shy Federal Republic out of its cautious inertia. German companies and products remain prominent throughout the world, and German diplomats can often go to places that American diplomats can't, because the Germans are seen as neutral and nonthreatening, while the Americans are seen as imperialists. A Bundeswehr officer on peacekeeping duty in the Balkans commented that he had grown up reading about the horrors inflicted on Europe by the Third Reich, and would never have imagined that the arrival of German soldiers in a town would be regarded by the locals as a happy event, bringing peace and safety, as well as medicine and food.

The year 2009 was crowded with anniversaries. Two thousand years had passed since Arminius defeated the Roman legions in the Teutoburgerwald. Ninety years had passed since the founding of the unhappy Weimar Republic. Seventy years had passed since Hitler launched the Second World War. Sixty years had passed since the founding of the Federal Republic and the DDR, in the ruins of that war. And twenty years had passed since the fall of the Berlin Wall. It was this last anniversary that was the most jubilant, even with a cold and rainy night that discouraged the faint of heart. Tens of thousands gathered in Berlin to celebrate. The federal president, Horst Köhler, describing the fall of Wall and the peaceful reunification of the nation, made no effort to summarize the historical events. He said simply:

"It remains a miracle."

Suggested Reading

Ash, Timothy. *In Europe's Name: Germany and the Divided Continent*. New York: Vintage, 1994.

Edinger, Lewis, and Brigitte Nacos. *From Bonn to Berlin: German Politics in Transition*. New York: Columbia University Press, 1998.

Funder, Anna. *Stasiland: True Stories from Behind the Berlin Wall*. London: Granta, 2004.

Hockenos, Paul. *Joschka Fischer and the Making of the Berlin Republic*. Oxford: Oxford University Press, 2009.

~

Notes

Chapter 4: What Is Enlightenment?

1. An excellent summary of the system of absolutism, the role of the increased military, and the state of historical analysis on the subject can be found in Guy Rowlands, *The Dynastic State and the Army under Louis XIV: Royal Service and Private Interest, 1661–1701* (Cambridge: Cambridge University Press, 2002).

2. This system is admirably explained in Peter Baumgart, Bernhard Kroener, and Heinz Stübig, eds., *Die preussische Armee zwischen Ancien Régime und Reichsbegründung* (Paderborn: Schöningh, 2008).

3. For an alternate view of Frederick and the war, see Franz Szabo, *The Seven Years' War in Europe, 1756–1763* (Harlow, UK: Pearson, 2007).

4. This story is noted by Lee Kennett, *The French Armies in the Seven Years' War* (Durham, NC: Duke University Press, 1967), 63.

Chapter 5: Imagining a Nation

1. Ilke Direske, *Die Herrschaft Schmalkalden im Königreich Westfalen* (Schmalkalden: Museum Schloss Wilhelmsburg, 2006), 58–62.

2. Walter Mönch, *Deutsche Kultur von der Aufklärung bis zur Gegenwart* (Munich: Hüber, 1971), 258.

3. Sam Mustafa, *Merchants and Migrations: Germans and Americans in Connection, 1776–1835* (London: Ashgate, 2001), 232.

4. An excellent summary of the choices for German emigrants can be found in Hans-Jürgen Grabbe, *Vor der großen Flut: Die europäische Migration in die Vereinigten Staaten von Amerika 1783–1820* (Stuttgart: Franz Steiner, 2001). See also the classic

study Theodore Hamerowe, *Restoration, Revolution, Reaction: Economics and Politics in Germany, 1815–1817* (Princeton, NJ: Princeton University Press, 1958), 21–55.

5. Robert Lee, "'Relative Backwardness' and Long-Run Development," in *German History since 1800*, ed. Mary Fulbrook (London: Arnold, 1997), 70.

Chapter 6: An Empire of Monuments

1. John Breuilly, "Revolution to Unification," in *German History since 1800*, ed. Mary Fulbrook (London: Arnold, 1997), 126.

2. Sebastian Haffner, *The Rise and Fall of Prussia* (London: Phoenix, 1998), 137.

3. Brent Peterson, *History, Fiction, and Germany: Writing the Nineteenth-Century Nation* (Detroit, MI: Wayne State University Press, 2005), 8.

4. Quoted in: Sieghard Rost, *Nationalstaaten und Weltmächte* (Frankfurt am Main: Diesterweg, 1961), 93–94.

5. David G. Herrmann, *The Arming of Europe and the Making of the First World War* (Princeton, NJ: Princeton University Press, 1996), 209.

Chapter 7: Modernity and Its Discontents

1. Modris Ecksteins, *The Rites of Spring* (Boston: Houghton-Mifflin, 1989), 56–59.

2. David Blackbourn, *The Long Nineteenth Century: A History of Germany 1780–1918* (Oxford: Oxford University Press, 1998), 462.

3. See, for example, Niall Ferguson, *The Pity of War* (New York: Basic Books, 1999), 174–211.

4. Blackbourn, 469.

5. Blackbourn, 426.

6. Volker Berghahn, *Modern Germany* (Cambridge: Cambridge University Press, 1987), 62.

7. Rudy Koshar, *Germany's Transient Pasts: Preservation and National Memory in the Twentieth Century* (Chapel Hill: University of North Carolina Press, 1998), 107.

8. Eric Weitz, *Weimar Germany: Promise and Tragedy* (Princeton, NJ: Princeton University Press, 2007), 135.

9. Weitz, 41–79. Among recent historians Weitz has offered perhaps the sharpest distinctions between these two worlds of Weimar Germany.

10. Sabine Hake, *German National Cinema* (London: Routledge, 2002), 32–51.

11. George Mosse, *Toward the Final Solution: A History of European Racism* (New York: Howard Fertig, 1997), 168.

12. For some classic examples in English, see Thomas Childers, *The Nazi Voter* (Chapel Hill: University of North Carolina Press, 1983), and Richard Hamilton, *Who Voted for Hitler?* (Princeton, NJ: Princeton University Press, 1982). An excellent analysis can also be found in Michael Mann's *Fascists* (Cambridge: Cambridge University Press, 2004).

13. In the 1930 elections the female vote for the Nazis trailed 3–5 percent behind the male vote in almost every region of Germany. By the end of 1932, however, there was virtually no difference. See Helen Boak, "Our Last Hope: Women's Votes for Hitler—A Reappraisal," *German Studies Review* 12, no. 2 (1989): 289–310.

Chapter 8: Downfall

1. Sauckel's memo and the images from the file are preserved in the Stadtmuseum Weimar.

2. Richard J. Evans, *The Third Reich in Power* (New York: Penguin, 2005), 13.

3. Paul Kennedy, *The Rise and Fall of the Great Powers* (New York: Vintage, 1989), 296.

4. The first historian to present a comprehensive argument against the conventional wisdom of a smoothly running Nazi regime was Ian Kershaw, whose *The Nazi Dictatorship: Problems and Perspectives of Interpretation* (London: Arnold, 1985) became the revision that transformed the debate about the Third Reich and is now considered a classic reference.

5. Evans, *Third Reich in Power*, 73–75.

6. The most persuasive argument of this nature has been made by Götz Aly in *Hitler's Beneficiaries: Plunder, Racial War, and the Nazi Welfare State* (New York: Henry Holt, 2005).

7. An exhaustive summary of the views of common infantrymen on the Eastern Front can be found in Stephen Fritz, *Frontsoldaten: The German Soldier in World War II* (Lexington: University of Kentucky Press, 1996).

8. An interesting summary of this debate among current historians can be found in several articles in the *Bulletin of the German Historical Institute* 45 (Fall 2009).

9. Evans, *Third Reich in Power*, 599.

10. The classic exposition of that argument—that German volunteerism equated to a nationwide eagerness for genocide—is Daniel Jonah Goldhagen, in *Hitler's Willing Executioners* (New York: Knopf, 1996). A more carefully nuanced analysis was put forward by Christopher Browning in *Ordinary Men: Reserve Police Battalion 101 and the Final Solution in Poland* (New York: HarperCollins, 1992).

Chapter 9: Zero Hour

1. Interview by the author with Anna Paapke, Wenden, Germany, July 2003; and with Heidi Hermann, Seattle, WA, September 1996. On Marianne Beutler, see Matthias Pankau, "I Thought There Was No Germany Anymore," *Atlantic Times*, May 2009, 28.

2. Interview by the author with Gerhard Hennes, Whitehall, PA, April 2005.

3. For an English-language summary of recent revelations in this case, see Luke Harding, "Menachim Begin 'Plotted to Kill German Chancellor,'" *Guardian*, June 15, 2006.

4. See, for example, Mark Roseman's essay "Division and Stability: The Federal Republic of Germany, 1949–1989" in *German History Since 1800*, ed. Mary Fulbrook (London: Arnold, 1997).

5. See Tobias Baur, *Das ungeliebte Erbe: Ein Vergleich der zivilen und militärischen Rezeption des 20. Juli 1944 im Westdeutschland der Nachkriegszeit* (Frankfurt am Main: Peter Lang, 2007). The quote from Adenauer is on page 140.

6. Quoted in Wolfgang Leonhard, *Die Revolution Entläßt Ihre Kinder* (Köln: Kiepenheuer & Witsch, 2005), 447.

7. For an excellent analysis of this policy see Timothy Garton Ash, *In Europe's Name: Germany and the Divided Continent* (New York: Vintage, 1994). The quote is from page 185.

Chapter 10: Ode to Joy

1. Charles Maier, *Dissolution: The Crisis of Communism and the End of East Germany* (Princeton, NJ: Princeton University Press, 1997), 66–71.

2. Gareth Dale, *The East German Revolution of 1989* (Manchester, UK: University of Manchester Press, 2006), 7–13.

3. Mary Elise Sarotte, *1989: The Struggle to Create Post Cold-War Europe* (Princeton, NJ: Princeton University Press, 2009), 33.

4. Interviews with border guards on ZDF Dokumentation, *Das schönste Irrtum der Geschichte* (October 28, 2009).

5. Timothy Garton Ash, "Britain Fluffed the German Question," *Guardian*, October 21, 2009.

6. Sarotte, 68.

7. An analysis of the link between far-right politics and the violence can be found in Ruud Koopmans and Susan Olzak, "Discursive Opportunities and the Evolution of Right-Wing Violence in Germany," *American Journal of Sociology* 110, no. 1 (July 2004): 198–230; and Gert Krell, Hans Nicklas, and Änne Ostermann, "Immigration, Asylum, and Anti-Foreigner Violence in Germany," *Journal of Peace Research* 33, no. 2 (May 1996): 153–70.

8. Dale, 212.

9. "Ich bin gern Deutscher, weil . . ." *Frankfurter Allgemeine Zeitung*, March 20, 2001.

10. For the latter quote, see: "Schroeder Startet Kampagne mit Bush Kritik," *Der Spiegel*, August 12, 2005.

11. Franz Müntefering, speaking in the Bundestag on October 29, 2002. Transcript: http://dip21.bundestag.de/dip21/btp/15/000/15004000.74.pdf.

12. Klaus Schroeder and Monika Deutz-Schroeder, *Soziales Paradies Oder Stasi-Staat? Das DDR-Bild von Schülern—Ein Ost-West Vergleich* (Regensburg: Ernst Vögel, 2008).

Index

About the Author

Sam A. Mustafa is associate professor of history at Ramapo College of New Jersey. He received his PhD from the University of Tennessee in 1999. A frequent participant in the Consortium on the Revolutionary Era, he is the author of *Merchants and Migrations: Germans and Americans in Connection, 1776–1835* (2001) and *The Long Ride of Major von Schill: A Journey through German History and Memory* (2008). His articles have appeared in *German History*, the *Journal of Central European History*, the *Yearbook of German-American Studies*, *Internationale Schulbuchforschung*, and elsewhere. Dr. Mustafa lives in the New York City area.